I'm Down

I'm Down

A Memoir

MISHNA WOLFF

St. Martin's Press
New York

I'M DOWN. Copyright © 2009 by Mishna Wolff.
All rights reserved. Printed in the United States of
America. For information address St. Martin's Press,
175 Fifth Avenue, New York, N.Y. 10010.

www.stmartins.com

Library of Congress Cataloging-in-Publication Data

Wolff, Mishna.
I'm down / Mishna Wolff.—1st ed.
p. cm.
ISBN-13: 978-0-312-37855-4
ISBN-10: 0-312-37855-6
1. Wolff, Mishna—Childhood and
youth.   2. Wolff, Mishna—Family.
3. African American neighborhoods—
Washington (State)   4. Comedians—United
States—Biography.   5. Models (Persons)—
United States—Biography.   I. Title.
PN2287.W55A3 2009
792.702'8092—dc22
[B]   2008046317

10 9 8 7 6 5 4 3 2

To my mom and dad, who gave me the best childhood I would never have been smart enough to ask for.

ACKNOWLEDGMENTS

OKAY, THIS IS IMPOSSIBLE. I have received so much time, guidance, effort, and encouragement on this book. Let me start by thanking all the amazing people at St. Martin's: Lisa Senz, Sarah Goldstein, Sally Richardson, John Murphy, Dori Weintraub, Stephen Lee, and everyone else who did the hell out of their jobs. And most important, Rose Hilliard, my fantastic editor, who brought so much to this book and just *gets* it.

Thank you, Erin Hosier, the best agent a girl could have, seriously. Sarah Thyre, for doing me a favor for no good reason and expecting nothing in return. My sister and best friend Anora, whom I am so proud of. The writers who pulled out a chair for me at the table: Jill Soloway, Maggie Rowe, Darcy Cosper, Josh Olson, and Claudia Lonow—thank you. The Fox family, especially Lauren Fox, my friend through *all* seasons. Virgina Scott, for your help with this story. Frank Hannah, a mentor who deserves a whole page. Hillary Malloy and the Malloy family, for filling a lot of seats and feeding me so often. Ira Sacheroff, my very funny and even-tempered stepfather. My stepbrother Sam, he-he. UCB Theater, Caliber Media, Eric King, Pat Healy, Jaclyn Lafer, Richard Potter, and the Doners; Linda, my stepmother, who makes life better. Lauren

Francis—I couldn't make it without you. Mrs. Romano, my seventh-and eighth-grade English teacher, who taught me about irony right when I needed it. Marc Maron, thank you for the risks you took and everything you shared with me. Lorca Cohen, you are truly a great friend who gave me a sanctuary to write in when my world got too chaotic. And thank you, thank you, thank you, Jeremy Doner, the most amazing man in the whole wide world. I promise I will make you so happy.

AUTHOR'S NOTE

EVENTS IN THIS BOOK may be out of sequence, a few minor characters are composites of more than one person, many conversations were re-created and names have been changed.

This book is from my perspective as I was growing up. I honored what I thought was true at that age, rather than what I might know to be true now. My memory is limited to what it is, and I didn't always have all the information as a child. Others might tell it differently.

I claim none of this as gospel. That being said, most of this stuff is totally true.

I'm Down

PROLOGUE

I AM WHITE. My parents, both white. My sister had the same mother and father as me—all of us completely white. White Americans of European ancestry. White, white, white, white, white, white, white, white. I think it's important to make this clear, because when I describe my childhood to people: the years of moving from one black Baptist church to the next, the all-black basketball teams, the hours having my hair painfully braided into cornrows, often their response is, "So . . . who in your family was black?" No one. All white.

However, my dad, John Wolff, or as the guys in the neighborhood called him, "Wolfy," truly believed he was a black man. He strutted around with a short perm, a Cosby-esqe sweater, gold chains, and a Kangol—telling jokes like Redd Foxx, and giving advice like Jesse Jackson. He walked like a black man, he talked like a black man, and he played sports like a black man. You couldn't tell my father he was white. Believe me, I tried. It wasn't an identity crisis; it's who he was. He was from "the neighborhood"—our neighborhood.

We lived in an area of south Seattle called the Rainier Valley that your average white person, at the time, wouldn't have gone to without a good reason. Not that there weren't plenty

of reasons to visit the Rainier Valley—there were. Right off M. L. King Jr. Way, I lived near the Langston Hughes Auditorium, not far from the Medgar Evers pool, close to the Douglass-Truth Library, down the street from the Quincy Jones Auditorium, which incidentally, was in the high school Jimi Hendrix went to. On the literary tip, Iceberg Slim had run a gang of hoes not far from where we lived.

But there were virtually no whites. There were the occasional middle-class white hippies who moved onto our street to escape bougie-ness, but they usually moved away when they had kids. And my dad always wound up hating them. Sooner or later they'd "be showing off" by throwing around their bachelor's degrees or fixing their roofs, and we'd be banned from any interaction with them. Even before it was hip, Dad was "keepin' it real."

He'd moved to our neighborhood as a child in the early sixties, back when it was a white and Asian neighborhood. That was before school busing programs, when middle-class white people started moving out of the cities and into the suburbs, because, "you know." My grandparents were too cheap to be racist. You don't sell when the market is down. And as the neighborhood got blacker—so did my dad. He was in high school when he started to help the Black Panthers with the breakfast program. He played sports and he made his friends. They were the brothers and he was cool.

But after a quarter of college football failed to make him a star, my dad reinvented himself as a hippie and ventured east to Putney, Vermont. He grew his hair long, wore leather pants, and roamed the halls of higher education selling weed. It was here that he met my mom. She was smart, pretty, socially conscious, and super needy. And when my dad talked about civil rights, she assumed he was a feminist. She immediately quit school and moved to Maine with him to live in the woods with no electricity and no running water. He had that effect on women.

They did the "back to nature" thing for a while, but once my mom had me, my dad convinced her to move into the house that he grew up in. My grandparents were finally moving to a better neighborhood. And eventually my mom agreed: women like free houses. But once my dad was back on his block, he began to change—or rather change back.

He cut off his long hair and got a short perm, he became obsessed with his shoes, and he bought us an African drum coffee table, and one of those high-backed wicker chairs—you know, the ones you always see Huey Newton in. And he was invited by all his friends from high school to join the Esquire Club, an all-black men's club. Within a year the man my mom had married had shed his crunchy granola skin, exposing a

bona fide soul brother—and they teetered on the brink of divorce.

Meanwhile my little sister, who was born in the Rainier Valley, took after my dad. She seemed to pop right out of the womb and into a dance troupe. She found so much love and approval in the black community, you'd think she'd invented beatboxing (see Doug E. Fresh).

So while my mom was busy planning her escape, my sister and father were cohorts—completely integrated into the community we lived in. And then there was me—the honky. I'm not saying that to be provocative or put myself down.

I *was* a honky. I couldn't dance. I couldn't sing. I couldn't double Dutch—the dueling jump ropes scared me. I didn't have great stories that started with "We was at . . ." and ended with ". . . I told her not to make me take my earrings off!"

Honestly, being a honky was A-OK with me. I wished my whole family were honkies. Big honkies! I wished we were the cover family for *Honky Weekly*. If I could have picked my family, they would have been honky professors that sat around in honky-assed tweed jackets reading the paper, stopping occasionally to say honky things about what was going on in China and how brilliant I was. They would talk in gentle honky voices and when they made a chicken they would THROW OUT THE GIZZARDS.

Instead I got my dad, sitting around playing dominoes with four large black men, who were all apparently my uncle, and who agreed that the only way to discuss affirmative action was—at the top of your lungs. They also thought kids were beer-fetchers crossed with remote controls and that there was something seriously wrong with my rhythm. I had a rhythm problem. This was not acceptable to my father, and so he began his crusade to make me "down."

I remember it starting shortly after my sixth birthday. Without looking up from his dominoes game, he said to me, "You need to stop tryin' to hang out with grown folk and get out and play with the neighborhood kids." The four learned black men he played with sat at the dining room table nodding in agreement, but I wasn't thrilled with the idea. I didn't really know the neighborhood kids, but they all hung out on the end of the block, being bigger than me and knowing each other really well. What I was a fan of was hanging out with my daddy. Mom drove a city bus and Dad took care of me and my little sister, Anora, during the day. Sometimes he would have a job doing construction, and we would go hammer nails and stuff until someone got hurt. But usually he was entertaining these four guys from the neighborhood: Reggie Dee, Eldridge, Big Lyman, and Delroy. And I just didn't get why he wouldn't want me there, too—I was fun.

My first birthday.

My dad put his dominoes in order as he continued, "You know what you need to do?"

I had a feeling he was gonna tell me.

"You need to get out and make friends with the sisters."

"You mean the girls out front of Latifa's house?"

My dad nodded.

"Why?" I asked.

"You may need those girls someday, and . . . your neighborhood is where you live."

"What do I do?"

"Just go introduce yourself," he said. Then, waving his hands around, he added, "But not like you're scared . . . like you're doing them a favor." I knew this had something to do

with being cool, but I was scared and I didn't see how I was
doing anyone a favor.

"Those girls out there would be lucky to have you hangin'
with them," Reggie Dee said.

"How come?" I asked. I liked Reggie.

"Well . . . ," Reggie said, thinking.

"I'm smart," I said. "Pretty smart for six."

"Yeah," Reggie said apprehensively. "But that's not something you want to brag about."

"Oh." I didn't get popularity at all. "Then what do I
have?"

"Well . . . ," my dad said. "You're my daughter, for one.
That's one thing right there." I waited for "two," but he just
looked angry that I was still there.

I walked out of the house toward the corner, where I saw a
group of kids. The clear leader of the group was a chubby girl
we called Nay-Nay. She had her honey-colored thighs shoved
into a pair of Day-Glo bicycle shorts two sizes too small, and
her fat piggy toes peeked out of a pair of matching plastic jellies. Jellies were a plastic ballet-style shoe that was popular in
the neighborhood, but my mom wouldn't let me have them,
because she said they were bad for my high arches.

"Hi," I said. "I'm Mishna. I live up the street. Do you want
to be my friend?" Awful—I didn't say it as though I was doing
them a favor. I said it like I was scared.

Nay-Nay looked me up and down and then said, "Do you
have any Barbies?"

"Sure," I said. Then asked, "What's a Barbie?"

Everyone looked at me like I was on crack, and Nay-Nay
condescended, "Barbie is a doll. Do you have any Barbies?"

"Yes!" I said defiantly. "I do!"

"Well, get them . . . and you can hang out." Nay-Nay said, putting her hand on her hip and blocking me from addressing anyone else in her group. But I stupidly stood there, not realizing that the conversation was over. I didn't exist until I had that doll. Nay-Nay smacked her lips.

"Oh," I said nonchalantly. "I'll go get my Barbie." And crept away.

I tore through the house past the dominoes game and into my room and began rifling through my dolls. I set them all on the bed in order to pick which of them, if any, was a Barbie doll. It was hard for me to tell what any brand-name toys were, because my mom didn't let me watch commercial television. She said it rotted my brain, but I half suspected it was because not seeing commercials made it easier to be poor.

Making a quick and instinctual decision, I grabbed my favorite doll to bring back to the girls, which was Tommy, a stuffed turtle that someone had made for me. I tucked him carefully under my arm being very mindful of his head, because that's where turtles are most vulnerable. And I hurried back upstairs—scurrying past my dad, who was in a shouting match with Lyman over whether or not he was cheating, and back out the front door. I didn't know if I had the right doll, but I was carrying the best doll I owned, and I was pretty sure that everyone would be impressed with my hot-shit turtle.

The neighborhood kids were all standing in front of Latifa's house fully into some sort of Barbie orgy. Hot, wild, Barbie-on-Barbie action, complete with sound effects like, "uh, uh, uh." And besides discovering lesbianism, I found that what I was holding could not have been further from a Barbie.

"What's that, whitey?" Nay-Nay asked, pointing to my doll.

"Tommy," I said. "He's a turtle."

"You thought you could bring your broke-ass turtle down here to play Barbies?"

I shrugged.

And with that, Nay-Nay began cackling in a way that quickly caught on with the rest of the group. I just stood on the corner holding Tommy the Turtle as five black girls holding plastic white women laughed at my stupidity.

I was desperate and argued, "Mine's a Barbie doll, too. . . . It's just a different kind of Barbie!"

To which Latifa, a girl a year older than me, exclaimed, "That ain't no Barbie doll! That's something out of the Goodwill goodie box!" And when I didn't walk away, Nay-Nay called me whitey again and gave me an embarrassing little shove in the direction of my house.

I marched back into the house and straight up to my mom, who had just gotten home from work. She was still in her work uniform, snacking on cheese and crackers at the kitchen counter, wearing her usual after-work expression of tired mixed with worry and coffee. She was deep in her cheddar and Ak-Mak, and looked surprised when I pounded the counter next to her and exclaimed, "Mom, I need a Barbie!"

"What about Tommy?" she asked, gesturing in the direction of my turtle. I threw Tommy on the ground.

"What about him?" I asked in a tone I hoped Dad didn't overhear.

"You know, now you'll never make turtle mother of the year."

"I don't care about my dumb turtle anymore!"

That got her attention. My mom turned to me and shook her head almost as if she knew this day had been coming and

My mother, father, and baby me—looking skeptical.

said in a calm and sincere voice, "Honey, oppressed people of the world make Barbie so a big corporation can get rich. Now, is it really worth that kind of karma for a doll?"

I tried to respond. "Um," I said. "Well . . ." But I knew I couldn't argue with karma and oppressed people in the Philippines.

A few days later, I walked out of the front door as my dad was putting the finishing touches on a tire swing in the front yard. "What's that?" I asked.

He finished his knot and said, "Tire swing. I thought it would bring some other kids over here to play with you." He added, "You'll see. This'll be *the spot.*"

"You think this will help me make friends?" I asked.

"Hells yeah," my dad said. And then pointing to the swing, asked, "Who wouldn't want to be on that swing?"

I guessed *me* was the answer, because *that swing* scared me.

But my dad really knew about this stuff. So even though *that swing* just looked like something that was too high off the ground and not really *clean* clean, I knew its secret would reveal itself. And, sure enough, before my dad was done testing out his knot, Latifa had come over.

"So," I said, looking awkwardly at Latifa. "You wanna go first?"

"Okay," she said, and got on the swing. She swung for a little bit and then helped hoist me up and pushed for a while. And I was surprised to find that hanging out with Latifa when she was away from Nay-Nay was pretty nice. I also learned that her favorite word was *daaang!* She started every sentence with it. "Daaang, you sure have some nappy hair." Or, "Daaang, why your parents dress you like a boy?" Or, "Daaang, you don't got no booty at all!"

Latifa and I spent an afternoon on the swing. I even tried throwing *dang* around a couple times, saying, "Dang, I like swinging—dang." Or "Dang, I'm swinging fast—dang." And when it started to get dark, I climbed into the house exhausted from fun.

But the next day, Latifa came back with Jason, Nay-Nay, Dorina, and three new kids. They immediately made it clear "my turn" was never again, and they found every way possible to turn a swing into a weapon. First they invented "swing bombing" where one person hurls the swing at a *friend*, causing them to bruise or fall over. And then they changed the game to twisting the rope up as tight as possible, and everybody piling on the swing and releasing it to let it spin. They spun at a nauseating speed while simultaneously trying to throw each other off onto the sidewalk. Then they would laugh and wipe their wounds and get back on to go another round. Nay-Nay pushed Jason so hard that with the added centrifugal force of the swing, he cleared the parking strip and landed in the street. "Dang!" he said. "I just got my hair cut!" Then he grabbed her by her shirt and tackled her to the ground. I stared as Jason and Nay-Nay took turns smushing each other's head into the parking strip. That is, until Jason looked up at me and said plainly, "What are you looking at, whitey?" And I answered his question by running into the house.

That was when Anora, my three-year-old sister, tottered out the front door, consumed with excitement, and began crawling down the front steps feetfirst as fast as she could. She was wearing a striped T-shirt and her curly dark hair was pulled in a ponytail over her head like Pebbles from *The Flintstones*. And, having cleared the stairs, she instinctively moved to the center of the action like a tank. Her blue eyes were ecstatic. I watched her from the dining room window, afraid that she would get hurt or banished or made fun of. But she just stood next to Dorina clapping her hands together, laughing, "Again! Go again!" In fact, she was being so adorable that Latifa walked over to her from the opposite side of the swing to try to help her up onto the swing. But Anora just screamed and hit Latifa's arm. And rather than getting angry, Latifa begged Anora to let her pick her up. And watching the scene in front of me I couldn't figure out how Anora was a sister and I wasn't, but she was my sister. And then Mom got home.

Her expression was already frustrated as she pulled her car up to a gang of rowdy kids playing king of the mountain on my tire swing. And as she parked, her face went from frustrated to frightening. She got out of the car, glared at the kids, and silently picked up my little sister as she marched into the house. She set my sister down in the dining room before she walked up to Dad.

"John, what's going on outside?" she asked.

"Oh . . . that's Mishna's tire swing," he replied, not looking up from his paper.

"How is it Mishna's?"

"Well, damn," Dad said. "It's not my fault that she's up in here!"

"John, those kids have taken over our front yard!" Mom was usually afraid of Dad, but the fact that he was still reading emboldened her. "Is that your idea of helping Mishna?"

"Listen," Dad said, "the girl needs to learn how to fight for her shit."

"There are six of them," Mom said. "And they are twice as big as her."

Dad looked up from the paper finally—to make a point— and said, "Yeah . . . that's how life is." And with that, Mom walked out the door, grabbed a saw from the garage, marched through the gang of kids, and cut down the tire swing. I guess she didn't care about popularity as much as Dad did.

This wasn't bad news to me. It meant the next day I got to stay in the house with my daddy, which was all I had wanted to do in the first place. And while Dad and his main crew sat and played dominoes, I tried to make myself as small and fly-on-the-wallish as possible, while still pretending like I was one of them. When beers were passed around, I shook my head as though I were declining their invitation. When they picked their dominoes, I was always, "Just sitting this one out." And when they yelled about football or politics, I scratched my chin as though they had a good point, but was still forming my opinion. There was also a lot of yelling at Dad for cheating.

Everyone knew Dad cheated whenever he could. He was a cheating machine—cheating at everything from cards to Candyland. And Eldridge, a huge caramel-colored man from Texas, was the loudest in the group—which made it his job to catch Dad cheating. That day he decided that the best way to get my dad to play an honest game was to teach me how to play dominoes. As he said, "No self-respecting father would cheat in front of his own daughter. So we just got to educate you!" So as the day went on, Eldridge showed me how he was playing, and how the points were counted. And when he wasn't teaching me, he watched Dad like a hawk.

But I wanted to apply some of this learning.

"Dad?" I asked "What if I just played one game with you guys?"

"You just sit there and be seen," he said, meaning, "not heard." And I shut my mouth. That is until a few minutes later when Dad made a questionable shuffling move.

Eldridge stood up and shook his finger, shouting, "Oh no, John! No way!" Then he turned to me. "Lil' girl Wolff, you saw that shit! You had to—you's right there." He got in my dad's face again with the finger. "You were done shuffling and you picked up some dominoes, decided you didn't like 'em and put 'em back in the pile like you was still shuffling!" He gestured to me. "Even your girl saw it! Shame on you!"

My dad retorted, "Eldridge! You trippin'!" Then threw up his hands like this was taking too long and said, "I thought we were playing some dominoes."

Eldridge turned to me again. "Lil' girl Wolff! Lil' Wolff! Did you, or did you not see your father pick those dominoes up, decide he didn't like them, and then put them back in the deck like he was still shuffling?" Then he said softly, like it was paining him, "Oh, your daddy cheats. He cheats so badly." He shook his head and looked at my dad again, but this time like he was worried about him and said, "When you go to church you oughta beg the Lord to forgive you for cheating."

"Are you done with your little performance, so we can play the game?" Dad said.

"No. I am not done," Eldridge said, turning to me, "So, lil' Wolff girl, did you see your daddy cheat?" He lowered himself so he was looking right into my eyes and said, "Jesus is watching."

Dad glared at me across the table—he might as well have been sitting there actually opening a can of whoop-ass. It was Jesus or a can of whoop-ass, and I didn't want to be one of the guys anymore. I wanted to take my chances with Nay-Nay.

"I didn't see anything," I said.

"See," my dad said to Eldridge. "You got nothing." Then he turned to me and said, "Mishna, why don't you come up here, play this round."

"Play dominoes with you guys?" I asked.

"Well, you know how," he said, and pulled up a chair next to him, which was the coolest thing that had ever happened to me.

I got my own dominoes and was playing at the table right along with the guys and my dad. I had died and gone to heaven. And I sat with the fellas, thinking, "Yeah, this feels right. Playing a game with friends—eating peanuts . . . I wish Nay-Nay could see me now."

Dad even gave me a few swigs of his beer—and I knew he was proud. I mean, these weren't the sister friends he had wanted me to have, these were better, these were his friends. And as I scored my points, I let my mind wander from the game to a fantasy of my dad taking me out for ice cream. He'd muss my hair and say, "You know I didn't think you were cool for a while . . . BOY WAS I WRONG! You are so fun and good at dominoes!"

But the tone changed when Big Lyman showed up, and the fellas started pulling out their money. My dad pushed my chair away from the table and said, "You need to sit this one out."

"Why can't I play?" I asked.

My dad rubbed his chin, trying to find a way to exclude me without having to have, "The Gambling Talk." But Eldridge took up the parenting slack, saying to me plainly, "You can't play, lil' Wolff, because you don't have any money."

"I have my piggy bank."

To which Reggie said, "Shoot, then, let her play."

But Dad wasn't having it. So instead of just sitting and watching idly, I decided to make myself useful and help my dad out by telling him what dominoes I would play if I was him. I saddled up beside him and surveyed the lay of the table before whispering in his ear, "Dad, play the one with the three and the five." I wanted all the other guys to be jealous, that they didn't have the same secret weapon as my dad.

But I guess I wasn't as quiet as I thought, because Reggie Dee turned to Big Lyman and said, "I heard that! John got a five!" Then he repeated himself, "I said, John got a five . . . sho' as a black man has dick!"

My dad's face soured, and he pointed angrily at the door. "Mishna, downstairs." And I slumped out down to my room.

From downstairs I could hear an argument start. There was shouting and banging. I wondered what was going on up there and if there was another version of dominoes with tackling. I sat on the floor of my room for the half hour while they were yelling, and I did some pretty bitchin' coloring. And when I heard Reggie's and Big Lyman's cars pull away, I switched to playing with Speak & Spell.

When I headed up later, one of the dining room chairs was broken and lying on the floor. And as I walked through the living room into the hallway, I heard Dad's voice.

"Mishna." I turned the corner and found my dad perched on the edge of his waterbed.

"Am I in trouble still?"

Dad and his buddy engrossed in a game of dominoes.

"No. I want to show you something," he said, and reached into the drawer underneath the bed.

"What?" I asked as Dad produced a shiny revolver.

He held it in his hand about one foot away from me. "Do you know what this is?"

"A gun?" I asked.

"Yes, it is a gun," he said, holding it up. "It's a three-fifty-seven Magnum."

"Oh," I said, a little intimidated.

"This is here for protection," my dad said. "It's always in the house and it's always loaded, you got that?" He put it in my hands and I had to fight the urge to drop it.

"Yes . . . But why is it loaded?" I asked. "Isn't that danger-ous?"

"It's dangerous to have an *un*loaded gun in the house," Dad said. "When you pick this gun up, it better be loaded and you better be ready to use it."

"I'm six," I said.

"I'm just saying it's not a toy."

"It doesn't look like a toy," I said.

"And know . . . if you pick up this gun and point it at someone"—Dad looked at me intensely—"you have to kill them."

"Couldn't I just shoot them in the leg or something?"

"No," Dad explained very analytically, "because now they're shot and they're angry, and they'll have a lot of adrenaline, which can overcome a busted leg, you know?"

It was then that Mom walked in, asking about the broken chair. She looked at me standing across from my dad. And when she saw the gun in his hand she turned whiter.

My dad saw this and smiled. "I was just showing—"

"I knew the girls were going to find the gun."

"She didn't find it," Dad said. "I was just showing it to her." For some reason this calmed Mom down a little. He continued, "I was just explaining that it's not a toy."

"Go play outside, please," Mom said to me.

"What's your problem now?" Dad shot back at her.

I circled the block three times, thinking about what a fun, exciting day it had been. And when I came back around the third time, there was Latifa. She was playing hopscotch by herself and I could not have been happier to see her alone and playing a game I knew.

"You want me to play with you?" I asked.

"Yes," she said, smiling. I took the key from around my neck to use as a marker. I was about to throw it down when Latifa shook her head and motioned to her mother, who was walking out onto the porch above the steps, carefully surveying our interaction. Her mom saw me with the marker in my hand and decided to stay outside. She took a seat in a padded metal chair, watching the two of us carefully.

"Um . . . you better go," Latifa said apologetically. But I just looked at Latifa, confused. She had a nervous look on her face and I followed it up to her mother, who had her arms folded and her lips pursed at me. When I looked questioningly at her mother, she looked away, avoiding eye contact—her disapproving face said it all. I was to go. As I walked away, the blood rushing to my cheeks, I finally realized what they meant by *whitey*.

One

I'M IN A CAPPIN' MOOD

I KNOW DIVORCE is supposed to be hard on kids, but when my parents finally did it, it wasn't really that hard on me. They were so mismatched that the year before they got divorced, I often wondered if Dad met Mom by mistakenly wandering into a poetry reading thinking it was a Parliament concert. Dad was cool. Mom was Mom. They were both attractive, but other than that, they didn't really make much sense. Their differences became louder every day. So when my mom didn't come home one night, my first thought was, "I hope Dad's new apartment has an elevator!" I was only seven, but I already knew how divorce worked. Dad moved out and got a cool apartment with a pool. We lived with Mom, of course—it was the mid-eighties and moms always got the kids. But we'd visit Dad on weekends, swim in his pool, and he'd buy us lots of stuff to make sure we still loved him. He would be there just to make sure that we were growing up to be cool, going to enough parties and dressing right. There would be two birthdays and two Christmases. And maybe Mom would move to a new neighborhood, and I would have new neighbors who liked me. Plus, if I was lucky, one of them might have a telescope.

But things didn't quite work out that way. Dad really wanted us with him. And Mom apparently had some "work" to do on herself—which meant she needed to cut her hair and cry a lot. She started dating a Jewish guy in Mensa, who also drove a bus and had "depression." And, since she worked full-time, and Dad had always taken care of us during the day, they decided Mom should be the weekend dad with the apartment.

The process happened so quickly that I didn't even get a vote on where I was gonna live. There was supposed to be a judge, like in the movies, who would take me and my sister into his chambers. Then he would clear all of the adults out of the room so no one's feelings would get hurt, offer us a Werther's Original, lean back in his chair, and say, "Okay, now level with me. . . . Who do you like better?" At which point I would say, "Mom." Not because I liked her better, but because I knew I was cool enough for Mom. And I felt that not being quite good enough for Dad might cause problems down the road—like I'd cramp his style and maybe he'd decide to leave me at a party. Of course, I assumed everyone wanted my little sister Anora—she was adorable. But when I asked Mom and Dad about the judge and the missing courtroom battle I was told that that sort of thing was for rich people and that normal people didn't ask their kids what they wanted.

The terms of the divorce finalized, Dad announced he was giving me an allowance. I had to take care of my sister, meaning quieting her when she got hysterical and keeping her from wandering off in public places. And for that I got a dollar a week, which was totally a fortune because I measured it in Now and Laters. Then my dad promptly got a summer job doing construction to "show that bitch," which left my sister and me without daily supervision. "Not to worry," Dad said. "You guys are going to Government Subsidized Charity Club." Which sounded really awesome—like the Mickey Mouse Club or the Nancy Drew Fan Club.

Okay, the place wasn't actually called "Government Subsidized Charity Club," but for now let's call it that, or GSCC for short. Our first day at GSCC, we all climbed into Dad's truck and drove down M. L. King, arriving at the side entrance of a building that was clearly used for something else. We walked up a rickety stairway to a side door and entered a dingy vestibule, where a counselor sat at a table picking lead paint off it. She had a clipboard and two jump ropes—which, combined with the two kick balls—brought the total number of toys in the facility up to four. In addition to the lack of toys, the entire place smelled like pee and cigarettes. I would not have been surprised to find out it was used as a low-bottom halfway house the rest of the year, and that every summer they kicked out people named Gimpy Carl and Staph-man McGee to make room for day camp. I peered from the entryway into a main playroom full of kids, and surprise! My sister and I were the only white kids there. I was also, from what I could see, the skinniest kid—in boxing, that's what they refer to as "shit odds." It was then I decided that either Dad was cheap or we were just stopping by on the way to the real day camp.

"Well," Dad said, signing a clipboard and cementing that we were, in fact, in the right place. "Looks like you guys are good to go." I guess by "good to go," he meant that we weren't standing on broken glass. But I smiled weakly, and I think he sensed my apprehension, because he got down on one knee, straightened my overalls, looked me right in the eye, and said, "Just, don't take any shit," before walking out the door.

We were then led into the playroom, and other than the counselor who had checked us in, there was not an adult in sight. I quickly got out of the way as two bigger kids threw the red rubber balls at a younger kid's head—some sort of two-on-one dodgeball. In the far corner there was a group of girls who were probably around nine, but looked like they were about sixteen. They laughed as they looked at a boy four feet away who was sitting on the ground crying. I decided to avoid eye contact and found a pole near the far side of the room to lean against. That's when I realized—everyone was staring at me.

I heard a wail from across the room that was directed at me, but loud enough to grab everyone's attention: "W'sup, marshmallow turd!"

I turned and saw it was coming from Caprice, a girl whose mother had braided half her head and then, I guess, moved on to something else.

"Nothing," I said, and went to grab my little sister's hand and lead her out of harm's way—thinking of my allowance. That's when I realized Anora was gone. Probably looking for something dirty or poisonous to put in her mouth. I was all alone and being surrounded. The boys with the kick balls, the girls from the corner—everyone closed in on me as Caprice walked over and got in my face.

"Nothing? Is that what you said, Wonder Bread?" Caprice put a hand on her hip. "You look like your mama's on welfare!" I desperately wanted to point out that that was like the pot calling the kettle white, but my lips had sealed themselves together with some sort of pussy glue.

Then a nine-year-old boy with an earring chimed in, "She's so white, we got to wear shades inside." And the group of kids that had been gathering started laughing like it was the funniest thing anyone had ever said. That's when I found my sister. She was next to another girl her age, laughing herself to death. It was around this time I began to seriously question my father's wisdom in sending us to this particular child-care facility.

At around noon, lunch arrived, which brought the promise of some order to the day. I took my government-issued sack lunch out of the cardboard box and took stock. The brown bag contained: a bologna-and-American-cheese sandwich that was smushed into a weird shape in transport, a fruit that was mutantly small—but big enough to smush a bologna-and-American-cheese sandwich—a bag of chips, and a milk—condiments on the side. It didn't seem so bad, but I didn't realize at the time that I would be eating it almost every summer for the rest of my life.

My sister sat with a girl her age, and as much as I wanted the company, I wasn't up for begging my little sister to let me hang with her. So I sat down in a corner behind a pole and began to eat my sandwich. I had just started on my sandwich when I got hit with what can only be described as an "arcing rope" of mayonnaise. I looked up and the boy with the earring was doubled over—pointing to my goo-covered face and shirt. And as I wiped mayonnaise off my cheek with a napkin, the boy with the earring threw the empty packet at me and said, "There you go, mayonnaise!" Then he proceeded to bend over and take my chips—the only part of the lunch that didn't taste like refrigerator.

Over the course of our first day at GSCC, my sister made two friends, and I managed to crawl into my skin, the way one does when experiencing third-degree burns. And when my father came to pick us up, I could no longer use words. I grunted hello to him, and got in his pickup. It didn't help that he was an hour and a half late, which meant that we were stuck waiting with the impatient counselor—and Darnell, the kid who smelled like pee.

On the ride home, my sister and I shared the passenger-side safety belt, which meant that I couldn't ignore her as she excitedly recapped the day's events to our dad.

"I have two new friends, Dad!" Anora said proudly. "Gitana and Rene. Rene and I made Chinese jacks and Gitana wants to do my hair."

"That's great, baby," Dad said. "What about you, Mishna? You meet some folks?" But before I could say, "No, Dad. People hate me. Why would you send me to that evil lair of cruelty and injustice?" my sister was chiming in.

"Mishna met some people." Then she laughed. "She got roasted." Dad looked at me disappointed, and he could see it in my face—I did get roasted.

"Mishna," Dad said. "You can't let people disrespect you. Get in people's face. Be like, 'Don't mess with me!' Remember, you're my daughter. Throw an elbow if you have to."

"Okay, Dad," I said. But what I was thinking was, *I know what he's telling me to do, but how come it's so hard for me to do it?*

I had to admit to myself that I wasn't the most articulate kid. In fact, if I needed to express myself, I had learned that my best bet was to break something and hurt myself to get my point across. Hurting myself was like my sign language. For example: Breaking glass and getting cut meant, "I strongly disagree." And hitting the wall until I broke a knuckle meant, "You have a point, but you aren't seeing the whole picture." And curling up into a ball in the fetal position and crying meant, "This isn't over."

But none of these devices seemed to work at GSCC. When I hit the wall with my fist because someone said my mother was so bucktoothed that she could eat corn on the cob through a fence—everyone just laughed at me more. Plus, the counselors got pissed at me for making them find the first-aid kit. So, I was defenseless and mute the rest of the week at Government Subsidized Charity Club.

And that week was hell. My whiteness was the butt of every joke. And with every public humiliation I became more sensitive, not less. So, as a last resort, I tried to avoid everyone. If someone looked at me, I moved out of their field of vision as quickly as possible. If someone looked like they were about to talk to me, I walked away. And at every opportunity, I found nooks to crawl into and places to hide. After a day or so of avoiding all human contact, I started to think of myself as stealthness itself, like a phantom lurking through the shadows—or better yet, like a ninja.

I had just settled into a broom closet with, *Are You There God? It's Me, Margaret* when one of the counselors flung the closet door open and stood angrily above me, tapping her foot.

"What's wrong? What are you doing reading in here all by yourself?"

"I'm really comfortable in here, if you just want to close the door."

But instead she said, "No! What you need to do, is you need to go join the rest of the kids!" I popped my head out of the closet and looked across the room. Rodney, an obese child, was setting his friend's jeans on fire. While Jamal, the boy with the earring, pointed out that a younger boy had a crooked dick.

"Please can I stay here?" I asked.

The counselor said without hesitation, "I can't watch you in no closet!"

But I just sat there unable to move, hoping she would change her mind and let me stay. I put on my most imploring face, but she just started looking at her nails. I tried opening my book again, and she cleared her throat and rolled her eyes. And while she looked at me impatiently, I slinked out of the closet and joined the rest of the kids.

Jamal welcomed me with a "skitch" to the back of the head. That's basically like hitting someone in the back of the head, but you graze it. So to the untrained adult eye, it looks playful.

Then Caprice belted out, "Her ass is so flat, it looks like two saltine crackers that done lost they box!" Kids cackled and pointed and grabbed their chins and said, "Cap" and "Roast."

"What are they doing?" I asked Darnell, because his pee smell made him accessible to me.

"Well," Darnell said. "You just got capped on. That roast is 'cause you're roasted."

"Capped on?" I asked. But I was too low on the totem pole for even the pee-kid to talk to me for very long.

He just said, "Yeah," as he walked away.

And so, I found out that day that what was happening to me was called, "getting capped on." And it wasn't about the intelligence of the insult. Caprice and Jamal were not particularly clever, but they had confidence and could work a crowd like Marc Antony. The one who needed to borrow some ears.

I became immediately fascinated with Caprice and Jamal's fearlessness. When I looked at capping as a skill, it was completely foreign and exciting to me. In fact, half the time, the caps didn't even make sense. Caprice came up to me on the side porch that day and said, "You look like a broke-down Teddy Ruxpin." And even though I didn't get it, people laughed. I wanted that kind of confidence. And later that day when Jamal said I was "a powdered dooky doughnut," a voice rang out clear as a bell in my head: *Hey, I'm funnier than this guy!*

I had no idea where the voice had come from, since I had never even told a joke. But the voice was uncanny, and for whatever reason, I believed it.

So for that next week at GSCC, I got taken down over and over again by their caps. But at night, I practiced capping like an upstart fighter training for a championship. I had seen that movie *Rocky* and I fancied myself kind of like Rocky, if he could talk. I practiced in the mirror, trying to place my hand on my hip just so, while rolling my neck for emphasis. I tried snapping in a *Z*. I tried closing my eyes and waving my hand in the air. And I tried every possible ending for a sentence that starts out: "Your mama."

The next Monday morning, as my sister joined her friends Gitana and Rene jumping rope. I walked into the playroom with my usual apprehension and took a seat on the floor with my copy of *Highlights*, Jamal, the earring-wearing terror, saw me from across the room and headed toward me with a self-satisfied look on his face. Caprice and posse followed closely behind him, as Jamal swaggered up to me and said with a smirk, "Morning, Mush-na."

The other kids laughed and said, "Ooooh," which hardly seemed called for. But it baited Caprice to one-up him.

"Look at her," Caprice said. "She's such a cracker, if she has a bowl of soup she dunks herself."

The crowd ate it up, and in an attempt to soak up some of Caprice's laughs, Jamal repeated her punch line as though he had come up with it. "She dunks herself!" The desired result was achieved—the attention returned to Jamal.

What happened next was one of the most magical moments of my entire life. I remember turning to Jamal and the words coming out of my mouth as if in slow motion: "*Am I being talked to by a burnt chocolate chip cookie?*" I had the neck roll and everything.

The cap came out of my mouth before I thought it through and was an amalgamation of things I had heard around, so it surprised me when a girl named Myvette shouted, "It's true! He dark!" And I realized I had just told a "He's-so-black joke."

The crowd was surprised and started roaring, and so I decided to push my luck. I took a second to regroup before striking again—this time at Caprice. I put my hand on my hip and said, "Your mama's so lazy, Jesus will come back before she finishes your hair!"

The laughs of the excited kids washed over me like manna. They grabbed their chins and cried "Cap!" and "Roast!" They pointed at Jamal and Caprice. Then something happened that I hadn't expected—something wonderful. Rodney slapped me five! Even with a messed-up knuckle it felt good.

That summer I learned Uno, and Chinese jump rope, and Chinese checkers, and Chinese jacks and double Dutch. I

learned hand-slapping chants that had the N-word in them—I
had no idea what I was saying. Like "Downtown Baby," which
was totally inappropriate for me to be chanting, but none of us
knew that. I went through the various hand slaps and acted out
gestures with Caprice and Gitana chanting along with them:

> *Downtown baby—down by the roller coaster* (roller coaster
>   with your hand)
> *Sweet sweet baby—I'll never let you go* (hugging yourself)
> *Just because I kiss you—don't mean I love you so*
> *I like coffee—I like tea*
> *I like the colored boy—and he likes me*
> *I say, Hey, white boy!—if you ain't shy*
> *Call me a n***** and I'll beat your behind!*

I also learned that if I wanted friends, picking up bugs was
a no-no. And I got better at capping every day. I was pretty
good for a white girl. But there were other cappers who were
better than me, for sure. At night I would lie in the top bunk
of my room and fantasize.

*Maybe if I come back every summer and really practice capping . . .
maybe one day, I could be the best.* Then it hit me, *Maybe I could
even find a way to cap for a living?* That seemed too good to be
true, so I second-guessed my own fantasy. *Nah . . . I'll just stick
with being an anesthesiologist,* I thought as I lay in bed sniffing my
Mr. Sketch markers. *Or a Solid Gold Dancer. Yeah, like the pretty
white one with the crimped hair.* I threw my head against my pillow as I contemplated my preferred order of things I wanted to
be when I grew up:

Solid Gold Dancer
Capper

Anesthesiologist

Governor (presidents have a tendency to get shot)

Assassin (someone needs to do all that shooting)

About halfway through the summer we started to have visits with our mother. I saw this down time as an opportunity to take my capping to the next level. Mom had moved into the top floor of the house of a solar architect and his family, and she was a Buddhist now—it was "part of her process."

So when we got to her house and checked out our room, I told her, "You ain't no Buddhist, you're a booty-ist."

"What did you say?" she asked.

To which I replied, "You're so dumb, you thought Buddhism was about booty." It wasn't one of my finer moments, but Anora laughed.

"What's going on?" she asked Anora.

My sister smiled and rolled around on her bed and said, "Mishna capped on you."

That was when Mom bent over, looked me right in the eye, and said in a very sincere voice, "I really don't like being capped on. It hurts my feelings." Hippies have a way of sucking the fun out of everything.

I couldn't really cap on my father, either. He was happy that I was getting along at GSCC, but my few attempts at capping on my father (the six-foot-four, two-hundred-pound ex-linebacker) were experiments in fear.

One day after day camp, I had swaggered up to him on the sofa where he was outfitting the broken TV knob with an adjustable wrench, and said, "You're so ugly, the itsy bitsy spider saw you at the other end of the water spout and decided to take his chances with the rain." That was when he pinched me in a place between my neck and shoulder, like a Vulcan, until I went limp.

But I assumed that the reason he Vulcan-neck-pinched me

was because the cap wasn't very good. So next day, I decided to make fun of his head shape, with a surefire winner I had stolen from Rodney. Dad, however, didn't laugh or high-five me. In fact, he didn't react at all. He just quietly grabbed some nuts from the nut bowl and began cracking them with his bare hands. He did this in silence for a while, looking me right in the eye before saying, "I'm not about to take it from my daughter in my own home. . . . I take it from the Man every day."

"Okay," I said.

Then his voice got really low and he grabbed my chin in order to look at me in the eye and said, "This shit stops here."

Which I assumed meant, "Go pick on your sister."

My sister endured all kinds of verbal abuse from me during this time. It didn't even bother me that "your mama" jokes directed at my little sister were "my mama" jokes. And I used her as a sounding board for all my new caps. I found I could measure the effectiveness of the put-down by how berserk she went. She would sit watching TV, and I would walk into the living room and make some declaration about how smelly she was or how much the ugly stick liked her. If she glared at me and went back to the TV, it meant the cap needed tweaking. If I got her to yell at me or throw something, I was definitely on to something. And if she whirled her arms, in a move that could best be described as "the windmill" and clubbed me about the head in a flurry of blind rage—I had a winner. I didn't hit back, though. Hitting her back meant facing Dad and the five fingers of death. So I happily took the licks as payment due for her allowing me to use her as a focus group.

Every day at GSCC Club I learned something new. Like Caprice taught me that throwing *psych!* on the end of a flattering comment was an awesome way to make a fool out of someone.

You could walk up to any unsuspecting person and say, "Nice shirt . . . PSYCH!" It was cheap, but it was almost more effective than a straight cap, because you couldn't brace yourself for it. The only way to brace yourself for a *psych!* was to already think you were a piece of shit—which, if you did, you were capping at a Jedi level. *Faggot* was also en mode, thanks in part to Eddie Murphy. None of us knew what a faggot was, but it rolled off the tongue like butter, and I used it as a comma.

When the end of day camp came, I found myself a little sad. I was really gonna miss everyone, especially Caprice, who had made me a very pretty Chinese jack as part of an alliance against Jamal. I thought it would be nice if just once all her hair was done, but I didn't have the skills to finish it, so I drew her a picture of Jamal with breasts.

The counselors announced that, for the last day of camp, we were required to do a performance for all of the parents. They suggested a song and dance number about our experience at Government Subsidized Charity Club. Which was strange, because all we did all summer was sit in a dank room and make fun of each other while they sat in an office and handed out the occasional kick ball. So, the number we wrote was called "I'm in a Cappin' Mood." We sat in a circle with a small Casio keyboard that someone had brought in, and wrote caps for ourselves to the prerecorded beats. Jamal and Caprice wrote for the younger kids like Anora, Gitana, and Rene, who couldn't write their own caps.

The night of the show we stood in a line on a makeshift stage, swaying back and forth as we sang the chorus;

I'm in a cappin' mood (clap, clap)
I'm in a cappin' mood (clap)

Then one by one we stepped downstage to deliver our own personal cap.

Jamal, who was standing next to me, was first. The room was filled with the twenty or so parents who had bothered to show up on the last day of camp. They watched patiently, knowing that it was penance for the months of almost free child care. Jamal fearlessly stepped forward and stayed on beat as he committed to the delivery of his cap.

Keep your shoes on
If you don't mind,
'Cause your feet smell like
A cow's behind.

Then the whole group did the chorus.

I'm in a cappin' mood (clap, clap)
I'm in a cappin' mood (clap)

My turn. I felt my stomach turn into knots as I stepped in front of the row of kids trying to keep the beat with my rhythmless body, while I delivered my cap.

You're so poor.
It's really sad.
I was at the junkyard.
And I bought your dad.

I got a laugh and it felt like coming home.

Through the rest of the performance I joined in on the chorus and watched the rest of the caps, thinking that they didn't quite measure up to the caliber of mine. And when we were all finished, the parents seemed truly impressed. But I was most excited for Dad to see how down I was, and how many sister friends I had made. And when I left the stage he smiled and said good job. Then he walked me over to meet Jamal's mom, who had huge breasts and very red lips—both of which Dad liked. Jamal's mom proceeded to tell me how great I was—and she was right.

Dad agreed with her, but then added, "Yeah, but I'll tell you one thing. You cap on me . . . you better not cap on me, 'cause I'll go upside your ass." But then he laughed at his own joke, so I knew it was just something he said so that I didn't get too big for my britches.

"Well, call me sometime," Jamal's mom said, writing something on a piece of paper and handing it to Dad. Dad wrote something on the other side of the same piece of paper and handed it back to her, "No, you call me."

And as we walked away, my dad said smiling, "She don't gotta know that the phone's off." We had missed a phone bill and gotten disconnected, meaning incoming calls only. I smiled back. The night just couldn't get any cooler.

As we drove home, Anora was bouncing in her seat and Dad was humming the chorus to, "I'm in a Cappin' Mood." And when we rolled onto our street, I saw the kids on the corner— Jason, Nay-Nay, and Latifa. And something had changed in the way they looked. Like somehow they seemed less intimidating, and much less cool to me. If I were to jump out of the car at that moment, I wouldn't be scared—I would be doing them a favor. And there was a new freedom in the air. In fact, I knew that I would never be afraid of them again—because I had the power of the cap!

Two

TEN-FOOT DROP

"GET DRESSED, we have people coming over," Dad said.

"Who?" I asked without looking up from the TV. I was still in my pajamas at eleven o'clock and had every intention of remaining that way until after my stories. GSCC had ended, but we still had a month left of summer vacation before school, which meant I had just enough time to catch up on *Days of Our Lives* and *Another World*. And by catch up, I meant on the outfits, not the story. I only watched soap operas for the style.

"What about breakfast?" Anora asked. She was sitting next to me, holding my old stuffed Snoopy doll.

"I don't know what you're talking about," Dad said. "It's almost lunch."

"I want breakfast!" Anora said, getting upset. "Then we can have lunch!"

"Shhh," I said, rubbing my sister's arm to earn my allowance. She calmed down a little bit.

"Who's coming over?" I asked.

"Big Lyman and his kids," Dad replied.

"Big Lyman has kids?" Anora asked.

"That's what I said," Dad said, walking up to the TV and turning it off—right as Kaylah, of *Days* fame, walked onscreen wearing the most amazing pink rayon overall-dress with shoulder pads.

"Why is Big Lyman coming?"

"We are gonna remodel! He's gonna watch over shit 'cause he's an engineer." I didn't know that word and rather than ask, I tried to decipher what that meant. *Remodel: to model again.* Yes, that sounded right.

"I'm hungry!" Anora said.

"Shhh," I said, feeling hungry myself. "We'll get some food in a little bit. . . . Right, Dad?"

"Yeah!" he said. "Don't you always get fed sooner or later?" *Later* was the answer to that one.

"Were they Big Lyman's kids before?" my sister asked.

"Yes," Dad said. "They was always Big Lyman's kids."

"But how come we never met them?" I asked. "Where were they before?"

And Dad said, as though it explained everything, "Texas."

An hour later Big Lyman arrived. His hair had its usual Don King vibe and his tawny skin had summer freckles as he ushered his two kids, Little Lyman and Zwena, into our kitchen. That's when he explained to Dad that they had been living with their mom, but with the event of his marriage to a woman named Lordess, Big Lyman wanted them all to be a family.

Big Lyman stood at the counter, talking loudly while absentmindedly tapping a Newport from his pack, unaware that every time he moved, his five-year-old son, Little Lyman, who was hiding behind his leg, had to reposition himself. From what I could see of him, he was much darker than his father and, when he wasn't hiding, his huge eyes were trained on Anora.

Meanwhile Big Lyman's daughter, Zwena, fearlessly struck up a conversation with me. Zwena was three years older than me and was light-skinned like her father but without freckles. She wore plastic glasses that slid down her nose and she seemed to have some sort of nasal problem that manifested itself in a runny nose, a nasally voice, and a hand I didn't want to shake. Because of that, she was a mouth breather, and watching her I noticed there was a crust in the corners of her mouth that she didn't seem too concerned with removing. She was also the unfortunate combination of sickly and energetic, which meant she would get so excited with whatever she was talking about, that she would run out of energy and have to take a second or two to recharge before she could finish her thought.

"We were on an airplane," she said, buddying up to me by starting a story in the doorway to the kitchen. "And it got a little bumpy, and there are these ladies that come out and serve you drinks that were running around, but the plane was really moving"—Zwena looked like she was gonna pop—"and the one lady fell on the other lady . . . and you know what the one lady said?" At this point Zwena ran out of air and started breathing in a way that begged the question: *Why doesn't this girl have an inhaler?*

It took Zwena about a minute to spit it out, and finally she whispered, breathing heavily through laughter, "Heifer."

"What's a heifer?" I asked. And she just threw her arms up, frustrated. But next to Zwena I actually looked cool, so I liked her right away. And Little Lyman was the same age as Anora, who was quickly able to coax him out from behind his father's leg by asking him, "Why you so scared of me?"

Within minutes of them arriving, the four of us had ditched the grown-ups and were outside sitting on Big Lyman's Ranchero. Zwena helped break the ice by asking us, "What if you won a million dollars?" And it was agreed that if we all were millionaires, we'd be spending a lot of time at McDonald's.

Then Dad and Big Lyman came outside and stood in the front yard looking at the house. As Dad pointed out various things around the yard, Big Lyman nodded and took the occasional drag off the Newport hanging from his long-nailed fingers.

I asked Zwena, "Does your dad ever cut his fingernails?"

"My dad cuts our fingernails," Anora said, whining. "It hurts."

I shared a look with Zwena—the "being a big sister is a tough job" look. And at that moment I hoped she would never leave our house and that she liked me as much as I liked her.

"I wonder what they're talking about," Zwena said, looking at Dad and Big Lyman above us in the yard. Then Zwena dared me to go see what they were talking about. Little Lyman reminded her that she had dared him to eat a rock, but I had never heard of daring.

"It's like, I bet you that you won't," Zwena explained.

Which surprisingly really made me want to do it. I ran up the front steps to where Dad and Lyman were in the raised yard.

"Dad?" I asked. "What are you guys talking about . . . modeling?"

"Can't you see we're in the middle of things?" he asked. "What's wrong with you?" He looked irate, and I wished I hadn't gotten all caught up in daring.

But Big Lyman got me off the hook by saying, "Hey, why don't you all go over to our house. I think Lordess is there, and we have a Slip 'n Slide."

We trekked the eight blocks from our place over to Big Lyman and Lordess's house—Zwena taking the lead. And the rest of the day was spent sliding on a sheet of clear plastic tarp that we wet with a hose. It worked just like a regular Slip 'n Slide but without the padding and a lot more bruising. But you could get a faster slide going and at the end of the day, that seemed more important than functioning hips.

While Zwena, Little Lyman, Anora, and I careened down the lawn toward the cement driveway, two kids from next door, Tre and Janella, watched us through the fence for a while, before changing into swimsuits and climbing over to join us. Tre and I instantly hit it off, because he was my age and we both liked candy. While Janella was so pushy that Zwena had to say, "Janella, you're not the boss of the Slip 'n Slide."

When the thrill of sliding wore off we all took turns prying the hose from each other and spraying everyone else while they ran screaming. There were so many fun things you could do with water. And when Little Lyman put the hose between his legs and said, "Look, I'm peeing!" I said he should be a comedian.

But when it was my turn with the hose, I sprayed Janella, and she freaked out. "Don't wet my hair!" she screamed, acting injured.

"But," I said, shaken, "we are playing with the hose. That's what you do."

I guessed that was the wrong thing to say, because Janella raised her voice instead of lowering it. "I just got my hair pressed this morning!" I nodded, but I thought pressing was something you did to a shirt. "So you best keep that hose away from my hair!"

I looked at Zwena, who said, "She did say she just got her hair pressed."

"Sorry," I said, "I'll be more careful." And dropped the hose, not wanting the awesome responsibility anymore. But the hose just jumped off the ground, spraying Zwena, Little Lyman, and Janella, who screamed like she was dying. I instinctively moved toward the other side of the yard.

"You best walk away, bitch!" Janella screamed.

"Ooooh," Anora said.

It sounded a lot like a cap. And being flanked by Zwena and Little Lyman emboldened me. I knew what I had to do.

I turned back to Janella and yelled, "You're so ugly, you saw yourself in the mirror and started barking!" Not very original, but I heard laughter coming from Zwena.

"Oh, burn," Zwena said, making Janella stomp her foot and pull on her little brother's arm saying, "Come on, Tre! Let's get away from this mixed-up, mixed-nuts group of white, black, yellow . . . who knows?" Then she climbed back over the fence to her house. Tre knew that being a little brother meant that he should follow after her, but he very politely came over and said good-bye to everyone and thanked them for the sliding, as though we had just finished a polo match.

That's when we realized how hungry we all were. Anora was still whining about breakfast even though it was four.

"Okay!" Zwena said. "We're funna go to the store."

"Cool," I said. "But, did you just say 'funna'?"

"Yeah," Zwena said. "It's like we're fixing to, but we're gonna. We're funna."

"Okay," I said. "We're funna go with you."

Zwena showed us how to look through all the sofa cushions and pants pockets to find loose change, explaining that it wasn't stealing so much as it was cleaning. We found enough money to hit the corner store and pick up some bologna and a box of Jiffy corn bread mix. Then Zwena amazed me by putting a batch of corn bread in the oven and then going to work frying some bologna. I couldn't believe she knew how to cook. She was only ten, but she put a pan on the stove, threw down the bologna in the pan, where it would puff up like a balloon. And she knew exactly when to flip it. She was like Julia Child for the food stamp set.

I headed home with Anora. I was full and still thinking

about how great Zwena was, when we turned the corner onto our street and noticed there was something going on in front of our house. A crowd of people had gathered, and orange cones blocked traffic. As I got closer I could see what all the commotion was about. Lyman, Reggie Dee, and Eldridge were watching Dad behind the wheel of the huge orange backhoe tearing our front yard out and putting it in a dump truck parked nearby. The rock garden my mother had worked on, the front steps—it was all being torn off and hauled away. I had no idea what he thought he was doing, but I had to stop him. I ran up to the backhoe and practically threw myself in front of it.

"Dad!" I screamed, but he couldn't hear me and just kept dumping dirt in the truck. He brought the claw back around, and that's when he saw me in front of what was left of the rock garden. He motioned for me to get out of the way, but I wasn't going anywhere. Finally he cut the engine.

"Get the hell out of the way!" he screamed.

"What are you doing to our house?" I asked.

"Remodeling!" he said, and then realizing I didn't understand, "I'm making it look better." There was dirt everywhere and a ten-foot drop from the front door.

"It doesn't look better!" I said.

"It's not finished!" he yelled. "Now, get out of the way!"

But I couldn't let him keep going. It looked like our front yard had been bombed. I sat down in the dirt, not completely unsure he wouldn't scoop me up with his next clawload.

Dad stood up and cut the engine and said, "Everyone take a little break." Then he climbed down the backhoe to stand next to me.

"Mishna. You gotta understand there's a project gonna happen here."

I folded my arms.

He bent down and explained, "We are building a second floor underneath." He pointed to the front door. "You see up there is where the deck will be, with stairs down to the street level." And he pointed to a corner area. "And over there is where your new room will be. It'll be done by the time you finish third grade."

"But," I said, "I liked the way the house looked before."

"Yes," Dad said. "But you don't know how good it's gonna look. Just wait and see." Then Dad bent over and dried my eyes.

"Can we have flowers again?" I asked. "Like the ones Mom planted?

"Pfft," he said, dissing her flowers. "Better flowers. Now, can I finish what I was doing?"

Then I watched him climb up the steps into the backhoe to continue fucking up our house.

The rest of the summer, I spent every day with Zwena, Little Lyman, and Anora. We were inseparable, and we almost never saw Big Lyman, Lordess, or Dad. We'd browse in Chubby and Tubby, the hardware store, till they kicked us out. Or sit on the overpass over Martin Luther King taunting passing motorists with rocks and middle fingers. We ate at Zwena's step-grandparents and we climbed fences to get everywhere, so I knew what everyone's backyard looked like and who had a pit bull. And on the days when I came home, our house had the same Fall-of-Berlin look it had the week before, just with new building materials in the yard. Once the cement was poured and Dad built some wooden steps up to the back door, nothing else really happened and all the materials just sat in the yard. And the front door remained where it was, suspended ten feet in the air.

When I brought Zwena and Little Lyman over, Zwena

said, "How do you get into your house?" And when I showed
Zwena the back steps she laughed, "Dang, your daddy ain't never
gonna finish your house!"

"That's not true!" I said defensively. "He's making a new
room for me that will be done by next year. He's probably
working on it right now!"

Then I led them into the house where Dad and Big Lyman
were sitting at the dining room table in front of three bottles of
hot sauce. They each had a beer and Big Lyman was laughing
hysterically as Dad cried and blew his nose.

"What are you guys doing?" I asked.

But Dad couldn't answer. He was bent over and his face
was flushed red as tears rolled down his cheeks. Lyman said
excitedly, "We're doing a hot sauce tasting. Went to China-
town today and bought some crazy shit."

I looked at the cryptic Asian labels on the jars and bottles
sitting in front of them. My father was still blowing his nose as
Lyman prepared a little hot bomb for himself.

"Is that stuff hot?" Anora asked.

Lyman said, "Let me put it this way . . . When was the last
time you saw your daddy cry?"

Dad regained his composure and his breath and said, "What
are you girls doing inside anyway?"

"I just wanted to show Zwena where my new room is
gonna be," I said.

"Nah, nah . . . It's not safe." This was from the guy that
had introduced me to bottle rockets. But I needed him to show
Zwena that the house was gonna be good.

"Can you just show us?" I pleaded. "We won't go in, we'll
just look."

"Not right now," Dad said. "We're busy."

He didn't look busy. He looked like he was giving himself
diarrhea.

"Why don't you go to Zwena's and Slip 'n stuff . . . Slide or whatever," he said.

I never should have gotten out of the way of that backhoe.

I was feeling bummed until Zwena suggested grits and hunger took over. She led the way back to her house, walking ahead while I lagged behind looking for lucky money on the sidewalk. Coming up the rear were Anora and Little Lyman—ten feet back holding hands. I looked up from what I thought might be a dime but turned out to be a wadded-up gum wrapper, and spied Janella in front of her house with two other girls. And the way the three of them looked at me gave me a bad feeling. But I passed them without incident and wrote off my bad feeling. Until they started whispering to each other, and that's when I got a *really* bad feeling. You know, the feeling you get when you realize you should have listened to that bad feeling. And I followed their stares to Tre running toward me from the side of their house at full speed.

He pushed me down and then darted a few feet away, taking a fighting stance. Janella and her friends surrounded Tre and me chanting, "Fight! Fight!" And I got excited, still not fully realizing I *was* the fight.

"Tre . . . I thought we were friends?" I said as he hit me in the ribs—not in a friendly way. But he didn't respond. Instead, he looked blankly ahead determined to avoid eye contact while he blindly swung at me. Anora and Lyman approached the small crowd while Tre continued punching me in my chest and head with more force than I would have expected. I was still bigger than boys my age, but judging by the pain in my ribs, I sure as hell wasn't stronger. The fighting finally made Anora cry, so on top of getting beat up, I was worried I wasn't earning my allowance. When I saw Zwena approach, I felt reassured.

But rather than defend me, Zwena coached me. "Hit him!"

she screamed. I made a lame attempt to swing at his head. "No, stomach!" she corrected me. Unfortunately I was already on the ground just trying to block as his fists rained down on my face. I squirmed out of his way and managed to wiggle back onto my feet. Then I took a swing at his face that actually connected. It hurt my hand and I was so stunned by the pain in my wrist that Tre got a square shot at my nose, sending me onto the ground. The fight was over.

The small crowd dispersed, leaving me alone and crying on the sidewalk. I watched Tre wipe his nose and march past his older sister and up into their house. My cheek was stinging and Anora was saying something to me, but all I could think was, *The sidewalk feels so nice and cool on my face.*

I rolled over onto my back and could feel the aching in my ribs. The white, white sky was quiet and peaceful, and I wanted to close my eyes and go to sleep right there on the street. Maybe because the blood rushed in my ears: *whoosh, whoosh, whoosh*—like a womb. Maybe I had a concussion. Either way, I liked the way I felt. I felt the serenity that comes when things can't get any worse.

Zwena walked up from where she had been standing a few yards away. She looked over me and said five words that made it worse: "That's a lot of blood."

I touched my nose. Sure enough—a lotta blood. Which meant Dad was gonna know I got my ass kicked.

When I got home, the blood had dried under my nose and my cheek was starting to bruise. I walked into the house and Dad looked excited. "Looks like you got into a disagreement."

I nodded.

"Did you let her know?" he asked.

I shook my head no and his smile faded. I corrected him, "It was a boy, and he won."

I watched Dad's face light up again. "My girl!" he said, picking me up in his arms. He was glad to see I was taking on boys and said that it would prepare me for dating. And for the next twenty minutes, he insisted on having me hit his fists and giving me fighting pointers like, "Move!"

Or, "Just keep moving and never stop."

Or, "You be everywhere and nowhere at the same time." And when he was done showing me his stance, we watched *Enter the Dragon* together—like grown-ups who get into fights.

As Bruce Lee coached a young student in the philosophy of fighting I asked, "Dad . . . when do you think the house will be done?"

"When I have the time and the money to finish it," Dad said.

"Oh," I said. "But it'll get done, right?"

"Of course it will," Dad said. "You just can't do it all at once.

I had to pay the lights this month . . . Watch and see what Bruce does to these six brothers with that stick!"

"Dad . . . ," I said, wanting to talk about the house more, but there was a knock at the door. And I went to get it.

When I opened the door, Tre was standing in the doorway. It was getting dark and I was worried that it was an ambush, but I figured, if he tried a sucker punch now, Dad would introduce him to the Vulcan neck grab.

"Hi, Tre," I said.

"Hey, Misushna," he said.

I didn't correct him.

"It took me a long time to figure out how you get up in your house."

"Yeah," I said, holding my cheek in an attempt to look lame and defenseless. "What are you here for?"

"Well, I just wanted to tell you I don't hate you." He continued, "I like playing with you. You are really fun and good at running, and clowning and junk."

"So why did you fight me?" I asked. But Tre was really upset and he started breathing hard like he was gonna cry.

"Janella. She said that if I didn't beat you up, she would beat me up."

"What?"

"I know. It's messed up," Tre said, actually crying now.

"It's okay," I said, feeling so sorry for him even though I could still smell my own blood in my nose. "Friends?"

"Okay . . . But not around my sister."

I returned my embarrassed hand to my side and said, trying to sound cool, "Yeah, okay . . . Well, I have to go watch Bruce Lee."

"Okay. But you should fix your front door," Tre said,

"Okay. Thank you," I said, and shut the door. And as I

returned to Dad and the movie, I kept thinking, *Why did I say thank you? I should have said fuck you.*

"Who was that?" Dad asked, still shadowboxing along with Bruce.

"The boy that fought me today, Tre."

"Did you let him know?" he asked.

"I didn't have to," I said. "He just left on his own."

"My girl!" my dad said. Then he looked at me for a moment. "Hey, you might want to grab some peas for your face."

Three

A LESSON-LEARNING MACHINE

ALL OF THE CAPPING I had done at the Government Subsidized Charity Club over the summer continued to pay off that fall at Kimball Elementary, my neighborhood school. It seemed third grade at Kimball consisted of capping or fighting, so I decided to major in capping and minor in fighting—knowing that I could switch it up later, should my left hook improve. My classes were crowded and rowdy, which meant I could use class time to come up with new caps. My teacher/warden, Mrs. Delgado, was a mean Filipina who thought *I* was retarded because *she* didn't understand sarcasm. Which was fine, because no one expected much from a retard. She stood at the front of the class writing down our spelling words while I sat in the back of the class thinking up fresh caps for recess. I covered my Pee Chee folder with notes on how fat the fat kid was, or how many times he was dropped on his head as a baby as I waited for the recess bell to signal one thing—it was on!

I was getting better at fighting, too. I wasn't strong, but I found that I was fast, which is important, especially in a running-away situation. And when all else failed, I had long nails that, when Dad didn't force-trim them, I filed into sharp points inspired by the X-Men character, Wolverine. And Fat Jehovah's Witness Naomi had given me beautiful cornrows with butterfly beads, which prevented easy access to pulling my hair. I was becoming a machine—or at least I thought I was. All I know is I had purpose:

1. Me ruling.
2. You sucking.

I had aspirations. I had goals. I had a lot of friends, and a lot of bruises.

About two months into the third grade Mom showed up one day to pick me up from school. Weird. I wasn't supposed to see her until that weekend, and in the afternoons she was supposed to be driving her bus, not picking me up at school. As I climbed into her car she said, "How would you like to go to Red Robin?" That was when I started to get a bad feeling. Red Robin was my favorite restaurant, so something was up.

"Sounds good," I said nervously, and I climbed into her VW beetle, "but um . . . what's going on?"

"Oh nothing much," she said. "I just thought we'd sit down and talk."

"Talk about what?" I asked.

"Well," she said. "Let's get some food and I'll tell you all about it."

I spent the rest of the car ride bracing myself for whatever "talk" inspired a trip for burgers. *Maybe we'll just talk about sex,* I thought. *Or maybe Grandma died.*

When we sat down in our booth and Mom said, "Just go ahead and order whatever you want," I almost wet my chair. Someone must have cancer.

As our waiter set down my strawberry and chocolate milk

shakes, Mom started, "Honey, I have felt for a long time that we could do better for your education, that you aren't really being challenged at Kimball."

That was crazy—I had many important challenges on the horizon. I couldn't get anyone into a headlock or anything. Secondly, what did that have to do with my cancer? And as I switched from chocolate to strawberry I told Mom, "You can tell me if it's bad news."

Mom stroked my face, which I liked a lot, and said, "No, I have good news, not bad news. Do you understand?" I decided to put my fears aside and hear what the woman had to say.

"Sweetie, you're moving schools!"

"What?" I asked. "Why?"

"Well," she said. "Remember all those tests you took?"

"No."

"At Marshall?" she reminded me.

"Oh yeah," I said. "Those were tests? You told me they were games!"

"Well," Mom said. "You tested very high, sweetie."

"I guessed on some questions. And I like my school."

"The program is called 'IPP.'"

"You want me to tell Zwena that I am going to pee-pee?"

"It stands for 'Individual Progress Program,'" she said.

"I don't care, it's embarrassing."

"Well, you're going." She said. "Your new school will be a chance for you to have experiences you wouldn't have at Kimball. Plus you'll meet new kids—all different kids, from *all different neighborhoods*."

"Listen," I said, knowing my mother was a reasonable woman, "I really think you have gotten the wrong impression of Kimball. I am learning sooooo much every day!" And when that failed I banged my fingers with the ketchup bottle.

But Mom brushed aside all disputes with one sentence: "Sweetie, I know you like Kimball, but I don't think you have what it takes to be a professional street fighter."

My mom was a sarcastic person. That's actually what led to the tests to get me into IPP. After my teacher tried to kick me out of kindergarten for sarcasm, Mom started taking me to get all these tests done—one a year for three years. I think it was her way of defending her personality. If I was sarcastic, I learned it from her. And while sarcasm being related to IQ is debatable, Mom felt it was now a fact. So, as I left my neighborhood school—my "behavioral problem" and "foul mouth" now a symptom of a frustrated genius (I preferred "wunderkind")—my mom couldn't get on the line fast enough to tell all my old teachers to go fuck themselves.

I, however, was inconsolable. I had just started to feel comfortable with the neighborhood kids and now I was moving. Plus there was Dad—I could tell by the way this was all going down that he wasn't happy with it. That night, when Mom dropped me home after Red Robin, he yelled at her and she got this tone in her voice like she was talking and getting electrolysis at the same time.

And when Dad came back in, he sat down next to me on the couch and said, "So . . . I guess your mom told you 'bout them tests." I told my dad how nervous I was to go to a whole new school where I didn't have friends like I did at Kimball.

"Well . . . ," Dad said. "You keep your friends at Kimball—that's called integrity. You go to school to learn. You don't need to be making all kind of friends when you're learning."

"Yeah," I said, unsure. "But you need people to play with at recess and stuff."

"You just need to learn there. You be you at recess."

"What about lunch?" I asked.

"You be you at lunch, too." I must have looked confused, because Dad explained it to me. "Okay. You're goin' to a new school, let me put it this way: Your neighborhood is where you live!"

Monday morning I decided my two-week-old cornrows were too messy and pulled them all out before I got in the shower. Then I put my wet hair in pigtails and got dressed in my best outfit to go to IPP—an outfit I thought was me being me. I headed up to breakfast in a pink sweatshirt with a super-cute quilted bear on the front, and a denim overall skirt with athletic socks and my real Nike tennis shoes. I felt confident.

Dad was quiet most of the morning as I hurried through a bowl of cornflakes and washed my bowl. Then he put my coat on me, which he never did. And said, "I love you," which meant he needed comforting.

"I love you, too, Daddy," I said as he zipped up my coat, but he just looked sad and bewildered. "What's wrong, Dad?" I asked. "I go to school every day."

"I know," he said.

Then he grabbed one of his ugly work hats and put it on my head emotionally. I decided not to say anything about the hat as Dad regained his usual face. "Don't you worry 'bout your dad, though. I'm okay."

Which made me worry about him, and I didn't even know why.

"Okay, Dad," I said, trying to sound as reassuring as possible. "I'll just be normal. And everything will be normal."

"Good," he said, and with that he sent me out to Mom, who was waiting in her car downstairs, unwilling to come up. I got in the car with her, fastened my seat belt, and looked up at Dad in the dining room window. And then Mom drove me across town, to a new school full of smart kids who were richer than God.

Nothing could have prepared me for the scene that morning: my classroom—a sea of shining white faces and brand-new clothes. In almost utter silence the kids dutifully worked individually and in very quiet groups while the teacher graded papers. No one was policing, yet there was quiet and order. Even Mom was weirded out by everyone's focus. And my new teacher, from what I saw, smiled endlessly for no apparent reason.

"Hello," she said, walking up to Mom and me. "I'm Mrs. Lewis." Then she extended her hand to me. "It's a pleasure to meet you, Mishna. I've heard a lot about you."

Mrs. Lewis got me settled at my new desk while she talked to me like I was thirty. "Mishna, I think you'll see that once you get used to how we work, you'll find it very satisfying. You can work at your own pace, and when you've finished one project you're free to move to the next . . . you don't have to wait for permission or for the rest of the class."

I needed to clarify. "So, um . . . If I just wanted to just do nothing?"

"I don't believe you really want to do nothing. Do you? I don't believe in laziness. If you are feeling bored with something you're working on, tell me, and together I think we can find a way to make it interesting for you."

I knew there was a catch. "So you really mean, I can work at the same pace as the class . . . or I can work faster?"

Mrs. Lewis looked at me as though I would understand better if I wasn't so poor and said, "You could look at it that way, but that's not exactly it."

Lesson number one, my teacher talked in riddles, and trying to make sense of what she was saying only made her talk more. Lesson number two, the more she talked, the crazier she sounded.

I spent my first week at my new school pretending to read a book and taking in as much as I could. And keeping my integrity was proving mighty easy, because everyone was so unusual to me that I was terrified to open my mouth and divulge any information about myself besides what I was wearing—which I found out early on wasn't good enough. I also learned my new classmates had boats and ponies, and they didn't have to go to the library to use the encyclopedia; they had their own! Their clothes were warm enough, and their parents packed ridiculously well-balanced lunches in their plastic lunchboxes with matching soup-filled thermoses. For the first time in my life I felt a weird feeling in my stomach like a pang—like hunger. It was jealousy. Not that I wasn't hungry, too.

I tried to bury my jealousy as best I could—I found just hating everyone worked a little and so did chewing on rubber bands. I also kept in mind that my neighborhood was where I lived, and that I wasn't supposed to belong with these rich white kids, which oddly made me feel a little bit better than everyone.

But as the days went on and I started to feel lonely, the lunches and recesses were brutal. Dad wasn't there and neither were any of my friends from Kimball. And on day three at my new school, I had my first little moment of sorta wanting school to be more than just class.

It was at recess. I sat alone on a playground structure near a group of girls playing foursquare. One of them, a redhead named Marylyn, said, "I'm tired of going to London, its just people doing the same stuff we do here."

I thought, *London! Wow! I want to ask her about London. Would it be bad if I just talked to her? I won't forget that my neighborhood is where I live. How can I live there!*

She continued, "We go, like, every summer."

"That's how I feel about Disneyland," said a brunette named Claire.

And I craned my neck farther in to listen to them.

"This summer I want to go to soccer camp instead," said Marylyn.

"I'm going to soccer camp," said another girl.

I was dumbfounded. Soccer camp over London? You gotta be kidding me! And at that moment I wanted so badly to be in proximity to people who could be blasé about Disneyland or Europe. I couldn't even be blasé about soccer. And there they were below me—kids that got to do stuff no one I had ever met had done.

It was then that the girls looked up at me sitting on my metal perch above them. I could have said something, could have asked them what other places they had been, but instead I pretended like I hadn't heard a word they said.

And I reminded myself, *you have friends at home*, while climbing down from the jungle gym and walking toward the school—careful not to let my filthy, peasant gaze soil the princesses on the foursquare court. *You come here to learn.*

Meanwhile, my sister had started going to my old kindergarten, and that afternoon when I got home she was sitting at the kitchen counter across from Dad, who was making her a sandwich.

"What's going on?" I asked. "What are you doing home?"

"Well," Dad said, licking the mayo knife, "I had to pick Anora up from school. She got in a little trouble today. No big deal."

"How much trouble could she have gotten in?" I asked. "She's in kindergarten!"

"S'true," Dad said, handing Anora her sandwich and NOT giving me information.

"So, what'd she do?" I wondered if she had been sarcastic, too.

Dad readjusted his Kangol and said slowly, "She got caught smoking. But she learned her lesson."

"I did learn my lesson, Dad!" Anora said, and dug into her sandwich.

"How did Anora get a cigarette?" I asked.

"I got some big girls to give it to me," she bragged. "They were in the bathroom."

God, she was already cool.

"Her teacher smelt it on her . . . ," Dad said, and then looking at Anora added, " 'Cause-it's-nasty! And-it-stinks!"

"I know that now, Daddy."

I couldn't believe my five-year-old sister could smoke, and I couldn't have white friends. And from what I could tell, her punishment was a sandwich. When I broached the subject of her punishment Dad said, "Why don't you keep your eyes on your own self. Or go outside, I think Latifa wants to play with you."

"I have homework."

Dad wrinkled his nose. "You know, I'd really like you to go out and play a little. All those kids you go to school with aren't really that well rounded. You got friends, you gotta pay attention to them."

I put my school bag on the counter next to my sister, who was happily eating her cheese sandwich and headed outside for some double Dutch.

The next day on the bus I decided that isolating myself at school was unreasonable. Anora was already making older friends and I was sure she had people to eat with. I should, too. I thought, *I'll just try to be like my family when I'm at home. And when I'm at school I'll act like school people.* I imagined that's what integrity was. I kept thinking about it as I picked at the black pleather bus seat in front of me. *If I could fit in at GSCC, I can fit in anywhere. When I'm around these people, I'll just pretend to be rich and normal in that white kinda way!* At the time it seemed feasible.

It wasn't like anyone at school knew where or how I lived, because the school bus didn't even go to my dingy neighborhood. It went to a good neighborhood that bordered it, and I had to walk a good ten blocks home. So that afternoon when the bus didn't pull away immediately, rather than let the kids on my bus see me walk toward my neighborhood, I crossed the street and walked into the good neighborhood. That's when Adam, a blond fourth-grader, who also got off at my stop, asked, "What are you doing?" He pointed to my neighborhood. "You walked from that way this morning . . . and yesterday."

"I'm going over to my cousin Jane's house," I said. A lie. "She has a Nintendo." Lie upon lie.

The bus pulled away, but Adam flanked me now, so I couldn't just double back to the ghetto, like I had planned to. I had to commit, and started walking up his street toward my fictional cousin's house. I watched him silently walking next to me. His perfect Lacoste polo sticking out of a cable knit sweater that matched his cords, hoping he would just mind his own perfect business.

"Where does she live?" he asked.

"Oh," I said, "Just, you know . . . up the street . . . I take a left up a bit." He was quiet, so I embellished. "She loves it when I come over, because I'm the only one who really gets her parrot talking."

Adam looked at me for a moment and after two seconds that felt like two years, he nodded and said, "I love birds."

"Who doesn't?" I said.

We walked another half a block until he peeled off to the left. "This is me," he said, and walked up the steps to the most beautiful two-story colonial I had ever seen. "See you around."

"Okay, cool," I said. "See you around the neighborhood." And I quickened my pace as I continued up the block. I decided then and there to hate him—but also to get invited over. That's the line I was trying to walk.

As I rounded the corner at the end of Adam's block I was relieved that lying had panned out for me so well—it actually made me feel a little classier. And on the way back to my neighborhood, I took my time. I walked down the streets of well-tended yards, and fantasized about fathers with tweed jackets, and mothers who stayed home and who had tons of Fruit Roll-Ups in the cupboards. I spent so much time picking out my dream house that I got home an hour late, completely forgetting that Dad and I had made plans. And rather than tell him I was late because I had been designing a new life for myself, I told him it was 'cause I was playing ninja with Tre's new nunchucks. He looked at me dubiously for a moment and then went back to jury-rigging the toaster.

As weeks went on, fitting in at school proved a little more difficult than I had originally anticipated. For one, my classmates did not appreciate a good cap. One day we were standing on the playground—all lined up to go back inside. And knowing that I had the ear of Zachary, Gavin, and Marylyn, I decided it was the perfect moment to say, "Gavin's so dumb, he saw a wallet in a store and tried to feed it grass." A surefire gem in the capping community, but at IPP it was worth nothing—just blank stares. I was amazed.

I explained, "Because wallets are made of leather." There was silence as Marylyn and Zachary looked at each other.

"Why would you say that?" Gavin said. "I couldn't possibly be dumb. I have an IQ in the top point-five percent."

"Oh," I said. "It's just like joking."

I thought about explaining what a joke was, but the look on Marylyn and Zachary's face let me know what they were thinking—I was too ghetto.

"You're kind of the dum-dum." Marylyn said, laughing a little.

"Yeah," Zachary said. "You didn't even know what algebra was."

It was then I really realized that I was actually the dumbest kid in the class. I mean sure I had passed some tests. But the tests I had taken tested logic, not information. And we all knew what time two trains that leave Chicago simultaneously arrive in Detroit. But unlike my classmates, I didn't know about algebra, or Shakespeare, or lacrosse, or Lacoste. I knew things like if you had fifty cents, and you stole a dollar from the slow kid, you had a dollar fifty. Or that the whipped cream canisters in the corner store across the street get you high. And overcoming these obstacles and making friends was starting to seem impossible.

Then open house came and Mom couldn't go and asked Dad to instead. I think she was partially hoping that if he saw my classroom and met my teacher, it would get him in the IPP spirit. It certainly got him in the dressing spirit, because the night of the open house Dad got sharp in a cream-colored suit and a shiny rope chain around his neck. And for his feet, there were new shoes. He took them out of a glossy bag labeled "B-A-L-L-Y," and they were so shiny, I wanted to cheer. When I went to touch them he said, "These are a two-hundred-dollar pair of shoes. I don't want you or your sister to even go near them." Dad also had on these socks that were like pantyhose for men. I had no idea he knew about all this fashion stuff from, but I thought he looked really rich. I thought maybe we had come into some money. But then again I had watched him siphon gas out of someone else's car the week before, and we hadn't exactly had dinner, so that seemed unlikely.

We got to my school late, and from the second we walked in the door of the building my dad wouldn't uncross his arms. I thought he looked so good that he was sure to impress and when we walked into the classroom, everyone looked at us. None of the other parents had dressed up, and as Dad walked through my classroom toward the presentations we had made about ancient Roman life, he said to me, "You know your classmates' folks could dress a little better." We walked around the room alone. The kids that were there weren't kids that I felt like I could just hang out with, and the other parents seemed to be in small discussion groups talking to each other. Dad and I just looked at everything in the room once and headed for the door. "Dad," I asked, "aren't you even gonna talk to any of the other parents?" To which my dad's response was, "About what?"

That was when Mrs. Lewis called, "Mr. Wolff." And he sighed before turning around. Mrs. Lewis chatted with him and did a quick round of intros to all of the parents and kids in the room. I was glad Latecia and Lanelle, the only black kids in class, were there because I thought it would reassure him about IPP. Then Mrs. Lewis led him to a group of parents talking as incessantly as she did. Dad held my hand tightly and looked at me as if to ask, "Is this lady for real?"

"We were just talking about working with flashcards," Marylyn's father said as Dad joined the conversation. "I found them very helpful when I was teaching Marylyn her multiplication tables. What do you think, John?"

"Uh-huh," my dad said. "I think, good parenting is about dicipline."

Donald Lin's mother said, "I used flashcards to get Don ready for the spelling bee last year."

"Well, it worked!" Marylyn's father joked, and everyone started laughing. That was when Marylyn's father actually turned his back to Dad and edged us out of the conversation as he started a story, "You know, believe it or not, Marylyn didn't always have the highest math scores."

Dad responded, "I know one thing. You disrespect me like that again, you're gonna feel it."

"Excuse me? I'm sorry. I don't think I understand what you mean. If I have managed to offend you . . ."

"You heard me," Dad said, staring him down for a moment before grabbing my hand and turning to Mrs. Lewis. "Thank you for your little show. I wish everyone here had some manners." Then he dragged me out. And as we walked out of the building he tugged at his tie and warned me about yuppies adding as we pulled up to the house that they were a, "Waste of good clothes."

A few days later, after coming the long way home past Cousin Jane's house, I walked in the house to find Anora sitting in front of the TV with a bowl of ice cream, looking dazed. Her head was completely bandaged in white gauze, and she seemed to be drooling into her ice cream.

"What happened to you?" I asked.

"I'm not supposed to fall asleep," she said.

"Why?" I asked. "What's up with your head?"

"I was playing," she said, and went back to *Care Bears.*

I knew Dad must be home and I screamed, "What happened to Anora's head?"

Dad entered from the bathroom with a newspaper under his arm. But rather than answer my question he looked alarmed as he saw Anora's ice cream dripping on the antelope-skin, African-drum coffee table.

"Shit, Mishna, get a rag!" Dad yelled as he hurried to set the newspaper under her bowl.

I hurried to the kitchen and wet a rag. And as I was wringing it out, I hollered, "Can I have some ice cream, too?"

"Is your head in a bandage?" Dad snapped back. I decided to skip the smart-aleck remark about how easy it would be for me to make that happen.

I brought the rag dutifully and asked again, "So, what happened to Anora's head?"

"Oh," Dad said, wiping the antelope skin with the grain, "she was playing a game with some girls and the bathroom doors."

"Tug-of-war," my sister said.

"Yeah," Dad said, looking at Anora. "With the bathroom door!"

Anora was dizzy, but still had the energy to brag, "With third-graders!"

To which Dad responded, "I guess you learned your lesson about messing around . . ." Then Dad got sucked into *Care Bears* and trailed off, "Her head went into the door . . . stitches. But she's a'ight."

"How many stitches?" I asked, awed that she was making friends with third-graders.

"Four," my sister said proudly, because four was a respectable amount of stitches. It wasn't anywhere near my record of nine stitches, but it was decent. My sister reached for her bandage to show me, when Dad pulled himself out of *Care Bears* and said, "What's wrong with you, Mishna? Anora, leave your bandage alone." I took a seat next to Dad and quietly started watching TV, even though I thought *Care Bears* was lame.

Dad suddenly shifted his attention to me. "Mishna," he said. "About your school." There was a pause during which I wondered how I had suddenly become the focus.

"It's been a few months, and I been wondering . . . How you getting along with the sisters?" This was a trick question. There were only two black girls in my whole class, Dad knew this from the open house. And I wasn't really "friends" with anyone. But rather than concede I said, "Well . . . I'm kinda friends with Latecia and Lanelle."

To which Dad replied, "Yeah, well . . . They're not *really* black."

I quietly crossed them off my list of people to beg for friend-ship.

I was increasingly desperate to make friends at school. And soon I lied again. I was standing on the playground butting in on a group of kids who were talking because they had no idea what to do with a recess. Gretchen, the tallest girl in our class, was talking about her weekend. "I rode at the Kirkland stable all day Saturday." She said, "I don't have my own horse yet, but my parents think we might get one in Germany next year."

"I have my own horse," said Catrina Calder, a girl with trendy glasses and an even trendier haircut. "But it's not Ger-man, it's just for riding." *As opposed to plowing?* Then she said in baby talk, "But, I love my Mastro. He's my handsome guy."

"I want to get a Hanoverian," said Gretchen.

That was when I said from out of nowhere, "I have a horse!" I was aware that it was a risky whopper, but everyone else was talking about their stupid horses.

"What kind of horse?" Gretchen asked.

"Coco," I said.

"That's the breed?" she asked.

"No," I said. "I mean Coco is her name. She's a dapple." I

had heard the word *dapple* when my mom sang the lullaby "All the Pretty Little Horses."

"Dapple is a color," Gretchen said. "What's the breed?"

That's when Catrina blurted out, "You do not have a horse . . . I mean, I thought your dad was a contractor?"

"He is," I said, not knowing what one was, and thinking that sounded more important than what he really was.

"So how do you have a horse?" she asked.

I told them we kept it on my uncle's ranch on the Skagit River, turning a rundown cabin into a ranch. And even I cringed at how thick I was laying it on.

But Gretchen just said, "That's cool. We should go ride together sometime."

And as the recess bell let me off the hook, I pushed my luck. "Coco has won prizes for her looks."

Catrina looked skeptical and repeated, "Your dad is a contractor," forcing me to look up the word *contractor* when I got back to class. Turned out even Dad's put-down job was kind of an exaggeration.

Then one day after school I was waiting to get onto my school bus. I was half watching an Asian boy named Donald Lin, who was obsessed with earthworms, explain to anyone who would listen about an experiment he was doing in a compost bin, when I heard the *thump—thump—thump* of a car stereo that clearly had its bass turned up to eleven. I knew immediately it was Dad. The blaring rhythms of Kool & the Gang came wafting up the block long before he did. And my classmates looked curiously at each other, wondering where the loud music could possibly be coming from. And then he came into sight behind the wheel of the car we referred to as "the boat" crammed with all his buddies: Big Lyman, Delroy, Reggie Dee, and Eldridge.

"Mishna!" he screamed from the driver's side window. "Hey, Mishna!"

At first I was overjoyed to get picked up by Dad and the coolest gang of guys I knew. But this pride was shattered when, walking toward the car, I noticed all of my classmates staring like they had never seen rust before. And when I got to the car, Christopher Scott and Stacey Leigh were practically falling over themselves laughing.

"Hey, Dad!" I said as I climbed in the car.

"Hey!" Dad announced to the car, "Look how beautiful my daughter is." He turned the radio back up and shouted over it, "Now isn't this better than the bus?"

"Yeah," I said, resisting the urge to step on the gas pedal myself.

Still, once we pulled away from the school and were half-way down the block—and I was riding on the hump between Dad and Reggie—and the tunes were bumping, I had to admit, it was way better than the bus.

But the next day Christopher decided it would be a good idea for him to spend recess making fun of Dad. And I decided it would be a good idea for me to pop him in his bitch face. It actually wasn't that conscious. I was near the wood chips when he walked over and said, "Hey, Mishna, where do you think I can get a car like your dad's?"

"Huh?" I asked.

"I bet I could get one of those at the Goodwill. Is that where you got your car?" He said it so sincerely, it was confusing.

"We didn't get our car at Goodwill," I said.

"Did you get your dad there?" Again with the sincere questions, but now Jodie, Ingrid, Marylyn, and Donald were watching.

"No," I said.

"I can't hear you," Christopher said. "I asked if you got your dad at Goodwill?" I didn't say anything. He was being tricky and I didn't know how to counter it, so I tried to ignore it.

"What's wrong?" he asked. "Cat got your . . ." Before he could say "tongue" my fist moved to his face on its own. It happened so fast that as I watched him holding his bloody nose, I honestly wondered what had happened.

Then, I learned the lesson of what happens when you pop a brat at rich school—they tattle like a fucking girl. I wound up in the principal's office sitting next to Christopher, who was holding his nose like a little bitch, and saying, "I don't know why she hit me like that for no reason . . . I didn't even have a chance to defend myself."

I begged them to call Dad and let him punish me, because I knew that the punishment in my house for fighting was Dad getting happy and saying, "I guess you let him know." But they didn't. They made me write an apology note to Christopher.

No matter, I thought, *I have some well-earned kudos coming my way from the classmates—I fully landed that punch.* However, said kudos were not forthcoming. In fact, at the next recess, Donald stayed fifty yards away from me at all times. And rather than invite me to play foursquare with her, Marylyn just looked at me like I was the wild woman in the attic from *Jane Eyre.*

I walked over to Gretchen and said, "Why is everyone being so weird?" and she grudgingly threw me a line because I was standing right there.

"Well . . . ," Gretchen said. "You kind of lost control."

"No," I said. "I let Christopher know."

"You actually let him get you upset," she said. "Which is what he was trying to do. And I sort of understand it, it's just a little weird to us here."

"Us?" I asked.

"Well," she said. "You're newer than some of us who have been here since first grade."

"Oh," I said. "That us." I scratched my head and said faintly, "Thanks for talking to me, Gretchen." And walked away to be alone on my playground structure, where things were simple and strength was rewarded.

On Presidents' Day we stayed home from school. Anora spent the day with her school friend Maybelline because she was popular, and I hung out with Dad because I was not, and because Zwena was with her mom. I still would have wanted to hang out with Dad either way, but the fact that our phone was "down" again, and we couldn't dial out, meant he couldn't pawn me off on anyone. People called in for Anora.

Dad and I were about to head out to the basketball court so that he could teach me about dribbling with my left hand and Malcom X, when he got a phone call. Dad got a little giddy as he answered it. Having our phone shut off made contact from the outside extra exciting.

"Wolff residence," Dad said. "Oh, hey, Candy . . ." Candy was Maybelline's mom and I knew instantly there was something up with Anora. Dad listened for a while before snickering and saying, "No . . . I'm not laughing." I got the feeling he was being yelled at as he listened more attentively and said, "Yes, I know this isn't funny." Followed by, "Okay, I'll be right there." Dad set down the phone and grabbed his coat. "Stay put, Mishna. I gotta get your sister, I'll be right back."

My heart skipped a beat: I knew Anora had done something wrong.

Maybe this is it! I thought, as Dad tore off down the street to get Anora. *The moment Dad will realize that every time he said,*

"Anora, I guess you learned your lesson about messing around," she hadn't learned her lesson at all. And that I was, in fact, a lesson-learning machine.

As I waited impatiently for Dad and Anora to return home, I decided I wanted to look extra good when they came back. And I scanned the house for ways to have them catch me in the act of being dutiful. I tried on "Caught in the act—sweeping" where I held the broom and looked up, like, "Hey, you guys are home . . . Oh, this broom? . . . I just got an uncontrollable urge to sweep."

Then I tried "Caught in the act—making them tea." That was where I look up from the teapot and say, "Hey . . . Tough day? . . . Who wants tea?" But in the end I just got really impatient that they were taking so long and put my head on the counter and thought about what I would buy at the corner store if I had a dollar, until I heard them drive up. Then I hurried to the sink to get caught in the act—washing dishes.

When Anora and Dad walked in I tried to ignore them—much too caught up in my dishes. They ignored me, too, and walked in laughing and carrying on.

"What happened?" I asked, trying to hide my eagerness.

"Why you so nosy?" Dad asked. "We just walked in the door."

"I was just curious," I said. "Because you guys are in such a good mood."

"Well," Dad said. "Candy took the girls on her errands today, and they all decided to play themselves a little game."

"It was a really stupid idea," Anora said, giggling.

"What was the idea?" I asked, trying to be cool.

"They stole something at every joint they went to," Dad said.

"Wow," I said "That's . . . wow."

Anora is the one in the middle, with child.

"Maybelline blamed Anora," Dad said, "and Anora blamed Maybelline." And apparently hilarity ensued, because Dad was acting like it was the funniest thing he had ever heard. I didn't get why it was so amusing that my sister was becoming a delinquent. And I wasn't letting it go.

"So . . . ," I said, looking at Anora and trying to seem sympathetic. "I guess you're punished, huh?" Then I turned to Dad. "She's punished, right, Dad?" My sister glared at me, noting that it was a dick move.

"Nah. I think she learned her lesson. We just have to return all this stuff." I looked at the stuff—a pack of gum, a nail file and three stickers—and I knew none of it was going anywhere, except in her mouth. I had learned my lesson.

Four

DOMINIQUE AND MORE LIES

"Mishna, what are you doing?" Mrs. Lewis interrupted her lesson, and everyone in class silently turned to face me. Based on the temperature of my cheeks, I was sure I was blushing.

"Nothing," I replied nonchalantly.

"Are you eating the paste?" she asked.

I was actually squirting paste out of my missing-tooth hole for two boys in my row. So I said, "Not really, I . . ."

"Bring me the paste now, Mishna."

I walked to the front of the classroom and handed her the round pot of Elmer's. Dave DeLuca and Andrew Tanaka, who had watched me with rapt attention only a few minutes earlier, looked down and away like they didn't know me.

"Why do you eat the paste?" she asked.

Everyone was looking at me, so I tried to look like I didn't care by licking any residual paste off my lips and smiling like it was delicious.

"Does that mean you don't know?"

I shrugged. But I knew exactly why I did it. I needed the attention.

After six months at rich school, it was obvious to everyone I wasn't going to fit in—so I fit out. I started doing the stuff other kids were afraid to do in exchange for an audience, like hemorrhoid talk. I harassed Mrs. Lewis with endless questions about hemorrhoids. I could work the word *hemorrhoids* into a question about any subject. For example, you may or may not know that the first president of the United States was George Hemorrhoid, or that four times twelve is hemorrhoid. For creative writing, I read aloud to the class my epic thriller "The Hemorrhoid That Lives in My Basement." And Mrs. Lewis stopped smiling as much as she used to . . . hemorrhoids?

And I took any dare. Besides paste, I ate glue, paint, and a rubber band. I was *Fear Factor* for third-graders. It didn't make me popular but at least I could get a crowd to spend five minutes watching me destroy my esophagus.

Mrs. Lewis continued to stare at me in front of the classroom, paste in hand for, like, a year.

"Can I go back to my seat?" I asked.

Mrs. Lewis disregarded the question. "I think you are purposely disrupting my classroom for attention."

Like, duh.

But rather than admit that—yes, sheer neediness drove me to eat the Elmer's, I faced the class and circled my ear with my finger—the universal sign for "Hey, is this lady is crazy, or what?"

"Do you act this way at home?"

"No," I said. The one time Dad caught me showing my sister how I could swallow a marble, he punished me for wasting a marble. And for the most part when I was at home I acted how Mrs. Lewis wanted me to, which was causing problems with with my friends at home. I had recently been left out of a very important game of Slam Charades (like charades, but meaner, and with words). And when I asked Jason about being dissed, he leveled with me. "Yo, you act kinda weird sometimes." When I asked him what he meant, he said, "You just say shit, and nobody understands what you're talking about."

I also knew I didn't have real friends at school. I could tell the difference between being liked and being a paste-eating sideshow.

Mrs. Lewis heard the titters from the kids who had seen my "crazy" gesture and her face went from bad to worse. And standing in the front of the class, while Mrs. Lewis scolded me, I started to think about a Sunday school class where we talked about limbo—and how much I connected with the idea. Except to me heaven was a crappy street where all the kids did after school was try to invent new ways to call me white, and hell was a room full of kids in French polos. It seemed that both heaven and hell sucked the same amount, but differently. But I'd have given up my teeth, my hair, my feet, and my education to be truly popular in either one. And I wondered if I would have friends after I died.

Mrs. Lewis was angry and ordered me to clean out my desk and move to the empty one in the back of the class.

"Next to Zachary?" He always had his fingers in his mouth.

"Yes," she said. "The empty desk next to Zachary Stein." Then added, "Facing the wall."

Over the course of the year I had been moved farther and farther back in the classroom, which from a feminist standpoint might have been something to be proud of. I was the only girl in "behavioral problem" row. But I took no pride in it. To me it was just proof that I was defective. It oddly never occurred to me to stop eating paste.

It was Friday, and Mrs. Lewis gave me a note for my parents to sign. I had the weekend with Mom, but I didn't want to give it to her, afraid she would freak out or be hurt or both. So I put it in my schoolbag to give to Dad to sign on Sunday night. On Sunday morning when I came down to eat, which I did a lot of at Mom's house, Mom was at the breakfast table holding the note.

"What's going on at school?" she asked.

"Dang," I said. "It's not a big deal."

"It is," she said. "Why are you misbehaving in class? Are they not challenging you?"

"No," I said. "Trust me, I'm plenty challenged."

"Well, you're not exactly making teacher's pet."

"Well, then, they'll just have to kick me out and send me back to normal school."

"It's not like that," Mom said. "They won't kick you out. They'll just ask how they can make it more productive for you."

"I'm just not that academic."

"*Academic* is a very academic word," she said.

"Well then, could I just live with you?" I asked for the first time.

"It's not the arrangement," she said. "You know your uncle is a lawyer, and has offered your dad limitless legal help." She was scared of him. "And your father really loves being a dad." I buried myself in my cereal.

"How are you feeling?" She searched my face, imploring me to open up to her. But I wasn't gonna open up to her on my three days a week. No matter what I was feeling, she was still gonna go to work on Monday, and I was still gonna go back to Dad's.

"Fine," I said.

" 'Fine' is not a feeling."

"Listen," I said. "I promise, I will try much, much harder."

"Really?" Mom said.

"Yes."

A few days later, after my sister and I got home from school, Dad called us into the bathroom where he was shaving, wearing a pair of jeans, work boots, and no shirt. I liked watching him shave because it was exciting. You never really knew what was gonna happen next. Every stroke could go exactly according to plan . . . or not. Those were the type of risks men took. He took a stroke up his chin that was a little too long, and the result was a tiny, bursting red blossom. I winced, but Dad didn't. He was a man. He just patted some Drakkar Noir on his face and took a last look in the mirror. His hair was cut short now but it still had enough length that he could feather it on the sides, and the top was so fluffy, it made him look even taller. He grabbed his chin and smiled like he was in an aftershave commercial. Then he slowly turned to face my sister and me—still in the commercial.

"You girls." This was important, so he kneeled down in order to be at eye level with us. Full eye contact—maximum impact. "I have met a real nice lady named Dominique."

"Like a girlfriend?" I asked.

"I don't wanna put labels on things," Dad said. "But she's gonna make dinner for us on Wednesday night 'cause you all gotta meet. I told her how important family is to me . . ." He turned to face me. "So, if you embarrass me . . ." He banged the bathroom counter, making a loud noise.

I didn't know why he was looking at me, but I nodded furiously. My sister threw her arms around Dad's neck and started laughing. "I'm so happy, Daddy!"

"Wait, how would I embarrass you?" I asked.

"Well, for one," Dad said. "You don't need to know everything about every little thing."

"How do you mean?" I asked.

"I mean you don't know everything, and you don't need to know about what you don't know."

"I think I understand," I said.

"Good," Dad said, returning to the mirror and making his most handsome face. "Good . . . Oh by the way," he added, "your mom and I talked and you gonna see her on weekdays, too, sometimes. When she's not working doubles."

"Cool," I said, even though it felt like there was too much stuff coming at me at once.

After chores and homework I walked over to Lyman's. Zwena had gotten a scholarship to private school that year. So now she was the only girl in the neighborhood who wore a uniform. I liked seeing her after school because she looked so rich in her white shirt with the navy plaid skirt. And when I told Zwena that Dad had a girlfriend the first thing she asked was, "White or black?"

"White," I said, unsure. "I think."

"That's good," she said. "I go to school with all these white kids and their moms are like servants."

"My school, too!" I said. "Don't you get jealous?"

"I used to," Zwena said. "But I'm the only kid at my school that knows how to cook."

"I'd rather have a servant."

On Wednesday night Anora and I got ready for dinner at Dominique's house and Dad put us in our gold chains that we were allowed to wear only to church. We had started going to an all-black Baptist church after the divorce and Dad usually let our gold out of his desk only on Sunday because he said, "If you wear gold every day, it loses its class."

Then we drove to Dominiques's four-unit apartment building on a busy street, not far from GSCC. We rang the bell, and a voice said, "Hello."

"It's us," Dad said into a metal box. "Buzz us up." And Dominique "buzzed us up"—which was the closest I'd ever had to a *Star Trek* moment.

It was the first time I had been in the apartment of a woman with no kids and upon entering I almost gasped at how neat her place was. It was full of bamboo and cream-colored furniture. In the corner sat a glass coffee table and the most real-looking fake palm tree you ever saw. And the whole place was covered in light cream carpet—which I tiptoed onto like it was hot lava. I knew that cream was for careful people, and no matter how Dad was acting, that wasn't us. We were the kind of people who needed dirt-colored things. In fact, our living room was home to a brown rug and a brown pleather sofa that was always just a little sticky.

Dominique heard us enter and ran into the living room with an ecstatic, high-pitched, "Hi!!!" And Dominique was black. I don't know why it surprised me, but I somehow assumed that if Dad had been into Mom, then he was only into white women. I assumed this because I was starting to have crushes at school, and I knew for sure I was only into Asian guys—and I was sure I would be till the day I died. But I guessed that wasn't true for Dad, which explained why all the women at church Dad made us stand around and talk to just happened to be pretty. And why we were always the last to leave church.

Dominique was also very pretty. Not Christie-Brinkley-in-a-Billy-Joel-video pretty, but definitely up there. She was wearing a huge smile—and perfect makeup that matched a perfect blue dress that showed off her perfect figure. She was also about the farthest from my mom's style that you could get. She ran up to Anora.

"You must be Anora!" she said, touching her shoulder.

"Is this your house?" Anora asked. "It's so pretty."

Dominique looked at Dad and put her hand to her mouth

like a lady getting proposed to. And turning back to Anora, gushed, "Well, aren't you cute!" Dominique then turned her attention to me. In fact, she looked me over for a while, like she was redecorating. "And you must be Mishna. Your dad tells me you're very smart."

"Really?" I asked excitedly. I looked at Dad, who had a stern look on his face. I turned back to Dominique, "I mean . . . it's a pleasure to meet you . . ." I didn't know what to call her so I said, "ma'am." And Dad gave me the old Vulcan neck pinch—just as a reminder.

After Dominique made us remove our shoes we sat down for dinner. The first thing we learned about Dominique was that she couldn't cook; some awful pasta creation with meat that tasted the way yak smells. But this didn't seem to bother Dad, who over dinner announced, "Dominique is a good woman, and I want you girls to listen to her. You should be so lucky as to grow up into a woman like Dominique!" He said it like it was important. But I didn't know what that meant—a "good" woman. I'd think he'd want to find a *great* woman if he could. I figured, based on church and forty-five minutes with Dominique, that being a good woman must have something to do with God and cleaning—because it sure didn't have anything to do with cooking.

And from what I could tell Dominique was all woman. After dinner while Dad and Dominique snuggled on the couch, I went to the bathroom—a beige room with magenta accents that smelled like a department store. It was full of perfume and makeup, and there was a mirrored tray with nail polish in every color you could ever think of—even purple. I picked up a bottle of perfume and smelled it. It smelled different from my grandmother's, and then I tried to set it down on the counter exactly like I found it. I thought about looking in the drawers, but decided that I had been gone too long already, and would save that for the next time. But on the way back to the living room I noticed Dominique's bedroom door was cracked and I couldn't resist peering in. I cautiously looked for Dad or Dominique before sticking my head in the door. The room was as neat as a pin, and all the furniture matched. And from her open closet door I saw a hint of what I thought looked like brightly colored feathers. I was so captivated that I hardly noticed Dominique behind me watching me look into her bedroom.

"What are you doing?" she asked, and I spun around like a top. I was snooping. And I was scared beyond belief that I had embarrassed Dad—and now he would put a hurt on me.

"I'm sorry," I said, "I was coming back from the bathroom and the door was open. . . ."

I was relieved when Dominique smiled and said, "You wanna see my room?"

I didn't know what the right answer was and at this point I was much more concerned with not getting in trouble than with seeing anything, so I just stood there sheepishly while Dominique opened the door wide and stood by her bed. And when she waved me over, I happily followed.

"Let me show you my closet." She beamed. She was very proud of it. And I was dying to see what another woman's closet looked like. I knew what my mom's closet looked like. It was filled with work uniforms, blue jeans, and sweaters that weren't particularly ruffly.

Dominique on the other hand owned two feather boas and had over a hundred pairs of shoes lined in perfect rows, including a fuchsia pair and a turquoise pair, because as she said, "You never know."

Dominique put me in her fuchsia shoes and threw the matching boa around my neck. By the time Dad walked over to see what we were up to, I was sashaying around her room like an extra from *The Cotton Club*.

Dad looked alarmed. "What are you doing?" he asked, hovering in the doorway while Anora gleefully ran in and jumped up on the bed with us. "Mishna, did you ask Dominique if you could see her room?"

But Dominique just said, "Oh John, you're just jealous." Then she slapped my shoulder like I would get it. "We're just having a little girl time."

Dad became sheepish and softly kicked the door frame before asking, "Well . . . how long does that last?"

But Dominique just giggled and went back to trying hats on me. I could tell Dominique and I were going to be great friends.

As weeks turned into months, and Dad and Dominique got cozier, she let Anora and I in on a little secret, something she no longer had the energy to conceal: she hated kids. A fact she managed to work into sentences like, "You Wolves"—that's what she called us—"You Wolves, go upstairs and stop making noise! I've got a headache, and you know I don't like kids!"

Or, "Who ate my cake? See, that's why I don't like kids!"

Or, "Who spilled Capri Sun all over the interior of my Prelude? See, that's why I don't like kids . . . always spilling shit."

Dominique would yell at Dad, too. She'd roll her neck like a cobra and say, "John, if you think you can come in here with your wolf kids, sleep with me, and not do a damn thing around here? Well, you can take your nappy-headed kids, and your big, lazy, no-TV-fixing ass, and get the fuck out of my house!" I found it oddly festive. And I absolutely understood why she hated kids. After two months with her, I hated kids, too. Little need machines that got greasy fingers all over everything and cost lots of money. And, like her, I had no clue why people had

Dominique is on the right, in a very casual look for her.

them. And even though I didn't get along that well with Do-minique, I really understood that she hated all kids and not just us. And I imagined she'd probably like me when I grew up. Nothing personal.

What Dominique loved was horror films. And though I had never seen a horror film before, I really couldn't under-stand the concept—why make yourself scared, on purpose, when there are electrical sockets to stick forks in? When we spent the night at her house sometimes I could hear bits of hor-ror coming from the TV in the other room. And one night, when she came over to our house, she was holding a VHS.

She no longer did her hair and makeup for Dad unless they were going out, so she had her messy hair in a scarf and a pair of jeans on as she went into the fridge and grabbed a beer. It was the first time she had brought a movie over to our house and as she walked over to the VCR, she waved the movie around as though it was important and kept repeating the word "classic." Dominique stuck the movie in the VCR, and plopped herself down on the couch.

"Mishna," she said. "You can watch this movie with me if you want. This movie is a classic!"

And as the opening credits rolled, she unwrapped a Blow Pop, put it in her mouth, and sucked it in between sips of her beer. She said it made her beer taste better, and I believed it did.

I walked over to the couch and remained standing as I checked out the opening credits. *Why not?* I thought. *If I don't like it, I can stop watching. Besides it's rated R.* At my school R-rated meant "Rated Really Cool." *I'll just see what all the fuss is about,* I told myself. *Like a rated-R scientist or a rated-R investigator.*

"Okay," I said. "But this is my first scary movie."

"Well, you picked a good one to start out with," Dominique said. "Have you heard about *The Exorcist*?" I shook my head as Dominique said, without taking the Blow Pop out of her mouth, "I've seen it seven times. Never gets old."

"How scary is it?" I asked.

"It's less scary," she said, "and more a classic."

"Okay," I said, and plopped down next to her.

I sat next to Dominique in the dark of the living room trying not to pee myself and by the time Father Merrin arrived at the MacNeil house, I was in the fetal position.

Dominique took the Blow Pop out of her mouth and laughed. "Girl, it's just a movie!" Which helped, but not enough for me to open my eyes. So she leveled with me, "Listen. There are no real demonic possessions." But I had seen Dad get mad in traffic and I was inclined to think that there were demonic possessions all the time.

Still, she had a point, it was just a movie and with some deep breathing I managed to calm myself enough to open my eyes and sit upright on the sofa. *I am a rock, I am a mountain.* But when Regan's eyes rolled back in her skull, I jumped up off the couch and announced, "It's time for me to go now!" and ran to the bathroom, locked the door, and stood with my hands over my ears, humming, "The Sun Will Come out Tomorrow."

When I got to school the next day I took a quick survey before roll call and deduced that no one in my class had seen *The Exorcist*, though everyone had heard of it. And by the time we had our first recess it didn't matter that I had seen only the first third of the movie. I had become an *Exorcist* expert.

At recess, I held court on the playground, halfway up the jungle gym, picking and choosing from the crowd below who was allowed to hear my recounting of the epic, and making up the parts of the movie that I was too scared to watch.

"So . . . ," I said as Matt Johnson, Zachary Stein, and Catrina Calder sat with rapt attention, "the girl Regan had a devil in her stomach. And it busted out and killed her mom."

"Dude," Matt said.

"I know," I said. "And there was this priest, who comes over to fight the devil in the amulet. The priest knew kung fu, and he wasn't afraid to hit a girl."

"That is insane," said Zachary. "I have to see this movie."

"Yeah," I said, "you do." Given his name was embroidered on the inside of his coat and his mom picked him up so he wasn't late to Hebrew school, the likelihood of that happening was pretty bleak. "But dang," I added. "Your mom would never let you."

"Mine, either," said Matt.

"My mother only lets us watch *National Geographic* and one hour of cartoons on Saturday."

"Bummer," I said. "That's harsh."

For the next week I fielded *Exorcist* questions like, "Can a grown-up be infected?" Or, "Did the priest have throwing stars?"

Even snotty Christopher Scott came up to me at lunch to ask, "So if she had a flying bed, why didn't she just fly away from the people that were trying to get the devil out of her?"

To which I casually replied, "Look, it's just a really cool movie."

And the scary movies just kept coming. Over the next month, I saw the first twenty minutes of *Hellraiser*, *The Omen*, and nearly half of *Prom Night II*. I would end each viewing in the same way: bathroom, hands over ears, *Annie*. But the next day, I'd walk into school, just busting with excitement. It was better than Christmas Eve. It was better than my birthday. I would wait till Mrs. Lewis had finished attendance and we were working "independently," then I would drop a bomb to whoever was close by.

"So . . . I saw *Hellraiser* last night."

Math was over. It was Mishna time.

I reassured myself that it wasn't lying so much as filling in the spots I missed. Besides, my renditions had to be at least as creative as the movies themselves—maybe more.

About a month after I first saw *The Exorcist*, I was approached on the playground by a girl in my class named Lilith Gardner. She wasn't the most popular girl in the third grade, but she was the leader of her group. She strode up with Violet, Kirsten, and the rest of her crew, who looked like normal eight-year-olds, but were about four to six years away from becoming the goth kids. They all thought elves were real, and they were a little too interested in the morbid side of science class—constantly buzzing about dissection.

I was alone on the turning bar when Lilith walked up. And when I saw them coming, I stopped spinning.

"Hi, Mishna," Lilith said.

"Hi!" I said.

"Can you draw?" Lilith asked, cutting to the chase.

"Draw?" I asked.

"Yeah, draw."

"Like what?" I asked.

Kirsten explained for her, "Like, elves or horses."

"Or lesser demons or wizards," Lilith continued. "That kind of stuff."

"I don't know," I said. They were asking for some pretty advanced stuff.

"Well . . . ," Lilith said. "Okay." She was just standing there deciding whether or not to walk away and never talk to me again.

"Okay . . . yeah," I said. But what I was thinking was, *Please ask me to join your drawing club. I will learn to draw whatever you want! I will work hard and practice till I know how to draw the best horse ever. I will learn what a demon is. Just, please don't walk away!* But Lilith stood there saying nothing.

It was Violet who said, "Draw with us next recess."

And Lilith shrugged. "You saw all those horror films, right?" Lilith asked.

"Yeah . . . ," I said. "Like *Exorcist, Hellraiser, Prom Night . . .* yeah."

"Well," she said. "Try to draw some of that stuff, too."

And I did, and every recess after that. Initially, I wasn't a good-enough drawer, and I couldn't even come close to drawing Pinhead from *Hellraiser.* So I traced things out of books, and added my own flourishes so that I could call them my own. And after a while, I could draw the two or three things that I traced. I sat with my new friends on the playground filling a notebook with eighty versions of the same brown horse. Brown horse as a unicorn, brown horse as a pegasus, brown horse as a brown horse. I was even invited to my first sleepover at Lilith's house, where we spent the night playing *The Legend of Zelda* and asking the Ouija board about math. And all of this added up to me sort of having a crew. Granted these weren't the princesses on the foursquare court, but I saw them as a bridge clique. Sort of a stepping stone on my way to bigger and better friends.

But soon my little bridge clique dropped a bomb on me. Lilith, Violet, Kirsten, and I were drawing what we all deemed to be a very important series of female vampires, when I said, "Hey . . . have you guys started this stupid book report?"

It got quiet for a second—like a needle scratching across a record player. And then Violet said, "I finished it last night." I thought I heard her wrong.

"Finished?" I asked.

"Yeah," Lilith said. "It's due Friday."

"Wow," I said. "I thought I'd just do it Thursday night, or something."

Violet rolled her eyes. Then Kirsten said under her breath, "That explains a lot."

"What?" I asked. I was getting really infuriated. "What, are you all mad at me or something?"

"Well," Lilith said. And by the looks of everyone's face, she was speaking for the group. "We all sort of think . . ." Nods all around. "Well, you kind of act stupid."

Kirsten softened it. "We don't think you *are* dumb, or you wouldn't be here."

Violet finished her thought, "But, you really act dumb and it's hella lame."

Wow! I thought. *Time to stop saying "hella."*

Lilith continued, "It's not that we don't like you, but we're all going to MIT and we don't want to get too attached to someone who's not also going to MIT."

Then I said the most honest thing I had said since I got to IPP. "You guys . . . I don't think I can do the work."

"What do you mean?" Kirsten asked.

"I mean"—I was trying not to let anyone see how upsetting it was to me—"I just look at like the instructions for the structure of our book report and I don't get it."

"Well, what don't you get about it?" Violet asked.

"I get none of it!" I said. "It's like looking at instructions on how to build a rocket ship."

"Listen," Lilith said, "just try."

What they were asking seemed impossible to me. We had like three hours of homework a night, and with the added burden of not understanding most of it, that translated to even longer.

"Well, why don't you ever call me?" Violet asked.

"Isn't that cheating?" I asked.

"Um . . . no," Violet said. "You should call me when you get stuck."

"What," I said sarcastically, "like every night?"

"Yeah, sure," she said. That was a great idea, but Dad hadn't paid the phone bill again so I couldn't dial out . . .

. . . But I could receive calls.

"Violet," I said. "Will you call me at night this week? And next week I'll call you, like a game?"

"Okay," Violet said. "Whatever you want."

"I want you to call me," I said. "This week."

So that week Violet called me every night, and the next week I spent at Mom's, under the new arrangement, and I called Violet every day. It was in those two weeks I started to notice that when Lilith, Kirsten, and Violet weren't talking about druids or trolls, they talked constantly to each other about what we were working on in class—I guess up till then I had sort of tuned it out. They didn't get all this schoolwork done 'cause they were magic—they had a really cool trick. When they didn't understand something—rather than close the book and run to the garage to sniff gasoline—they *asked* each other for help. And sometimes we even sat and worked on schoolwork during recess. Although I felt like deadweight in the group, I was starting to find ways here and there to contribute. And occasionally, when the teacher asked for an answer, I raised my hand with everyone else. And, surprise—our schoolwork wasn't completely boring. And I started to think, *Hey, I'm not terrible at this school stuff. And this school isn't totally awful either. . . . Too bad my stupid neighborhood is where I live.*

Then one night, I was over at a barbecue at Dominique's parents' house with Dad and Anora. Dominique had a huge extended family and her parents lived in a big old house that was able to fit tons of people. It was the kind of house that I thought was beautiful, if only it weren't covered in plastic.

I asked Dominique, "What's the plastic for?"

"My mom keeps it on the carpet and furniture to keep it nice."

"How would they know it's nice," I asked, "if it's always under plastic?"

"Oh," Dominique said. "They take it up for company."

I wasn't sure I understood. I kinda thought we were company.

"Who comes over for company?"

"Why you so nosy?" Dominique said. "Jeez."

And I walked off thinking, *I just wanted to know who I have to be to get into the living room.*

Anora was doing her thing. I watched her walk up to Dominique's sister, blink her eyelashes, and say, "Do you like my dress?"

To which she responded, "Oh yes."

A minute later she was saying to Dominique's sister-in-law, "I wish I had pretty long nails like yours."

Or to her dad, "Do you want to see me do the running man?" and Dominique's relatives pulled candy out of their asses to give to her. Dominique's uncle, who didn't have any candy, reached into his wallet and gave her a dollar. That's how cute she was.

I made my way across the room and stood next to Dominique's older brother, trying to look like I wasn't thinking about how I looked. He was sitting in the La-Z-Boy surrounded by Dad, Dominique, and a couple of other adults, telling everyone about his time in 'Nam.

Dad said, "I almost lied about my age to go."

"Serious?" her brother asked.

"Oh yeah," Dad said. "A veteran in a wheelchair talked me out of it."

Dominique's brother shook his head and said, "It was the dumbest thing I ever did—get on that plane. I'm telling you, if you offered me a million dollars today to go back to Saigon, it'd still be no."

I jumped in. "Especially since there's no Saigon anymore." We had been studying Southeast Asia in school and I was sure the grown-ups would think that was interesting. Nope, silence and stares. I backpedaled, "'Cause it's not called Saigon anymore." Still silence, still stares.

"What was that?" Dad asked in his scary voice.

It was then I realized I was talking way out of turn. And I practically whispered, "Ho Chi Minh City."

"Why don't you go on downstairs? The grown folks are talking."

"Okay," I said, and I slumped away, both embarrassed and unsure of how much trouble I was in. I headed to the basement where Dominique's nephews were playing video games.

I sat down in the wood-paneled TV room with three of Dominique's nephews and one niece, who ranged from my age up to fourteen. They were playing Nintendo, and I knew there wasn't a snowball's chance in hell of them giving me a turn. So I decided to watch. They were laughing and carrying on and having more fun than I had ever seen any kids milk out of a one-foot-by-six-inch machine. When Dwight the twelve-year-old died in *Super Mario Brothers*, he jumped up and acted out his death.

"Ya got me!" he said as his Mario died of a giant bullet.

And when Jordan the fourteen-year-old's Luigi was killed by a fireball he jumped up and said, "I'm burnin'! I'm burnin'!" Meanwhile, Michaella, Dominique's ten-year-old niece, laughed and laughed till I thought she was going to die of exhaustion.

"Daimon," she said to her nine-year-old brother, who was also sitting out. "Do your Mario dance!" At which point this fearless nine-year-old did a little dance of ducking and jumping that he had worked out to the theme song on the video game. It was like a spontaneity convention. The whole scene was amazing to me and I could not have felt stiffer.

That's when Daimon stopped dancing and asked, "What are you looking at?"

To which I responded, "I was just watching." And I decided to head upstairs to see if Dad would take me back yet.

I crawled up the carpeted stairs because I thought that that was the way to handle sneaking back to Dad's side. When I reached the top of the stairs and was about to head across the hallway to the dining room, I overheard a conversation going on around the dining room table.

Dominique was saying, "They are not gifted kids, unless *gifted* is another word for bad. That girl is *b-a-d*." I knew she was talking about me.

Dominique's brother added, "That girl is no more gifted than any of my kids, and she's disrespectful, thinking she knows more than grown folks."

I waited for Dad to jump in and defend me.

"Yeah," Dominique said. "Where do they get off filling that girl's head with all that crap about being smart? It's just gonna mess her up when she gets to the real world thinking she's better than other people."

Dad finally jumped in, "Yeah, that school is full of uppity brats . . . ," he said matter-of-factly. "But even before she went there, Mishna thought she was better than everyone. She's just snotty like her mother. She's her mother's daughter. . . . Now Anora . . ." Dad got a pride in his voice. "Anora is my girl."

I had to grab the railing of the stairs. I couldn't breathe. *Anora is his girl?*

She hadn't even tried! I was the capper. I learned dominoes. I hit Christopher Scott for him! How could I not be his girl?

I couldn't even keep my head up and collapsed lengthwise on the plastic covered steps and slid back down them into the basement—enjoying the way each step felt hitting the back of my head and taking me out of my thoughts.

I certainly didn't think I was better than anyone! In fact, I was pretty sure I was worse:

I was not as smart as my classmates.

I wasn't cute like my sister.

I *always* said the wrong thing.

I couldn't dance or rap or be spontaneous like Dominique's nieces and nephews.

And I embarrassed Dad constantly.

I sucked and I knew it. I never asked to go to rich school,
but as bratty and uppity as those kids might be, they were
easier to please than Dad. So I hit my funny bone as hard as I
could against the railing.

Five

THE JESSE OWENS STORY

WHATEVER RESISTANCE I still had to my school vanished in the stairwell of Dominique's parents' house. I was a changed girl. Not that Dad noticed—over the next week he was much too engaged with my sister's newest undertaking. Anora and her best friend Maybelline had formed a six-year-old song-and-dance duo called the Sweet Beats. And Dad's friend Reggie Dee was managing them—figuring he could do it as a side gig while he was growing his Amway business.

The Sweet Beats were conceived by Anora and Maybelline while they were taking African dance. They both studied at a studio called Ewajo, where Anora was the only white student—and didn't seem to care. *Ewajo* was a Yoruba word from Nigeria and meant, "people, come dance." Which made Ewajo a command, like "halt" or "pull my finger." I really couldn't figure out how exactly Ewajo led to the R & B-based Sweet Beats. She and Maybelline somehow managed to turn a dance relationship, fostered in traditional African pageantry and ceremony, into doing the running man and the cabbage patch in our shared room to their dope tunes like: "I'm Not Giving You My Digits" or "Somebody's Triflin'."

I didn't go to Ewajo and wasn't asked if I'd like to be included. I had already taken community center ballet when I was Anora's age, which was like regular ballet but cheaper and oddly, more Asian. And after learning that tall people didn't become prima ballerinas, I couldn't really see the point of standing at a bar and pliéing till my eyes fell out next to the petite Vietnamese girl who, unlike me, would never have to play a prince or an animal. Maybe this was why I didn't catch Sweet Beats fever like everyone else. Or maybe it was because the group jettisoned my sister from someone who sang and danced for fun into "a professional," which was basically like asking her to never ever stop making noise. She was so empowered by her newfound status that she found the courage to keep me up at night—singing in bed.

"Let me sleep!" I would beg.

"I need to practice," she would say. "I want to be on MTV."

I would ball the pillows over my head and try to tune her out, but I had to admit, "Somebody's Triflin'" was catchy. Which only made the whole affair more irritating.

My irritation with the Sweet Beats didn't just come from being constantly annoyed—this was something more: I wanted nothing to do with the Sweet Beats fervor that was infecting everyone around me. Anora was Dad's girl, so let her be. I was slowly finding that I wanted to act, I dunno . . . uppity.

A couple weeks later, we got to pick out our music instruments in school. If your parents signed a slip, you could participate in orchestra or band, and it was free. Not only that. They gave you a musical instrument—free. The word *free* caught Dad's ear when I broached the subject over Monday night football. He kept looking at the TV, but I could tell by the way he stayed in his chair through the rest of the quarter that he was entertaining the idea of me playing an instrument.

And during a time-out he looked up and said, "You should get a saxophone."

"I dunno," I said. "I was kind of thinking of something else."

"Like what?" He asked.

Anything else, I thought. But what I said was, "I don't know, something more classical."

"You know . . . ," he said, returning to the game. "You're kind of too small to handle a tenor sax, otherwise that would be cool. I think alto sax is a good choice for a girl." Then he screamed at the TV. "Run, motherfucker! Run!"

I couldn't handle the idea of playing sax—not in my house, not now that I knew how much I embarrassed Dad already. I could already see Dad's shame at the dominoes table with his buddies—the sounds of me practicing my sax wafting in from the other room, and him blaming my lack of soul on my mother. Not that he could play any musical instrument, but he was a skilled air trumpet player, which made him an expert on all metal instruments.

The morning I was supposed to get my saxophone, Dad was in a hurry to get out the door. I presented the slip he was supposed to sign saying that I was taking home a musical instrument and if something happened to it, he would be responsible for it. He perused it for a second then made a face at the word *responsible*. He looked at the paper for a while, scratching his chin, and then slowly signed it.

He handed me back the pen, and said, "When you get home today I'll play you some Charlie Parker . . . the Birdman!"

"Birdman. Birdman. Birdman," my sister said.

"Okay," I said, picking up my slip and putting it in my backpack. "Sounds great."

"Oh yeah," he said. "You don't know what great is yet. But your dad's gonna take you to school."

"I want to hear the Birdman!" my sister screamed, crumpling in a heap on the floor.

"Take care of your sister," Dad said.

Of course, at school the event of the day was music class. All day there had been chatter about getting our instruments, and once we were all actually in music class there was no controlling the excitement. We waited in line while Mrs. Hathaway, a fifty-year-old woman who dyed her short white hair purplish, took our slips and one by one gave us the instrument we wanted. More than anything people were walking away with violins. Christopher passed me with a violin and a bummed out look on his face.

"Hey," I said. "You're playing violin?"

"Yeah," he said. "I wanted to play sax, but my dumb parents are making me." He looked really disappointed, and at that moment I thought about bragging about how Dad actually *wanted* me to play saxophone. But instead I put on my most disappointed face, shuffled my feet and said, "Yeah, my parents are making me play violin, too."

Christopher gave me a sympathetic look and a smile. And I had never been more interested in the violin.

"God," I said. "Why are parents so dumb?"

"Exactly," Christopher said. "It's like they have to be involved in everything, all the time."

"I know!" I said, trying to sound like I was gonna barf. "It's like, I'm my own person, right?"

That afternoon, as I walked in the house with the beat-up violin case in my hand. I decided to lie and tell Dad they had run out of saxes. He stood at the kitchen counter, shirtless with a basketball in his hand, and went through a litany of other in-struments I should have chosen while trying to spin the ball on his finger, "Trumpet, trombone, clarinet . . . tenor fucking sax!"

I shrugged, and he dashed into the living room,

"Follow me!" he said, throwing the ball at me for me to catch, and not noticing it bounce down the front of my chest.

"I'm gonna teach you a little something about jazz." He was already leafing furiously through a stack of cassettes.

"So, Mishna," he said. "What about you get on the wait list or something for a sax tomorrow?"

But I knew I wasn't giving my violin back. No matter how many times he played me John Coltrane.

"I think maybe we should stick with this for a year and see how things go," I said. "Let's just try it."

"Fine," he finally said. "Have it your way."

Which was his way of saying, "I will get you back soon . . . and when you least expect it. . . ."

The next day, I walked my new violin home from school again feeling proud—and free. I had no idea what to do with it yet, but it felt so good to have something so wonderful and foreign in my hand. It was a cheap violin that had been abused by doz-ens of students' greasy fingers, but as I walked with it into the corner store to buy a ten-cent pack of Now and Laters, I imag-ined it made me look both smarter, richer, and like my parents were really overbearing. I didn't even mind when an older black woman in a Monte Carlo pulled over beside me outside and asked if I was lost.

But the second I walked in the door, I could tell by Dad's face he had an announcement. He was wearing that look he always wore when he had just made a decision that involved all

of us. His face said, "I have great news—we are starting a skunk farm!"

I set my violin down on the counter just as he said, "I have great news!" I set my bag down. "I signed you up to run track!" If he had finished the thought, he would have said, "You'll be the only white person on the team, and probably the slowest."

But he didn't. He looked at me excitedly until I said flatly, "That's great, Dad."

He got more animated and started to move his hands around as he said, "You gotta be more physical, too, you know. You go to school for your head"—he pointed to his head—"but that ain't everything, you know. You need to be well rounded." I looked at him blankly as he traced a circle with his hands to represent "well rounded." But I knew now what *well rounded* meant. It meant, "We need to balance all that uppity white shit out, because you're embarrassing me."

———————

When I arrived at my first practice at CDAC, Central District Athletic Club, it felt like I had accidentally walked into gladiator training. Everyone was huge and strong, and they looked like grown-up Olympic athletes. I had never seen twelve-year-old boys whose muscles were cut like Ben Johnson, or fourteen-year-old girls who moved like Jackie Joyner-Kersee.

As I walked across the field, holding my father's hand, I saw a girl my age take a long jump. She raced to the line and sailed into the air, pumping her feet until the final moment when she thrust them out in front of her to grab those extra inches on the landing. She smiled like crazy as she picked herself up from her jump, and ran to where the rest of the team was running laps. And as she folded back in with the group, a teammate laughed and slapped her back almost as if to say, "You just can't get enough long jumping, can you?"

In the middle of the field a line of boys were pole vaulting, something I had never seen before, and reminded me of Evel Knievel. I watched amazed as they flew through the air and then landed softly like cats. It was like they were bionic.

Everywhere I looked huge majestic dark bodies jumped and sped through practice with perfect skill and grace, chests out, legs pumping. I was witnessing physical excellence for the first time—gods in training. I was totally fucked.

And then I saw Zwena. Zwena was like this wonderful oddity on the team. I spotted her loping on the other side of the field wearing her glasses with an elastic head strap and carrying an inhaler in her shorts pocket. She ignored all the coaches yelling and smiled as she remained completely in her own world, oblivious of the people dashing by her and the fact that we were supposed to be competitive. There was hope.

———————

The ages on the team ranged from seven to seventeen so I was put with the younger kids because I was nine. The few older kids, from what I could tell, were stars and got their own personal workout from the coach. Not that we didn't all share the same track, which meant if one of these stars was coming up behind you, they had the right of way. The muscular person moving at the speed of sound always has the right of way.

After school I immediately left my new school friends who were really starting to like me, and took a bus to a field full of neighborhood kids who would jump on my dead body if they thought it would add spring to their high jump. I know that because I slowed once on the track and didn't move out of the way quick enough for twelve-year-old Jada to lap me. She body-slammed me to the ground and then, angry that her stride had been broken, pointed to her spikes and saying, "Next time, I'll stomp your face and not think twice about it."

Running at CDAC also seemed to have some weird association to a man named Jesse Owens. Jesse Owens was the meet we sponsored and the guy on the medals. Zwena didn't know who he was, but I thought we might be his team. We both had the sense not to ask the coach who Jesse Owens was. My coach was a six-foot-three bulldog with a whistle. And I worried if I asked him who Jesse Owens was, he'd say, "You're on his team, dummy!" Then he would call Jesse Owens over and Jesse Owens would karate chop me in the neck. Or worse, kick me off the team, which I would have no way of explaining to Dad.

One night, Dad came to watch the last half of my workout. I had really tried to hold my own on the field so he would be happy, and as we left practice I was truly exhausted. We got in the car and were at least five blocks from the track. "Dad, who is Jesse Owens?"

Dad looked at me quizzically and said, "I never told you the

Jesse Owens story?" Then he scratched his chin, "Okay," he said. "Jesse Owens was a black man who won the Olympics, but he took a lot of shit for being black. I mean a lot of shit."

I tried to imagine what that looked like. I said, "Did people throw rocks at him?"

"Well," Dad said. "I don't know all that, but he had to eat at different restaurants than the other folks on the team, and he couldn't do all the stuff white athletes did. And he really pissed off Hitler."

I was confused. "I thought Hitler hated Jews."

Dad said, "Oh, he hated black people, too, a lot. Hitler hated all people who were different. And when Jesse Owens won all the Olympic races, it was in Germany, and Hitler got so mad he went off."

"That must have been scary," I said. "I mean Hitler is already scary. Was Jesse Owens afraid that Hitler would kill him in an oven?"

By now, my father had zoned out and he muttered, "Definitely."

I looked at Dad proudly. I bet Kirsten's father "the professor" didn't know as much as Dad did about Jesse Owens. I was always amazed how much he knew about social injustice. I remembered when we had Dad's friend Carl living with us for a while, who I hated until Dad explained to me that I didn't know what it was like to be black and out of work. Then Carl stole our TV, but Dad didn't get mad, he just said, "If Carl took that beat-up old TV, the joke's, on him."

I looked at the road and noticed we were driving past the turnoff for the house. "Dad, where are we going?"

He snapped back to attention and said, "Oh. We gotta get your sister from rehearsal."

"What rehearsal?" I asked.

Dad looked at me like I was retarded. "The Sweet Beats."

I didn't realize we were taking them that seriously.

I had a lot of homework, plus we had seating tests for orchestra the next day, so I had to practice my violin. I asked Dad, "Dad can you just drop me home? It's pretty much on the way and I have a lot of work for school."

"You can hang out for a little bit. We have to support your sister's endeavors, too."

When we got to Maybelline's house, I saw Reggie Dee's car parked out front—so he was really managing them. Maybelline's mom, Candy, was at work. We walked in to find the Sweet Beats hard at work in the little TV room while Maybelline's socially awkward older half-brother, Carlos, holed up in his bedroom in silent protest. Reggie was sitting on the couch with a beer half watching the girls, who were in front of a mirror doing a dance routine that involved twirling an invisible hula hoop to Salt-N-Pepa.

I watched for a minute, trying to understand if there was some sort of order to what they were doing, but there didn't appear to be any real throughline. Anora would do the running man, and Maybelline would follow. Then Maybelline would shake her butt and Anora would copy her. It was like dance class in the amnesia ward. I turned to see what Dad thought of all this, but he already had a beer open and was stretched out on the couch next to Reggie, like he lived there. The song ended and Maybelline asked, "What now, Uncle Reggie?"

Reggie looked up from the conversation he was having with Dad about the Raiders defensive line and said, "Um . . . just do it again."

Two hours later, we were still there. Sweet Beats practice had dissolved into Anora and Maybelline in Maybelline's room playing with her hair stuff. And Dad and Reggie were still on the couch, only now the game was on. Candy, Maybelline's mom, was nowhere in sight and I was nowhere closer to getting my homework done or learning the stuff I was supposed to learn on my violin for seat assignments for orchestra.

"Dad . . . ," I asked. "Are we close to leaving?"

I used my quiet voice, hoping he would magically hear me. He didn't. He just continued looking straight ahead, lost in the TV.

"Dad . . . ," I repeated, whining a little.

"What?"

"Dad, I have a lot of homework to do. And I have to practice my violin."

"So," Dad said, "no one's stopping you. Do what you gotta do."

"But—"

"Oh, stop," Dad said. "Everyone's having a good time. Just get your stuff and do your homework."

I stomped out to the car and got my violin and schoolbag—seething. Every step through the dirt yard was an angry thought. *What the hell . . . why couldn't he just drop me home? Sweet Beats, my ass! I have very important things to do!*

I wound up sitting on the kitchen floor and finishing my homework. It was clean enough for a girl who just ate dirt at track practice, but not as clean as a chair. Every now and then Dad would come in to grab a beer.

He looked at me with my books spread around me on the floor. "I guess I'm supposed to feel sorry for you, wif' your little show! You look like a goddamn orphan!"

It didn't take me long to finish my homework, but practicing for the seating in orchestra was gonna be a little more difficult. I walked back into the TV room where the game was over and, once again, the Sweet Beats were rehearsing. "Push It" was playing for the fifteenth time that night, and Reggie and Dad were smiling and laughing. Dad got up off the couch and started shaking his hips to the music.

"Let me show you girls a thing or two," he said, doing an exaggerated version of what Anora and Maybelline had been doing.

"Dad," I said. "I really need to practice. I need to go home."

"Practice in the kitchen," Dad said, moving into the chicken dance. "You do every other goddamn thing in there."

"But," I asked timidly, "when are we leaving?"

Dad stopped dancing and looked at me like I was the world's biggest buzz kill. "You better stop your whining. . . . You just do what you need to do. We'll leave when I'm ready to leave." That was his final word.

I started to unpack my violin, saying to myself as I set up, "Fine! If he wants me playing my violin here for the whole house full of people, violin he shall get!" I put the resin on my bow, set up my music on the counter and put my chin in the chin rest—Salt-N-Pepa still blaring in the background. I lifted my bow. I put my bow down. I lifted it again, and squeaked out a very quiet note. I put down my bow again. I tried to play the piece very quietly. It sounded like shit. I worried that Dad and Reggie heard it and were making fun of me in the living room. I popped my head in the living room—nope, still dancing. But I couldn't take any more chances. One day I would be a real violinist and I would play loud and well and fill a house with sounds so beautiful that everyone would stop what they were doing and listen. Today was not that day.

I packed everything up and sat next to Reggie on the couch with my arms crossed where I remained until ten thirty when Candy came home and we finally left.

———

The next day at seating tests for orchestra I ate it. I walked into the little room where Mrs. Hathaway auditioned us, and forgot the piece I barely knew to begin with. Mrs. Hathaway just sat there with a pen and notebook writing furiously with an angry face. When I finished she looked at me over her glasses and said, "Mishna, that was terrible." Mrs. Hathaway was one of those old-school teachers who didn't know that she was supposed to coddle my developing self-esteem. "Really . . . just one of the worst performances I have ever seen. I don't know why you are wasting my time." She stuck out her bottom lip and blew her bangs off her forehead. "You know, a lot of these kids have been playing since they were five. If you want to participate, you have to really apply yourself." At the end of class, she put out the seat assignments. I was last chair, last violin. And someone was gonna pay for it.

At track practice I was too angry to run. I couldn't find it in me to put one foot in front of the other. I took a lap, and I was done. But I couldn't leave. I had to find a way to make it look like I was working out without actually working out. I began to sort of move around the various events on the field in a way that made it look as though I had just finished up that particular event. I moseyed away from the long jump brushing sand off my shorts, before making my way to the pole vault, which I left rubbing my sore pole-vaulting arms. This was working so well that I hid under the bleachers for the rest of practice and either nobody noticed, or nobody cared. Either way it felt great to completely play hooky from track practice.

As the weeks went by, I got lazier and lazier. My only real goal became to escape notice. I was almost a ghost on the team. I even began to think I had the same powers to disappear in plain view that I had had at GSCC. When I wasn't doing that, I just ran with Zwena and we'd keep up a pace that was comfortable to have a conversation at.

"How's it going at smarty school?" she'd ask.

"I feel pretty much like the weirdest person there all the time," I'd say. "How's it going at private school?"

"Rich and white," she'd say, but always adding, "But I like my classes."

I was surprised when one day when we were walk-running and I asked, "I guess your dad pretty much made you run, huh?" And Zwena told me he hadn't at all. She'd wanted to run and she thought it was fun. I just looked at her for the next lap, baffled. I couldn't figure out why she would want to do anything that she wasn't immediately great at.

Zwena and I had a good thing going, and then Dad reappeared at practice. He started by marching over to the head coach and having a long conversation with him. I could tell by the way they were looking at me from across the field that I was not as invisible as I had thought. From then on Dad came to every practice and coached from the sidelines. He even took to coaching Zwena, too, and suddenly she didn't think running was so fun.

"Mishna," he'd scream, "you still got half an hour left of practice—hit that like you mean it."

I'd roll my eyes at Zwena just in time to hear Dad tell her, "Zwena. You, too! Stop actin' like you're dying. Neither of you two is gonna die from some wind sprints." And the more involved Dad got in track, the more exhausted just thinking about a track made me.

Every weekend for the rest of the season Dad dragged me and Zwena to track meets, and I tried to invent injuries in the car on the way. I wasn't that good a runner, I could imagine I was injured so deeply, I could actually cause swelling. I would limp into the car at 7:00 A.M. on a Saturday morning whining, "Daaaaaad, my calf has a cramp . . . and on top of that, I think

I twisted my knee coming down the steps. It might be my rotator cap." But Dad would just grin and say, "When we get to the meet you can take a few laps—walk it off."

One night I was in my bedroom practicing my violin. My sister had made her usual show of running out of our bedroom with her hands over her ears.

"What?" I asked. "Am I that bad?"

"I just have to go," she said. "That kind of music messes with my rhythm."

"Fine," I said. "I'll be done in a half an hour. Just listen to one side of your Salt-N-Pepa tape."

"Ooh, good idea," she said, and slammed the cheap pressboard door on the way out.

I had been practicing for thirty—or five—minutes when Dad walked in. I nervously stopped playing.

"I didn't kick Anora out," I said. "She left on her own."

But Dad just looked at me for a moment before saying, "I think at the next meet we're gonna enter you in the four-hundred-yard dash."

"That's a long way," I said.

"It's nothing," Dad said. "And I really think that it's the right distance for ya."

But I was pissed. At the time I was doing fifties and hundreds, and four hundred yards—that was like miles.

"But, Dad," I said. "I'm a sprinter."

"First of all," Dad said. "You're too young to know what you are, and second of all, the four hundred is a sprint."

"It is?" I asked.

"Oh yeah," Dad said. "There's no pacing yourself around the field. The four hundred is an out-and-out sprint."

I really hated this idea: run longer at the same speed. But Dad was sure that was the distance for me. And even though the whole next week I begged not to, I was running that stupid race.

By the day of the race I had convinced myself that if I ran the four hundred, I would die of a combination of exhaustion and embarrassment. I don't know how I knew, but I felt like the old wise people who die in movies—I just knew it was my time. I glanced at my competition: six hesitant-looking white girls and Yolanda, a teammate. Then I looked at Dad who, from the look in his eyes, was trying to make my legs faster with the sheer power of his mind. I got up to the blocks wondering how I could not run this race and avoid an ass-whooping.

I thought, *I just don't feel like trucking those four hundred yards to the other side of the field.* I looked at the finish line. *It's just so far. . . .* Then it hit me. *Wait a second, if I fell, no one would look down on me for not running.* People fall. I could even be hurt. Then Dad would shake his head and say, "Why? Oh Lord, why? I'm so so so sorry ever let her run the four hundred!"

So I got on the blocks, and I knew I needed to make the fall good or no one would believe I was hurt. And so the gun went off. And I fell. And it was good.

But the dumb lady with the gun had some investment in me making it to the other side of the field, 'cause she screamed at me, "Get up! Get up!"

I ignored her, and decided to look at the dirt. Like, *This is an interesting pebble. Has this always been here?*

But she kept screaming, "Get up!" So I grudgingly picked myself up, and as long as I was running I wanted to do it fast, so I could get the stupid race done with and get into a bag of Fritos. And all the while I'm running I thought, *What does this bitch care whether I run or not? I've never seen her in my life. She needs to mind her own business is what she needs to do.* And I'm embarrassed, and in such a hurry to get off the field, that I accidentally come in second, meaning I lost to Yolanda. And I had to admit, four hundred yards wasn't as long as it looked and it actually was a sprint.

I imagined Fritos were out now, though. *I'll be lucky if he ever feeds me again,* I thought as I made my way over to the stands where I was sure Dad was waiting, pissed. But when I got over to him, he was with a group of parents. Rather than being mad, his eyes were full of tears and he was beaming with pride. He grabbed me by the shoulder and held his arm up pointing to me while exclaiming to all the other parents, "My girl!" And that was just the beginning.

That night he sat with his buddies, and during a lull in their arguing Dad began to recap the day.

"Mmm . . . It was at the Jesse Owens invitational. Mishna was running the four-hundred-yard dash. And that gun went off, and I don't know what happened, but . . ." He got really singsongy, like a preacher as he continued, "I think there was something wrong with her shoes, 'cause she tripped and fell and she had lost a lot of distance. And I knew she was gonna be disappointed 'cause she had been looking forward to the four hundred for a long time, and she wanted a piece of that race. You know that's life, right? You try to get yourself going and . . . you know the politics and such. But Mishna is on the ground, and she sees these girls getting ahead of her, and I saw a look in her eye, like a tiger who sees a fish. . . . This girl picks herself up, and she's chasing these girls like a pit bull. She comes around that first turn and she's already caught most of them. The girl comes in second. . . . Second, from being out of it—down—finished . . . second."

He took a pause to gauge the attention level of his listeners before adding, "I raised 'em tough but fair. They don't have to be number one but they have to try. You got to or, you know, the Man takes you down without a fight."

The first recounting of the four-hundred-yard-dash story was to the fellas. The second was to anyone who made eye contact—neighbors, grocers, total strangers. And even though I felt kind of bad for not setting the record straight, I was now officially well rounded. In fact, I was almost a hero. And though I had given up on it, Dad's approval felt good. So good that I forgot about the Sweet Beats or that I had taken a dive in the first place.

A week later we went over for dinner at Maybelline's house. Candy had cooked and Reggie Dee was there. Anora and Maybelline sat side by side, practically eating off each other's plates. Dad helped himself to seconds of everything and was so into the food that he didn't notice when Candy and Reggie kissed in the kitchen. And after dinner as Dad told everyone the four hundred-yard-dash story, Maybelline's half brother Carlos seemed truly impressed. But what I noticed was that Candy was practically in Reggie's lap, which was weird because I thought Reggie was always over at Candy's because Anora was in the Sweet Beats. I looked questioningly at Carlos, who was sitting on my left. He looked annoyed as he whispered, "Reggie lives here now."

After dinner we ate ice cream while the grown-ups had another beer. Maybelline asked, "Uncle Reggie . . . when are you gonna get us some shows?"

But Reggie was staring at Candy, his hand on her shoulders, and just said, "What?"

"Some shows . . . The Sweet Beats," Maybelline repeated, annoyed. "What did you call them?"

"Gigs . . . yeah," Reggie said, without taking his attention off Candy. "I'm gonna get on that."

Anora clapped her hands excitedly. But Maybelline, who knew better, just pushed her ice cream around. She knew there wouldn't be any gigs or any more managing.

I took a couple more bites of my ice cream and looked at Maybelline and Anora sitting across from me. I nudged Carlos and said, "You guys can do a show for me." Maybe I was just earning my allowance.

"Really?" Maybelline asked.

"Yeah," I said. "Carlos will watch, too." Carlos gave me a nasty look for volunteering him. Maybe I just wanted to protect Anora from the news that hadn't reached her yet.

"Yay!" Maybelline said, throwing her arms around her older brother. He rolled his eyes, but I knew he wouldn't say no.

"I haven't seen you guys in a while," I said, looking at Anora. "I bet you're really good now."

"We are!" Anora said, getting up to set things up in the family room. "We really are!"

"Where do you want me to sit?" Carlos said. "And how long is this gonna take?"

"Oh stop being so weak, Carlos," I said as Anora finished setting up a couple of chairs and told Carlos where to sit. The truth was, I liked it when Anora was happy.

So that night, Carlos and I watched as the Sweet Beats performed their first and final show. They did all their big numbers: "Push It," "I'm Not Giving You My Digits," and "Somebody's Triflin'" with the skill and grace of six-year-olds who have had too much root beer. And when they finished they smiled and bowed, and Carlos and I clapped really loud. And then we beat the shit out of them with the couch pillows.

Six

VALUE VILLAGE

AFTER PE at rich school we had lunch, during which I made an elaborate production of trying to hide my subsidized lunch ticket. We would all line up in front of the desk of an ancient Polish lady with a mustache, and one by one we would tell her our last name so she could give us our ticket. When it was my turn, she would file through the perfect aqua-colored tickets until she got to my ghetto peach-colored ticket, while I used my body to hide our transaction from the rest of the kids. Then I would palm the ticket till I got to the lady who punched it, hoping to God she wouldn't make her usual show of holding it up to make sure there were no hanging chads.

My special different-colored ticket served as a reminder that the city thought I needed some extra parenting. It was such a thorn in my side that I would actually skip lunch on days I wasn't feeling strong enough to answer the question, "Hey why is your lunch ticket a different color than EVERYBODY ELSE'S?" Or simply, "What's up with the pink ticket?" Once, in frustration, I told Catrina Calder it was because I was allergic to raisins, to which she responded, "Bummer . . . raisins are good."

I made my way through the line, getting my well-balanced meal, then found a seat at the fifth-grade oddball table with Lilith and Violet. Lilith was pushing her spaghetti with meat sauce around her plate like maybe it was poison. She took a few bites of the salad, which she deemed "edible" so that she wouldn't catch too much flack from the lady that scraped the food off our trays while reminding us about the drought in Ethiopia. While Violet just looked at her spaghetti and meat sauce and let out a long low sigh, Lilith speculated, "It's gotta be horse."

"No way," said Violet. "I know it's cat. It smells just like my cat's box." Then she turned to me and said, "Mishna? What do you think they used in the sauce?"

My turn. "I think maybe it's just really bad beef."

"Beef?" Lilith said amazed that I was defending the meat. "No way that came from a cow." And as she glared at me I felt myself slowly becoming the mystery meat. So I changed my answer to rabid raccoon meat.

"Ewww!" the two girls said in unison and pushed their trays away, signaling my redemption.

The truth was, I loved my lunch and would have eaten two lunches if I could have. And not just spaghetti. I loved it all: turkey tetrazzini—delicious. Salisbury steak—warm and juicy. Tacos—did I just die and go to heaven? I lived with a single man who liked to go out; my sister and I had literally been living off a Costco container of minute tapioca for a week. (It deserves to be noted that minute tapioca takes over half an hour to prepare and requires eggs.)

Yet sitting there with my friends, I was agonizing over the fact that I would have to throw away some food no matter how much it killed me. One lunchtime, I scarfed down my entire portion of ravioli and used the roll to sop up the sauce. And when I looked up, Lilith and Violet were looking at me as though I had just become Chef Boyardee. Even though I had washed my hands, the running gag all day was how much I smelled like ravioli.

I looked at my tray. I knew not eating my coffee cake was not an option. I'd rather lose an arm than throw away cake. And the salad had yummy ranch dressing on it, which went so good with spaghetti sauce. It was like a scene out of *Sophie's Choice*. I decided I would mix my salad into the pasta and eat half of each, but wound up eating three-quarters.

Then I set my fork down and said, "God . . . This food sucks!" Lilith nodded. And Violet gagged on her finger.

Then changing the subject, Lilith turned to Violet and said, "Are you guys going to Sun Valley this Christmas break?"

"Yes," Violet said, rolling her eyes.

"Well," Lilith said. "We might go, too."

"That would be good. I get stuck skiing with my little sister and she always gets stuck in the powder. When will you know?" Violet asked.

"Well . . . ," Lilith replied. "Dad doesn't want to fly so he thinks we should go to Whistler. But my mom doesn't want to leave the country, and she'll probably win. She always does."

"Awesome!" Violet said, and they shared a moment. I did not share that moment.

"What's Sun Valley?" I asked. Lilith and Violet were my friends, so they didn't laugh at me. Instead they talked to me slowly—like I was a slow person.

"Sun Valley . . . ," Violet said. "Is . . . a . . . ski . . . resort."

Then Lilith said, "It's for skiing."

"Lilith and I ski," added Violet.

"Well," I said, "I want to ski, too." Neither of them said anything. So after a minute I asked, "Why can't I ski?"

"We're just really good," Lilith said apologetically. "We've been doing it for a long time."

"Oh," I replied.

And then to soften the blow Lilith added, "I really liked your science diorama. That moon—looked so real."

"I just spraypainted a golf ball," I said, looking up sadly. It was at that moment I realized I had accidentally eaten the rest of my lunch.

When I got home from school that night, my sister was walking around the house in a pair of shiny new track spikes. She clomped around the kitchen floor enjoying the sound her spikes made on the linoleum.

"New spikes?" I asked, setting my bag down on the counter. She responded by beaming. "I'm gonna run track, too."

"It's November," I said. "Track season isn't till the spring."

"So," she said, and went back to listening to her feet.

"They're on sale now!" Dad said, walking in from the bathroom. "That's how you do it."

"But what if her feet grow?" I asked.

"You think I'm stupid? I think of everything."

"They're a size too big," Anora explained. She was now trying to tap dance in her track spikes.

"Okay," I said, and grabbed my bag to head downstairs to the basement. "I'll be downstairs."

"Where are you going?" Dad asked.

"My room?"

"Nah, nah, nah," he said. "You gotta change for dinner."

I didn't know we had special dinner plans and asked, "Are we going to McDonald's?"

Anora started jumping up and down, clapping her hands, but her track spikes made her lose her balance and she had to steady herself on the counter.

"No," Dad said, "you don't worry about where we're going. Just make yourself look nice." Then he added. "And find a dress for your sister, too."

There was enough time to change and get a little homework done before we left, but unfortunately I had to get my sister out of her new spikes, which she refused to remove.

"Just take them off," I begged. "You can put them back on the second we get home."

"NO!" she snapped. "You're not the boss of my feet!"

I insisted that I wasn't trying to be the boss of her feet, I just wanted to preserve the sharpness of the spikes, but she wasn't buying it.

Reason having failed me, I resorted to trying to tickle her out of them. And although it got me mortally gouged in the leg, Anora finally gave in and removed the weapons from her feet herself.

Holding the spikes, I examined my leg. There wasn't any blood, but my calf looked as though it had been aerated. I sat on the matted red carpet on the floor of our room firmly holding the track shoes in either hand. But Anora came after the shoes again, and when she couldn't wrestle them out of my grasp she proceeded to sit on my stomach and bounce up and down. It hurt a little but I wasn't giving in. She angrily bounced on me over and over, getting more and more frustrated until finally the frustration on her face was replaced by calm resolve. That's when she proceeded to pee on me—wet, hot, ample, vindictive pee. I was drenched. But even as I threw her off me and stood up in shock, I kept the track shoes high above my head.

"Now I have to change!" I screamed.

"You had to change anyway. Now, give me my shoes back!"

"No!" I said, getting on a chair and placing the shoes on top of the homemade plywood bookcase. Then I grabbed her arm to march us upstairs and into a shower. But halfway up the stairs she went limp, forcing me to drag her into the bathroom, mimicking Dad as I went, "What's the big deal? . . . Just get your sister dressed. Your dad can't be looking out for every little old thing."

Needless to say, I didn't get any schoolwork done before we left the house, and as we drove to God knows where, I started to get the knots in my stomach I always got when I knew I wasn't gonna be adequately prepared in math.

However, my fears were eased a little by the fact that the houses were getting better as we drove, and I sort of stopped worrying about where we were going, and started to get excited.

"Hey, Dad?" I asked. "Will you tell us now where we are going?"

He had a smile on his face and a wicked look in his eye as he said, "Jackie's house." I had no idea who Jackie was. This was the first I heard that Dominique was out.

"What happened to Dominique?" Anora asked.

"She's still in the same house," Dad joked. "But that's enough talk about Dominique."

And my sister started singing, "Dominique, Dominique, no more Dominique."

"I told you that was enough," Dad said. "Mishna, don't let your sister talk about Dominique in front of Jackie."

"How do I do that?" I asked.

"By any means necessary."

Jackie's place was like a dream come true. For one she didn't live in our neighborhood. She lived in a nice neighborhood where people didn't have their old dryers on the lawn. And when we walked into her house it was immaculate and smelled like food—good food—professional non-yak food—food, glorious food. It made me giddy—Mishna was gonna get her eat on. We were greeted by a tall slim woman around Dad's age with a belted shirtdress on that gave her the appearance of one of those fifties TV moms—only black and less funny.

"Hi," she said with a huge Donna Reed smile. "I'm Jackie."

"I'm Mishna," I said.

"Mishna," she replied. "It's a pleasure to meet you." Then she smiled like it *was* a pleasure and said excitedly, "I can't wait for you to meet my son Zaid. He's only a year older than you. I think you'd really get along." She looked to the hallway. "He's on his computer. Let me get him off, and we'll have dinner."

Fuck Zaid and dinner, I thought. *I wanna get on that computer!*

My sister tugged on Jackie's dress and said, "Do you have a kid my age?" But Jackie was too busy calling Zaid and didn't pay attention to Anora. This woman was scoring points all over.

Zaid lumbered into dinner unimpressed with all of us. He was a tall boy in sweatpants who was a little doughy from the four to ten hours a day he spent on his computer. Dad noticed Zaid's lack of physique and asked, "You do any sports, Zaid?"

Zaid didn't see the need to answer, so Jackie chimed in, "Zaid is a really good skier. We both ski."

I just about dropped my fork. They skied just like cool people I wanted to hang out with.

But Dad was unimpressed, and said to Zaid, "I'll throw the football around with you sometime. Put some muscle in those arms."

Zaid looked at Dad and said blankly, "What do I need arm muscles for?"

"Well," Dad said, "to be strong, for one. That's a pretty good reason right there." Then he reached for seconds on potatoes, not noticing Zaid's shit-eating smirk. I was really beginning to like this Zaid guy.

Dad had his mouth full when I said, "I'd really like to learn how to ski."

Jackie smiled. "We'll all go! It'll be fun." She looked at Dad. "Right, John?" He was faking a smile and began to cough a little. Jackie instinctively handed him a glass of water. He took a big swig and the coughing subsided, leaving his face red and flushed.

"Oh my God, John!" she said. "What did you choke on?"

Dad took a deep breath and said, "Just a little mashed potatoes."

"How do you choke on mashed potatoes?" Zaid asked.

"Zaid!" Jackie threw her napkin down.

"What? I really want to know," Zaid insisted.

But Dad just looked around like he didn't know where he was anymore. Within minutes of meeting him, I could tell Zaid was smarter than Dad, Anora, or me, and he knew it.

The rest of the evening Zaid was forced to entertain me on his computer. He put me in front of an intricate role-playing game while he sat on his beanbag occasionally looking up from *Popular Science* to tell me how shitty I was doing. I walked into a room full of orcs and heard an "uh-oh." from the beanbag chair.

"Uh-oh, what?" I said.

"You're screwed," Zaid said, and went back to his article.

"What do you mean? What should I do?"

"Die," he said.

"Isn't there something I can do?" I asked.

"I'll say this," Zaid replied, annoyed. "There's something you could have done. But it's too late, now. You're dead."

"What?" I demanded.

"Well . . . ," he said, replacing his magazine meticulously on his shelf. "You might have changed your weapon. Oh well. Them's the breaks, huh?"

"No!" I said. "Them's not the breaks! You couldn't have told me earlier?" Onscreen, orcs clobbered my human character.

I started the level over asking, "So when I get to the orcs, what weapon?"

"Just try them all," Zaid said, sitting back down in his beanbag with a new magazine.

At that moment Dad and Jackie popped their heads in. Jackie looked at Dad and smiled. "I knew those two would get along."

"Get your coat," Dad said. "Your sister's being a pain in my ass."

I heard my sister bellow from the other room, "Why do I have to put on a stupid coat!?"

"But Dad," I whined. "Do we have to go already?"

"Aww," Jackie said.

"What did I say?" Dad said.

But I didn't want to go home. I wanted Dad and Jackie to get married right away. I wanted to move in. I wanted to beat the orcs. I wanted Jackie to take me to school in her New Yorker and I wanted a healthy breakfast. In that order.

On the car ride home I kept looking at Dad. I had clearly underestimated him. I mean, this was a cool guy—look at his girlfriend. She was a nurse and she cooked—now that's good people. And she seemed to like Dad, which meant something. And as Dad tucked us in that night, I squeezed his neck and said, "I love you, Daddy."

"I love you, too," he said. But he was distracted as he gripped the top bunk where I was lying. "Do you smell pee?"

"Well," I said nervously. "Anora peed on me because I took off her track shoes." Dad's head disappeared from view as he got in Anora's face down in the bottom bunk.

"Why did you do that?" he demanded. I leaned out of my bunk and hung upside down so I could see what was going on. "Why would you do that to your sister? That's nasty!"

"Well," Anora said, tears filling her eyes. "She tickled me, and she took my track shoes so I couldn't wear them, and put them up there." She pointed to the top of the bookcase.

"I was just trying to get her dressed."

"Mishna, you don't need to defend yourself," Dad said. This was news to me. Then he got back in Anora's face. "You're supposed to listen to your sister. You hear me?"

"But, Dad . . . ," my sister cried. Dad wasn't hearing it and told Anora she'd be cleaning the carpet in the morning.

"I don't know how."

"You'll learn." And that was Dad's final word. He turned on his heel and walked out of the room.

What an awesome night.

The next day at lunch I sat with Lilith and Violet in front of a plate of uneaten Stroganoff telling them all about the computer game I was on the night before. I couldn't remember the name of it, and I kept mixing up orcs and ogres, but they were impressed. I was about to choose what food to throw away that day when Violet said, "Mishna, my mom wants to take you skiing with us this weekend."

"What?" Lilith and I asked in unison.

"Yeah," she said. "If you're still interested. She said she'd teach you on the bunny hill while Lilith and I ski."

"Oh," Lilith sighed. "Me, too. You meant with Mishna *and* me."

"Yeah," Violet said, but her focus was still on me. "So, what do you think? Do you want to go?"

"Yeah," I said. "But I have to ask Dad. What do I need to bring?"

Violet started brainstorming, "Well, we have an extra bib. . . ."

"Bib?" I asked.

"Yeah," Lilith said. "They're just ski pants."

"You should bring a hat and gloves and a ski jacket," Violet added.

"What's a ski jacket?" I asked. I was worried now.

"Like a warm coat!" Lilith said impatiently. "That's water-proof."

"Maybe just some goggles, you can buy them there. And you'll rent skis." This was starting to sound expensive.

"How much money do you think I'll need?" I asked, knowing it might be a deal-breaker.

"God," Violet said blankly. "I have no clue." Then she had a better idea. "I'll just have my mom call your dad."

As I strode home down our street that afternoon I was a little bit giddy. I couldn't believe I had been invited skiing. It was a cold day, and my violin kept me from pulling my hands into my coat sleeves. But, despite the cold, Jason and Tre were out on the street. They had found a large piece of cardboard and were using it to hone their break dancing skills. Jason spun on his head and almost knocked Tre over as he managed to turn the fall into an upward flip and landed in a freeze.

I took on a bit of a strut as I passed, fearful that if I didn't look "ready," they would beat me up and I would drop my violin and it would cost three hundred dollars. But my violin case was screwing up my strut with its centrifugal force, so rather than looking tough I looked disabled. Tre saw me and stopped dancing.

"Hey, violin!" he said. "Where you going, violin?"

I tapped my chest with my free hand and set the violin down to let him know that if need be, I was ready to go.

But Jason just laughed and said, "Shoot, she ain't worth the trouble." And they went back to their dancing and I turned the corner toward my house, still daydreaming about my ski trip.

———

After dinner my sister and I were doing the dishes when the phone rang. Dad answered, and I knew by the way he immediately corrected his posture, he was talking to a woman.

"Mishna, your friend's mom called," he said. "Viela."

"Violet," I said.

"That's what I said! Anyway . . ." He paused. "They want to take you skiing this Saturday . . . if you want to go."

"I do," I said. "But I think I need some gloves and a hat and I don't know if I have a warm enough coat."

"Her mom told me exactly what you need," he said, scratching his head to remember. "You need some gloves and a hat . . . and what else? Oh, you need a ski coat."

"When can we get me the stuff?"

"We'll hook you up by Friday," he said, looking easy and relaxed. But I was worried, and suddenly, I got a flash of myself in the snow, my ungloved hands turning a shade of purple I had never seen before on human flesh.

"Oh," Dad said, remembering, "that's right. You also need lunch money. We'll just pack you a lunch." I went back to my vision of the frostbitten hands and added hungry to the mix.

By Friday, I still had nothing to ski in. We didn't get my gear on Wednesday, because the game was on. We had been over at Jackie's house again on Thursday. And when I got home on Friday the fellas were over playing dominoes. And I was so concerned about my ski stuff that I wasn't even excited that Dad's good friend Delroy was there, which I normally would have been stoked about because he was so smart. Delroy had the Queen's English, a law degree, and most important, a briefcase. And the fact that he hadn't passed the bar, after seven years—and three tries—had less to do with the fact that he wasn't smart and more to do with the fact that he smoked pot every day. Which meant he could totally pass if he really wanted to—and he would become a lawyer as soon as he was done being stoned.

"Hey, genius!" Delroy said as I walked in the door.

Big Lyman was up, which meant he knew everything. "Little Wolff—"

Eldridge corrected him. "It's lil' girl Wolff."

"Little Wolff! Why don't you come over here and watch me take your daddy to school?"

Dad wasn't about to take that insult in his own home, and asked in a low voice, "You about ready to go home, Lyman?" Big Lyman was not, and piped down as Dad added, "That's what I thought."

"Dad," I said. "I still need some ski stuff."

"Ski stuff?" Lyman said, surprised. "You rich or something?"

"Her friends are taking her," Dad said, as if excusing himself.

"Well," Reggie said, scratching his chin, "I don't know what kind of a sport skiing is. The hill does all the work. You just slide. Where's the ath-let-i-cis-m?"

Almost automatically Dad said, "Did I ever tell you the four-hundred-yard-dash story?"

Lyman spoke up, "I think we all heard about Mishna in the four hundred yard dash."

Then Delroy chipped in, "I thinks it's great to ski. Leave her alone." I was grateful for Delroy's two cents, but I just needed a coat. I wasn't up for a whole pro-anti ski debate. Then Delroy added, "I went skiing a few times when I was at Lakeside."

"You would ski!" Lyman said.

"What's wrong with skiing?" Delroy asked. "Is it a white sport?" There was silence from Lyman and Reggie Dee. Delroy continued, "You brothers play tennis all the time. That's a white sport."

"Well," Reggie explained, "tennis is a hot-weather sport. You play when it's hot, and you get hot playing. No brother volunteers to be cold."

"Oh," Delroy said, "so, I'm not a real brother. Is that what you're getting at?"

I was in a hurry for this argument to be over with and said, "Dad's new girlfriend skis."

There were looks from all the men at the table. Dad hadn't told them yet about Jackie, although I couldn't imagine why.

"Here," Dad said, handing me ten dollars. "Go to Value Village and get your shit worked out." I was almost out the door when he said, "And take your sister with you."

"Hey! Hey! Hey!" Big Lyman added as I headed back out the door with my sister. "Stop by see if Zwena wants to go, too." So I guessed it was an expedition.

The way my sister walked, stopping to pick up garbage she found interesting, it took us a half hour to Zwena's and another half hour to get to Value Village, the local neighborhood thrift store. Walking into the store and the glaring fluorescent lights I was reminded again how huge it was—and what mildew smelled like. But Zwena and I loved it there because we could always afford something. It was much better than expensive-ass Salvation Army, where they seemed to think all their junk was made of gold. At Value Village they knew they sold garbage, and it was priced accordingly. And people who shopped there made a joke of pronouncing the *village* with a French accent, and it was endearingly referred to as "Value Vee-lahge."

Holding my sister's hand, I followed Zwena to the kids outerwear where Anora promptly broke free and wedged herself into the middle of a rack of clothes. Zwena found me a green wool hat without too much trouble and it actually had a skier on the tag, so I knew it was the right kind of hat. But the only gloves I could find were bright pink mittens which felt a little young for a fifth-grader. There were only two coats that really fit the bill. One was black, which I liked but not with pink gloves and a green hat. The other one was red and blue, which I also didn't like with the other colors. I held them both up for Zwena.

"Hmmm," she said through a head cold, "I think they're both pretty good. But I don't know anything about skiing."

I turned to Anora. "Which one?"

A little head popped out from between faded rayon. "The red one!" she said, smiling.

"You sure?" I asked.

She thought about it and said, "The black one."

"You're not helping," I said as she climbed back into her rack.

"I'm a caterpillar."

"You are not!" I said. "You're my sister and you're crawling on the floor when I took you someplace."

"Fine," she said, and popped her head back out. "What are you wearing underneath?" Zwena and I looked at each other stumped.

An old black lady with plastic bifocals was putting some dusty paperbacks on a shelf nearby and Zwena jumped into action asking her, "Excuse me. Do you know anything about skiing?"

"Well . . . Not too terribly much, but what can I help you with, sweetie?"

Anora pointed to me and said, "My sister is going skiing for the first time and she needs to know what you wear under your coat."

"You're going skiing? Well, isn't that exciting." The lady

looked at the red and blue coat. She studied it very carefully and said, "I think I know." She went over to a rack of girls turtlenecks and picked out a bright red one. Then she put the coat over it on the hanger. They looked great together—very professional.

"That's it!" I said.

"Oh, yes." The lady nodded. "You're gonna look sharp." I was sure I would, too. We thanked the lady and I counted my items to make sure I had enough money. Zwena did the tax in her head and we scraped through checkout with fourteen cents to spare.

The next day Violet's mother showed up in their minivan.

I ran out of the house and got into the van and Lilith laughed and said, "None of us could figure out how you were gonna get out of your house."

I had almost forgotten about the ten-foot drop from the front door. "There's a back door," I said dryly. It was too early for laughing.

We drove to a ski area about an hour away. And while Violet and Lilith headed for the slopes, Violet's mom brought me to the bunny hill and showed me how to use the rope tow. And I fell, and fell, and fell. A half hour into the day my ski pants were already wet and I felt like I had been beaten with oranges. The one thing I was not, was cold—simply because getting back up with all that gear on, and hiking to where my skis had gone flying off me, required so much energy that I felt like skiing was actually making me old.

After about an hour of this, Lilith and Violet skied by to check on me in my crumpled pile next to Violet's mom. Their parallel skis skidded to a stop, spraying beautiful ski wake into the air. Their matching one-piece ski outfits were dry as a bone and they didn't wear hats but rather precious woolen headbands that covered only their ears.

"How is it going?" Lilith said. "Is she skiing yet?"

"Yes," Violet's mom said. "She's looking good." I had no idea who she was talking about. I was sitting like a pretzel where I had fallen under the rope tow. And I was done skiing. I was just too much of a pussy to tell anyone.

Violet suggested, "Maybe me and Lilith should take her on the lift."

"Hey, guys!" I said shakily. "Let's not do anything to put me in danger."

But once I got on the lift I actually enjoyed skiing for the first time all day—or at least the chairlift part. Apparently there were rides in skiing, like at the fair—but slower so you don't throw up. And, from the lift-ride, I could see snow covered hillsides and trees—basically a full-on winter wonderland. It was beautiful. And when we arrived at the little house at the top of the hill, and I patiently waited for them to stop the lift so that I could get off. But they didn't stop the lift and then I noticed Violet skiing off the lift and calling to me, "Come on!"

I thought, *Surely she's not asking me to get out of my seat while the ride is still in motion.* I didn't think anyone could possibly expect that from me.

No sooner had I thought that, than an alarm went off and there was shouting and the man operating it came running out of the little house waving his arms and screaming, "Get off! Get off! What's wrong with you?"

And I answered honestly, "I dunno."

I arrived home that evening never wanting to ski again. Dad and Anora were out and I peeled off my wet socks and lay down on the brown vinyl couch. I felt good for the first time all day. I would sleep until the aches and the humiliation were gone.

The next thing I knew Jackie's voice said sweetly, "Look.

Poor thing is all tuckered out." And I hurled myself out of sleep, only now realizing my cheek was soldered to the couch by drool. I wiped my cheek and looked up. Jackie, sweet Jackie. I was even happy to see Dad and Anora. Then I noticed Zaid frozen in the entryway gaping at the unfinished cement landing and the picture of black Jesus in the dining room.

"Hey, skier!" Dad said excitedly. "How was the ski trip?"

It was awful, so I said, "It was awesome!"

"Wow," Anora said. "I want to ski."

"It's pretty complicated," I said.

"Well," Dad said. "You can teach us a thing or two next weekend."

What the hell is he talking about?

"We are all gonna go skiing . . . I decided," he said. "As a family. With Jackie and Zaid."

Jackie cooed, "Oh, John. You're gonna be a great skier. I just know it. I'll show you some stuff, and by the end of the day you'll be beating me and Zaid."

Dad smiled at the idea and said, "That's probably true."

The next week I set out with my family to the exact same mountain I had been on the week before—knowing full well that the odds of running into people I knew was a solid 97 percent. Jackie was behind us in her car because Dad insisted on driving us in the boat. Which was super, because the holes in the floor allowed us to monitor the climate change as we drove into the mountains. Anora and I watched through the missing floor as we passed from cold draft, to really cold draft, to snow. And when we skidded onto the shoulder, that was the first we heard that Dad didn't *exactly* have snow tires.

"Don't worry," Dad said. "I lived on the East Coast. I know exactly how to drive in this shit."

The rest of the way up, I sat in the back of the boat, was

going five miles per hour and swerving all over the place, as speedsters in their four-wheel-drive vehicles honked past us. And, just to make sure none of my friends could possibly see me from their passing vehicles, I got as low in my seat as I could.

When we got into the parking lot of the ski area, I made sure the coast was clear before getting out. We needed to get our rentals and our lift tickets, which left me chained to Dad and my sister for an hour in the very busy lodge that could be home to any number of my schoolmates. This was a melding of worlds I had not bargained for. Jackie and Zaid looked great, but my father was wearing blue jeans, work gloves, a long-shoreman's hat, and a coat about a size too small. He looked like a ski lumberjack. And my sister had on a metallic Value Village one-piece that was about a decade out of style. As we walked the halls of the lodge collecting the things we needed to start our day, I became more and more terrified we would run into someone I knew. Sure enough, we were just leaving through the rental shop when I ran into Violet, her mom, and her sister. Violet waddled up to me in her ski boots.

"Oh, awesome," Violet said. "I'm about to meet Lilith on Bonanza. Come with me." But when I looked at Dad he gave me *the look*.

"I'm gonna ski with my family," I said. Violet gave my family the head-to-toe once-over: Jackie, Zaid, the ski lumberjack, Anora the disco skier, and me. We were like nothing they had ever seen on the mountain. While Violet's mother started chatting with Dad and Jackie, I took the opportunity to lean against the lockers and look like I wasn't with them.

We hit the slopes, and Zaid went off by himself, having had just about enough of us already. I was actually a little disappointed he didn't want to spend some time laughing while I fell. My sister, Dad, and I went to the rope tow with Jackie. And I had to admit it, Dad was a bit of a natural. In fact, so was Anora. So much so, we were off the rope tow and onto the lift after about two runs.

At lunch, Jackie pulled out a homemade picnic and I decided to set aside the embarrassment of sitting with my family and pay homage to the glory of food. I was famished, and Jackie was such a good cook—she had made fried chicken and macaroni salad, and she even packed juice boxes for us, just like a mom.

As we finished I saw Violet again and got excited. She was sitting across the room with Lilith and Lilith's mom and sister. Violet's mom was standing in line with Violet's little sister getting some drinks. And when I finished my food, Dad said smiling, "Why don't you go over and hang with your friends?"

The next day, I felt confident enough in my skiing to talk about it a little at school. I went over to Violet's desk before PE and brought up some of the runs we had been on in front of Catrina Calder, who I knew also skied. Catrina, of course, joined in the conversation and we chatted a little about the conditions as we lined up and headed out the door to the gym. I was a skier, and I stood next to Gretchen who also skied and recounted my Saturday until we got into PE and sat down. There was always a lot of speculation about what we would be doing in gym and I was hoping for Wiffle Ball, because I could use the time on the bench to talk about skiing more. It was then Mr. Tully, our PE teacher, announced we would be break-dancing. My class of twenty-one white kids and six "others" went crazy with excitement. I, on the other hand, was queasy. I wasn't sure which was disturbing me more: the fact that Mr. Tully was trying to "hip up" gym class or that he was dressed like an extra from *Roller Boogie*.

He faced a class of elementary school students in a pair of shorts so short that the only reason his junk stayed in was because they were also skintight. His polyester shirt was half unbuttoned to show off his insanely hairy chest. His upper lip disappeared into his well-combed mustache as he described the break-dancing "moves" we would be working on. He almost drooled on himself as he pointed to three large poster boards, with step-by-step instructions on how to do the six-step, the backspin, and the worm. I could tell by his excitement that he was sure he was blowing our young minds the only way a PE teacher can—by bringing the street into the curriculum.

Mr. Tully put Run-DMC on the sound system, and I watched in shock and horror as Chaim, a chubby Jewish kid moved along the gym in a motion that can best be described as floor-humping. I walked up to Donald, who was waiting for his turn to try the windmill.

"Hey, Donald," I said.

"Hi," he said cautiously.

"So, I went skiing this weekend."

"Oh, it's my turn!" he said excitedly. Then he took something out of his coat pocket and put it in my hand. "Will you hold my mealworm while I go, I don't want it to get crushed."

"Okay," I said, not feeling like I had a choice.

But it was all too insane to me. My class of preppy intellectuals had break-dancing fever, and they were trying to act like little Jasons and Tres as they did their pop-locks and freezes. When it was my turn, I didn't want to do it; I wanted to brag about skiing. I waited for Donald to finish and pushed his mealworm back into his hand. Then I asked Mr. Tully for the bathroom pass and didn't come back until just before the class bell rang. Instead, I locked myself in a bathroom stall and counted square tiles on the floor. Then my fingers skied down the large white sink and defied gravity by skiing back up.

After PE we had lunch, which meant more opportunities to talk about skiing with anyone who would listen. I tried to strike up a conversation with Chaim, who was ahead of me in line.

"Hey," I said, "I went skiing this weekend. I took a couple of runs down Bonanza."

"Did you see my moves?" he asked.

"Skiing?" I was confused.

"No," he said as though I was the stupidest girl who had ever lived. "Um . . . break dancing. I think I'm gonna really try to practice and get dope."

"I'm sorry, Chaim," I asked, "did you just say 'dope'?" That's when I realized I had just gotten my lunch ticket, and Chaim was watching me palm it.

"Hey," he said, pointing, "why is your lunch ticket a different color?"

I deflated and said, "I'm allergic to raisins."

Seven

ARE YOU STUPID?

"ARE YOU STUPID?" Zaid asked as I walked into a room full of goblins without putting on my cloak of invisibility.

"No," I said, and it was then that I realized what I had done wrong. "Uh-oh."

"Oh well," Zaid said. "Guess it's my turn."

"You did that on purpose!" I screamed.

"I made you stupid on purpose?" Zaid reasoned. "Do you have any idea how illogical that sounds?"

"Well . . . you have stupid hair!"

"My hair doesn't have a brain at all, it has style."

"I'm going!" I threatened. But a threat has to scare someone. And Zaid, unfazed by a potential lack of me, just grabbed the game controller and ignored me as I stomped out of his room into the living room—right into an argument between Dad and Jackie.

"All I'm saying, John, is that there are some ways you aren't really taking responsibility." I stopped in my tracks against the hallway wall.

"Jackie," he said. "Are you in my head? No. I don't think so."

"John. You aren't listening."

"Just get off my back already," he whined. "Let's just be where we are at, okay?"

I didn't know what Jackie wanted, but I wished he would just give in to the woman who had only hours before made us dinner.

"But, John," Jackie said, "I'm just trying to help."

"Well," he snapped, "when I need your help, I'll fucking ask for it."

"Please, John . . . ," Jackie started, but then she saw me in the hallway and stopped. I tried to pretend like I wasn't eavesdropping and, instead, acted like I was just walking into the living room unaware there was a disagreement in effect. I summoned all of my courage and plopped down nonchalantly on the couch. Dad just watched, baffled.

"Hi," I said, trying to act casual. "What are you guys talking about?"

"Stay out of grown folks' business!" Dad snapped, adding, "I think it's time for you to go back into Zaid's room."

"But he doesn't even want me in there."

Dad waved his hand as if dismissing me. "I don't care. You got to go." I nodded my head and got up to leave.

"Well," I added, turning in the doorway, "I really hope you guys can work it out." At which point Dad removed one of his shoes and threw it at me.

The rest of that night I was worried about Dad and Jackie. They had been dating about a year now and I had seen them unhappy with each other before. On the car ride home I tried to do what I could to assure Dad that Jackie was the best thing that had ever happened to him.

"Dad," I said. "Jackie's house is sooo nice, huh?"

"It's not all that."

"I mean," I adjusted, "she keeps it really clean."

"Well, if you and your sister could organize yourselves a little better, and learn how to do a complete job on that kitchen, our house could be that clean."

"I just think," I said, "it would be super cool if you married Jackie."

He looked at me next to my sister, who had fallen asleep on my arm, and said, "That's my business, not your business! Dang, why can't you be more like your sister. Not so nosy!" He said it so loud, he actually woke Anora up.

As we pulled into our driveway that December night, I felt my sister's drool cooling on my shoulder. I also saw the Christmas lights shining in our window, and I knew why it was so hard for me not to be nosy. In the months since Dad had started seeing Jackie, our lives had seen a lot of improvements. For one it was mid-December and we already had a Christmas tree, and the sight of those lights through the window was a sign to me that we had our shit together. Not just the tree part, it also meant our electricity was on. And on top of that we had a full fridge and Dad had even bought me tickets to the symphony! I also just liked Jackie. She was a nurse, she was sweet, and she taught Dad stuff. Like she knew that if you got cut you should clean and dress the wound. She knew that there were three meals in a day. And she knew that kids had homework every night not just to inconvenience your shit.

Christmas break came, and Dad and Jackie seemed to be doing better. The week before Christmas, they even went Christmas shopping together, leaving Zaid in charge at our house. Zaid, who was working on a project for science extra credit showed us how to take the motors out of most household things and use them to make a really lame car, or a crappy paper electrical fan that works about a quarter as good as a really cheap one you didn't need to destroy an electric can opener to buy.

And that afternoon Jackie and Dad came home laughing and smiling, and Dad didn't flip out when he saw Zaid in the living room desperately trying to put a can opener back together. Dad was also carrying shopping bags, which, even if they weren't for me, were just so exciting. I drooled over the glossy paper of the fancy bags. It was like Dad dating Jackie made us richer, and I made a mental note to snoop though them later.

That night when everyone was upstairs watching TV, I said I needed to put wash in the dryer and crept down stairs to Dad's basement office, convinced that's where the shopping bags had gone. Dad spent a certain amount of time in his office, but we were strictly forbidden to enter. He said he had some very sensitive projects going on and that he needed us not to be fucking shit up in there. But seeing Christmas bags from real stores come into our house was too much for me. If I got punished for the rest of my life, it would be better than not knowing what was in that Toys "R" Us bag. I knew I had to be quick, and I past the washer and dryer to the pressboard door of the makeshift office that my dad spent so much time in.

As I cracked open the door, I was immediately blinded by bright light. And when my eyes adjusted I saw that the floor of the "office" was a forest of marijuana plants. Thirty or more marijuana plants in perfect rows with grow lights poised over them like it was time for their close-up. Whatever I thought of my dad's parenting abilities with us, he certainly knew how to daddy some weed.

So that's why Dad's so happy and everything is taken care of, I thought. It wasn't because Dad had gotten his shit together at all. He'd just gotten better at selling drugs. I thought about a series of items that had been around the house for as long as I could remember. The scale in Dad's bedroom. The plastic baggies everywhere. The fact that we always had extra electronic equipment lying around that people had brought over. How many people had a Betamax, a VCR, two Walkmen, and three stereo receivers? God, I felt so stupid. The anger welled up in my feet and worked its way up to my head, which I thought might pop off. And I started to cry. I stood there crying for a minute.

And then suddenly I stopped. It was as though I realized I wasn't really sad, I was fake sad. I didn't really care where the cold cuts and the lift tickets came from. I cared because I was supposed to, but I didn't actually care. I was glad there was heat and food and Christmas. And I wiped my eyes on my sleeve, walked out of the grow-op and closed the door. It was then I decided to forget I had ever been in that room and I went back upstairs and sat on the couch, cuddled up with Dad and Anora and watched the end of *The Cosby Show*.

Christmas Eve, we spent with Dad, and we were to go to our mom's for Christmas Day after presents. So Christmas morning Dad made a fire, and when we came up to the living room we found our stockings filled with candy from See's. Dad got so happy watching us take down our stockings and fill our mouths with junk, maybe because our mom didn't like us having sugar, or maybe because he ate half of it. But either way, he was stoked. And as he made his coffee, he called Jackie to wish her a Merry Christmas and I felt reassured in every way.

While Dad was on the phone I had a weird moment. I looked down at my stocking and imagined it filled with pot. Not literally—I wasn't hallucinating. But I wondered how much candy one plant could buy and if anyone ever bought candy that way. And when my dad hung up the phone and returned to the living room, I cleared my mind by stuffing my mouth with caramel.

At gift-giving time I had a certain amount of apprehension—mostly because Dad had a habit of harshly judging his gifts if they weren't good enough. This year, my sister and I had gone halvsies on a shirt from Frederick & Nelson. The shirt was on sale and not particularly nice, but it was in one of their pretty boxes with tissue paper. And this was very important, because if it wasn't in a good box, Dad would think we had gotten the shirt at an off-price store and call us selfish.

Dad smiled as he peeled back the wrapping paper to reveal the department store box. "Let's see what we have in here . . ." and Anora and I watched in anticipation as he lifted the shirt out of the box. But the smile slid off his face as he saw the shirt and then turned it around to see if the back side was any better. "I guess you ladies aren't really doing a good job saving your money," he said. And, as though physically repelled by the shirt, he stood up and went to the kitchen for another cup of coffee—and, I guessed, to decide whether his selfish daughters were present-worthy after giving him that shitty shirt. After an ungodly amount of time, he reentered the living room, sat down on the sofa with his coffee, and took a sip. Then he silently handed Anora a present.

She tore though the wrapping paper, her eyes bugging out of her head as she revealed a spanking new Cabbage Patch Kid. She squealed and jumped up and began running in circles with the box over her head.

"I can't believe it! I'm a mother!" She jumped up on the couch. "I'm a mother!"

Dad finally smiled, letting us off the hook, and joked, "So I did okay?" And Anora ran up to him and started kissing him all over his face. "Thank you, Daddy! Thank you! This is the happiest day of my life!"

I was super jealous at this point and sat on the couch sulking. I knew we couldn't both get good gifts. There couldn't be that much pot. I didn't even see anything for me . . . *Bah, humbug.*

"Well," Dad said, looking at me, "aren't you a sulky little baby."

"No, I'm not," I said, "I was just resting my head."

"Well . . . I'm afraid I didn't have time to get you anything. I hope that's okay."

"That's fine," I said. "I understand. Don't worry about it." Then he started laughing and laughing, and Anora, who was tearing the Cabbage Patch box open with her teeth, looked up and laughed at me, too.

"What's your problem?" I said, embarrassed. "Stop laughing at me!"

But Dad just walked into the other room and when he emerged, he was holding the most beautiful pair of K2 skis wrapped in a big red bow.

I

Was

Floored.

"Wow!" I said.

He handed me the skis to examine. "Did you really think you weren't gonna get anything?"

"I didn't know," I said. Then, examining my skis, I said, "These are long!"

"I think you can handle them," Dad said, slapping my back. I didn't know if he was right, but I was sure as hell gonna find out. Or just ski like a pussy till I got used to them.

"Wow!" I said to myself again. "Wow."

"Yeah," he said, rubbing his stomach and smiling. "Maybe next time, you all won't be so selfish at Frederick and Nelson's."

———

We spent the day at our mom's having a Christmas dinner and opening her little presents, but I couldn't wait to get back to Dad's house where my skis were. And I spent the majority of the afternoon trying to remember details of what they looked like. And that night, I lay in bed with my ski poles, thinking that things might actually work out okay for us. I hugged my poles close to me. *Maybe Jackie will keep being a good influence on Dad, and he won't mind so much that I'm not down. He'll stop trying to make me be like him, and just be happy with the person I am.* And at that moment if there was a God, I thanked it for bringing Jackie and weed into our lives. . . .

A few weeks later, Dad introduced us to his new girlfriend, Yvonne.

I had no idea what had happened to Jackie. She was just gone. Poof.

Damn, I thought. *I guess she finally wanted a man who was more like her.* I tried to accept it, but I just couldn't believe she didn't say good-bye to Anora and me. Or at least just to me.

Yvonne arrived at our house on a Sunday. I watched from the window as a tall beautiful black woman got out of a seven-year-old Honda with an air that made the car seem like a loaner while her Rolls was getting fixed. Her rayon blouse was tucked into a matching pair of rayon pants, and her hair was french-braided into a clip with a bow on it that matched the rest of her outfit. Her features were so delicate, she looked like a doll. And as she got out of the car she looked up at the ten-foot drop from our front door before helping her two kids out of the car. Then she walked them directly to the side steps that led inside, letting me know she had been over before.

Yvonne walked into the house and took it all in and then smiled—not a thoughtless smile that comes out to meet you, but a controlled one that if she were a baby might be mistaken for gas—before saying to my sister and me softly, "Hello, I'm Yvonne."

Dad pointed eagerly. "This here is Mishna and Anora."

And in an even softer voice she said, "How do you do?" I thought we might be in a movie or something. Yvonne then introduced us to her kids as though they were wines. She pointed to a four-year-old boy and said, "This is my son Andreus. . . . That's Russian for 'Andre.' He's four years old and very playful." Then she pointed to the most beautiful two-year-old girl I had ever seen and said, "And this is Yvette. Her name is French and she's two and a little shy at first." Her kids clung to her as we all enjoyed a super awkward moment. But Dad was beyond excited as he held Yvonne's hand and led her by the arm to the breakfast bar in the kitchen, the only room that was done being remodeled.

Within the first few minutes of meeting Yvonne, I found out that she was a dental assistant studying to be a dental hygienist and that's why she was so sophisticated. She was crazy beautiful, and spoke very softly and laughed at almost everything Dad said. But something seemed off with her, and no matter how hard I tried, I didn't feel like we could connect, not like I could connect to Jackie anyway. It was like there was no *her* there, just this young feminine thing that had too much mystery to mother me.

But her kids seemed normal. And the four of us were thrown out into the yard of hazardous materials to get to know each other. As we sat down next to the pile of glass Dad bought two years before to build a hothouse, Andreus immediately put his arms around me and lay against my side. I was amazingly flattered and put my arm around his four-year-old shoulder as Yvette and my sister picked at building materials in the yard.

Yvette picked up an old screw and made a face at how dirty it was before throwing it toward the house. "S'up, moose!" Yvette said. And Andreus broke free of my side and laughed.

"What was that?" I asked.

"W'sup, moose!" Yvette repeated, giggling to herself. She was clearly aware of how cute she was.

"Oh!" Andreus said. "Uncle Frank calls Mom that 'cause she was fat."

"When?" I asked.

"I dunno," he said. "Mom hates it."

"S'up, moose," Yvette repeated.

"What's up, homey!" my sister said to Yvette slowly. "What's up, homey!"

Yvette looked at Anora for a second before trying it, "S'up ooohhh-meee." And Andreus, Anora, and I laughed and laughed. This game was a little bit too much fun and a little too tempting. And I decided we'd save the curse words for later.

When Dad and Yvonne came back out, Dad said, "Mishna you watch the kids for a couple of hours while I take Yvonne for a drive."

"Okay," I said. And Yvonne leaned down and gave her kids a little kiss before saying, "You guys listen to Mishna," and got into Dad's van.

As Andreus grabbed my waist and Yvette said, "I'm hungry," I quickly got a sinking feeling.

The next day when Dad and Yvonne took off for the evening and left me with Anora and the babies, my worst fears were confirmed: just when I thought my life was about to get easier, it was getting harder.

Later that evening, I woke up in what felt like the middle of the night but in actuality was only like eleven thirty. I heard voices coming from upstairs and got up hoping that they had restaurant leftovers with them. I padded up the cement stairs toward the kitchen, and from the landing I could see the scene in the dining room.

Jackie was back and she was arguing with Yvonne. And as I listened I realized they were fighting, OVER MY DAD!

Dad explained, "Jackie, you gotta understand . . . I'm with Yvonne now." Then he looked at Yvonne to see how he was doing.

Jackie did not look like Donna Reed that night. In fact, she was wearing a lot of makeup and a tight red dress. And Yvonne stood there looking unimpressed, but mad as hell at Dad.

"John," Jackie said. Then she wrapped her leg up around my father's waist from the front. "This . . . *girl* can't make you happy. You need a woman. I can make you happy." It was like something out of a soap opera.

"I think it's time for you to go home," Yvonne said sweetly, "before you embarrass yourself any more."

"John," Jackie asked, "are you really throwing all this away?" And Dad was quiet. That's when the piece of mail under my foot made a noise, and Yvonne craned her neck.

I quickly raced back down the stairs, mortified. I had no idea what I had just walked in on, but I knew it was not for me to see. I also couldn't believe that Jackie wanted him. I just assumed she had kicked him to the curb. I was actually a little confused.

Is Dad really picking Yvonne over Jackie? Does he not care what I want at all?

The next morning, as Dad made Yvonne and her kids pancakes, she insisted on playing a Janet Jackson cassette. But I was so bummed about Jackie that even the idea of pancakes wasn't cheering me up. *Why is Dad trading my one chance for a normal life for this young woman who doesn't do much?*

When the song "Nasty" came on, Yvonne jumped up from

the table and started dancing next to the stereo. She lip-synched the words, "Oh you nasty boy," and entreated Dad from behind the breakfast bar and into the living room. He slowly began to move his hips in unison to her. And emboldened by her laughter he went for it. In nothing flat, he was throwing his body around looking like a teenage boy as he tried to keep pace with a girl thirteen years younger than him. Anora jumped up, too, and joined in, which made Dad even more fearless. He started grinding and thrusting in a way that made me wish I had a stun gun so I could zap the Patrick Swayze out of him. The babies laughed and clapped and I just watched in silence, feeling like an eighty-year-old. Then the song ended, and Yvonne said, "Girls, your dad sure knows how to move his thing." And though he looked happy, I was sure I didn't ever want to hear any more about Dad's thing.

Eight

HERE AND NOW

ON THE NIGHT of Yvonne and Dad's wedding, I stood trembling in a rented A-frame hall holding my violin. My dad stood across from me at the altar, looking down in order to stay serious and not start mugging for the audience. My skinny eleven-year-old body floated in a cream-and-black rayon dress with huge shoulder pads that I wouldn't have bought off the dollar rack at Value Village, but that Yvonne paid top dollar for in the women's section at Kmart. It was meant to look like a cream top tucked into a black skirt, but what made it so badass was that it was really just one piece. It was also at least two sizes too big.

Yvonne thought it would be really smooth if I played the wedding march on my violin. I was to play the traditional march first, and then she would walk down the aisle to a Luther Vandross song. Which was fine for her, but I had a little stage fright about playing solo for a room full of people I knew, especially on the day Dad was making such a big mistake. Still I agreed when Yvonne said, "Well, then, maybe you don't need violin lessons anymore . . . right, John?" And Dad proceeded to nod like a bobble head.

Anora was across the room, next to Yvonne, in a dress

similar to mine but with a vest. Her hair had been done by Yvonne's hair guy that morning and she was sporting three french braids. She was waiting to go down the aisle in a sort of ill-defined bridesmaid/fashion show capacity and salivating over the audience of relatives she would get to mug for on her way to the front of the hall. In the months since Yvonne and my dad decided to get married, Anora had been so into the wedding, you'd think she was getting married. As Yvonne dieted up until the big day, Anora discussed in intimate detail the different wedding picture combinations that would happen and what angles they should avoid posing in. And seeing Anora studying Yvonne, it was clear she dying to be a bride soon, and maybe several times.

Yvonne cued me from offstage and I put my violin under my sweaty chin and began playing one of the easiest songs ever written. But besides being sweaty, my hands also shook almost uncontrollably. I raced through the short piece, but no matter how fast I played, the wedding march seemed to go on forever. I finished and tucked my violin under my arm and ran to my seat to hide from her and everyone else in the room just as Luther Vandross kicked in.

I was sweating and staring in my rayon dress as Yvonne and Dad stood at the head of the hall and gazed into each other's eyes as "Here and Now" played in its entirety. It was the longest five minutes and twenty-two seconds of my life. Dad shed a single tear, which trickled down his right cheek and glistened in the light. And I discretely sniffed my armpits.

In a show of things to come, Yvonne elected to have no food served—just cocktails and passed hors d'oeuvres. She said it seemed "cleaner" than serving a messy dinner. So I walked around the reception unable to reach the hors d'ouvres and feeling quite clean in the stomach, as my relatives walked up to sell me on how great it all was.

"Your dad's married!" my aunt Alice said, her eyes about to pop out of her skinny head. "Aren't you excited?"

"Sure," I said. But she wasn't satisfied with my level of my excitement and repeated, "Isn't it exciting?"

"Yes, Aunt Alice. I'm so excited. Just like the song."

"Are you happy to have a new lady in the house?"

To which I responded, "I think I see Uncle Dick. . . . I really should go say hi to him."

I walked through the crowd as people mingled and smiled and my father and Yvonne danced and danced. But I wasn't mingling, I wasn't smiling, I wasn't happy.

I approached my uncle Dick, who was bartending.

"Hi, Uncle Dick," I said.

"Hey, kiddo," he said. "What are you drinking?"

I felt sullen, and I must have looked it, because when I said, "Champagne?" his response was, "I guess this is as big an occasion as there is." But he poured me only a tiny sip for the toast. Still, it made me a little happier. So happy, in fact, that when Dad and Yvonne opened presents, I began drinking whatever was left in the clear plastic party glasses that had been left behind on the tables.

And by the end of the night, I had a much brighter outlook on everything. I walked right up to my new stepmom to tell her how much I loved her. Dad was very happy with this outcome and said, "We are all gonna be a family. It's gonna be like a real dream come true, and stuff." I nodded furiously, agreeing with all my might. I wasn't sure if he could tell that I was wobbly, but when he tried to get me to take a dance with him, I talked him out of it, unsure about my coordination and knowing I would be better at sitting.

Instead, I watched him and Yvonne dance all night, happily telling anyone who would listen: "My dad just got married!" And explaining, "That's why I'm dressed like a waitress."

Nine

DUCK-BUTT

"LADIES"—THAT'S WHAT Yvonne had taken to calling my sister and me—"men are just big dumb animals that need you to control them."

Yvonne stood rifling through a clothes rack at Kmart, explaining to us how she "caught" my dad.

"First of all, you can never tell a man what to do. . . . You can only steer him." She grabbed a 50 percent cotton miniskirt and held it up to herself.

"How do you do that?" My sister needed to know, even though she was only eight.

Yvonne paused for effect and then said like it was a magic word: "Mystique."

"What's that mean, *mystique*?" I asked skeptically.

"It means something you don't have any of, Duck-Butt!" Duck-Butt was my new nickname, because Yvonne said my backside looked like a duck's.

Anora laughed, repeating, "Duck-Butt." And then said, "Hey . . . do I have mystique?"

"Well," Yvonne said, picking out a purple rayon dress with gold buttons and dolman sleeves. "It's too soon to tell, because mystique is about secrets, and you're too young to have any secrets."

"What kind of secrets?" I asked.

"It doesn't matter," she said. "What the secret is, is not important, ladies. It doesn't matter if it's big or small or what. The only thing that is important is that they can never totally know you or have you."

"But don't you want the person you're with to know you?" I asked.

"Of course," Yvonne said, "but you have to fight that urge."

"But if you get married, they're gonna find out eventually, right?" I asked.

"No," Yvonne said, "because, there's always something that you can withhold from a man." She waved her hand as if to demonstrate. "For example, I didn't let your dad kiss me for our first four dates. So, he had to *wonder* what it was like. . . . And I didn't tell him I had kids until after he said 'I love you.'"

"Oh, I get it," Anora said, nodding.

"Isn't that like lying?" I asked.

"Ugh, God!" Yvonne said, exasperated. "You're not lying! You're protecting your mystique!"

"But what about stuff people need to know?" I asked.

"A woman knows what a man needs to know," Yvonne replied. "Plus, you can withhold lots of other things, too: your time—you can be real busy and stuff . . . sex, secrets, doesn't matter. What matters is that you're almost available, but not quite."

"That makes sense," my sister said maturely.

"How is that good for my dad?" I asked.

"Your dad doesn't know what's best for him." She held up a pink rayon blouse. "I do."

She put the blouse back and then grabbed one next to it that was even more hideous. It was mustard-colored rayon with three-quarter-inch sleeves and matching pants with an elastic waistband. She looked at the outfit and handed it to me. "Duck-Butt," she said, "why don't you try this on?"

"That's for grown-ups. I wear kids or juniors, but that's for women."

"So?" Yvonne said. "You're almost a woman."

"I'm twelve," I said.

"Well, you're very tall," she said. "Besides you can't imagine what I was doing at your age. I was almost out of the house."

"I don't like shoulder pads," I said.

Yvonne was aghast at my disobedience. Her nostrils flared and her eyes got vicious. "But your clothes never match! And they look so old . . . and they smell!"

"That's because they're secondhand," I said, grabbing the wool V-neck sweater I had on. "This is really good quality, though. Feel it. It's Nordstrom brand."

Yvonne's anger was replaced by coldness. She took a deep breath and when she exhaled, I didn't even exist. She looked over at Anora, who was trying on a felt hat, and said, "Drop the hat, we're going now." Then she grabbed Anora's hand and began dragging her out of the store.

"I'm sorry," I said as I marched behind her out of the store, trying to keep up as she dragged Anora into the parking lot. But Yvonne wasn't responding; instead she said to my sister, "Do you hear something, Anora?"

The second my father and Yvonne had gotten married, Yvonne decided that she would mold me from a twelve-year-old tomboy into a sophisticated young black woman. And even though I seemed utterly ungrateful, she would benevolently share everything she had ever learned about being a lady in her twenty-three long years of life. By now she had convinced my father that my general weirdness reflected poorly on the family, and that it was his fault for not knowing about periods and such.

But no one in our house was particularly consistent, including Yvonne, so her charm school was intense and intermittent, and usually ended with Yvonne calling me Duck-Butt and leaving the room. I was what she described as "unteachable," because I just couldn't believe most of the things she told me about men and women. It depressed me to think that love was like steering a mule with a rubber carrot. Besides that, she was hymen-obsessed, and everyone's virginity was constantly suspect. She insisted that my friend Violet was promiscuous because "virgins couldn't wear tampons," and Violet used them. And that turned into a big production with Dad about what kind of girls I should and shouldn't be hanging out with. I insisted, "Violet is in the math club! Trust me, we'd all know if a boy even looked at her!" But then it was Lilith, and then Kirsten, and as time went on, I noticed that Yvonne just thought every twelve-year-old was a whore. She also had all these feminine taboos about what men could and could not see, and when we were doing laundry she went to great pains to make sure Dad never saw her underwear or bras. Saying, "Ladies . . . the only place a man should see your panties is on your body. They lose their power if men see them lying in a drawer." She would even hide drying bras in closets and other weird places to keep their power charged while they were drying. It was like I was learning about adolescence from the mom in *Carrie*.

Dad seemed content to step aside and let Yvonne mold me. Even though, if he was as gullible as she made men out to be, he was a total tool.

Among my chores were new womanly endeavors, as well. My allowance went up for the first time in years and now part of my new responsibilities was the job of looking after my step-brother and -sister. This included a range of activities, from feeding them to doing their hair before school.

The first time I was asked to do the babies' hair I was baffled. Their hair was soft and curly yet completely different from my sister's hair. I had no clue what to do, so I just treated their hair like white hair. I ran a brush through Andreus's flat-top, and pulled Yvette's hair into a ponytail. I stood back and took stock of my work, thinking they looked pretty good—paired down, but playful in a "kids being kids" kind of way. And seeing that Yvonne and Dad had already left for work, I walked Andreus and Yvette to day care.

But that evening when we picked them up, Andreus's hair looked like a sheep's back, and Yvette's had popped out everywhere except where the hair tie was. It was worse than I expected. I mean I knew that black hair was unruly enough that Zwena was willing to subject herself to hot pressing combs and scalp-searing relaxers to maintain order. But Yvette's hair defied gravity. She looked like she had spent the day in the dryer.

Yvonne was quiet as the two kids got in the car and started chatting about what they did at "school." She listened to them adding an "uh-huh" here and there or a "That's nice," and I thought maybe she hadn't noticed their hair. But as soon as they piped down, she looked at me and said under her breath, "What the hell did you do to my kids' hair?"

"What do you mean?" I asked. "I think it looks good."

"What's good about it? My daughter looks like a Troll doll."

"I mean . . . it's a different look," I said, hoping to defuse the situation. "It's a more natural look."

"What the hell are you talking about, 'natural'? Her hair's sticking up all over the place! Is that 'natural'?"

"I don't know," I said.

"So . . . what exactly do you mean by 'natural'?" Yvonne asked pointedly, and glared at me for an uncomfortably long time. I avoided eye contact.

"What was that, Mrs. Natural?" Yvonne asked. "That's what I thought."

The next day I was eating breakfast while Yvonne tried to get ready for dental hygienist school. I always tried to steer clear of the frenzy that was her getting out the door. She kissed Andreus and Yvette, who were sitting next to me, and then on the breakfast counter, next to my bowl of cereal, she angrily deposited two products: a tub of something called Bone Strait, and a bottle of Luster's Pink oil.

And as she walked out the door she pointed to the products and told me, "I think you can do beaucoup better on the hair than yesterday! Beaucoup!"

I hated that she pronounced the *p* on *beaucoup.*

I sat Yvette down in the living room and opened the tub of Bone Strait. It smelled familiar, and my immediate reaction was, *Oh, that's what that smell is.* As I started to brush it into her hair, Yvette got squirmy and kept trying to get up, so I turned the TV on to *DuckTales.* Yvette was only three, so her vocabulary was limited to what my sister and I taught her when no one was looking and food words. But she knew how to say, "*DuckTales* ooh-hoo, ooh-hoo." And as she mumbled-sang to the opening song, I pulled her hair back into a ponytail at which point Yvette stopped singing and started hollering at the top of her lungs, "Ow! Ow! Ooooww!" as though I were killing her. In fact, even after I had completely stopped touching her hair, she was still screaming as dramatic tears streamed down her face.

"Oh, come on," I said.

"It hurts," Yvette sniffed, and stood up, stopping me from continuing.

"I'm not even touching you," I said.

"Don't pull, Duck-Butt!"

"Okay, okay," I said. "Now can I finish your hair?"

Yvette sat back down warning me, "Don't pull, den."

So, giving in, I pulled her hair as tight as I could without her screaming, which wasn't very tight. And rather than leave it as a ponytail in the back, I braided it, closing the end with a poodle barrette, and then smoothed on a touch of the Bone Strait, which made it look much less frizzy. For Andre, I rubbed some of the product into my hands and then worked it into his hair as I brushed it. I felt confident that the product would keep their hair looking perfectly styled for the whole day and that I had done a fantastic job.

But that afternoon when we picked them up from daycare, Yvette's hair was worse than the day before. The barrette was long gone and all her hair was sticking out except for one clump with the hair tie hanging on to the end for dear life. And as they got in the car, Yvonne looked at me and said sarcastically, "good job on the babies' hair . . . very natural." I didn't know what it was gonna take to make those kids' hair look neat for more than an hour, and I clearly wasn't the person for the job.

"Maybe I shouldn't do their hair," I said. "I'm not very good at it."

"You just need to try a little harder. Not half-ass it," Yvonne said. "Yvette wants to look her best, same as you. I mean, don't you want to look your best?"

"I don't know," I said. "I never really thought about it."

"You might want to think about it," Yvonne said.

That night while Yvonne got ready for a date with my father, I worked on my homework at the kitchen counter. I was in the middle of an essay question when Yvonne called, "Mishna, come here." I got up and followed her voice into the bathroom.

"What?" I asked.

"Just come here," Yvonne said.

She stood at the bathroom sink in a bright blue silk dress, and her hair and makeup were flawless. She looked so good, it actually startled me.

"Yes, Yvonne?" I asked.

"Just come here," she said.

I walked over to where she was standing by the mirror. The bathroom hadn't been remodeled yet, so you had to steady yourself between where the linoleum floor ended and where it was just uneven plywood. The wall she was standing next to was torn up exposing the fiberglass and beams. But Yvonne in her blue dress and heels transcended that. And looking at her all made up in the light of the clamp-on work light, she seemed to glow. I wondered if this was how Dad always saw her. I walked across the bathroom and stood next to her.

"Look up," she said, suddenly producing an eyeliner. I backed away. "Don't be afraid. Look up." She was so pretty.

I silently obeyed her as she held my eyelid open and shoved the eye pencil into my eye and started drawing. It was so uncomfortable, it actually answered the question, "Why do we have eyelids?" I teared up and I was dying to rub, but as she let go of my lid, Yvonne said, "Don't rub your eye." And it took all my will to resist. Then she stood back and said, "Wow."

"I can't believe you do that every day. It hurts so bad."

"It's not so bad!" she insisted. "Beauty isn't free."

"Does it look good?" I asked.

"Almost," she said, reaching for the blush. She put blush on my cheeks and smoothed on a bright red lip liner, which she blended with Vaseline. I had to stand perfectly still as she curled my lashes and put on thick black mascara, warning me the whole time not to blink. And she finished it off by running a curling iron through my bangs and making two soft curls to frame my face, burning my ear as she did.

When she was finished, my eyes and lips felt weird, and my ear was burning, but I just focused on the way Yvonne's dress gathered around her waist and flattered her shoulders and how pretty her red lipstick looked against her skin tone. Ultimately the pain seemed negotiable.

"Let me see," I said.

But Yvonne teased, "No," and walked me away from the mirror. "I want you to see yourself how everyone else sees you." Yvonne walked me out the door and into the dining room where Anora was sitting with Andreus and Yvette. And like a needle scratching across a record player, everyone turned their attention to me. That was when my six-year-old step-brother wolf-whistled.

I scolded him, "Andre!"

"But, you look like a babe!"

And Anora just threw up her hands and said, "Finally!"

Yvonne was beaming as she said, "Okay. Look in the mirror, Mishna." I was glad she didn't call me Duck-Butt, and I got on a chair and checked myself out in the mirror over the fireplace. It was too much makeup, but I definitely looked like hot shit. I was immediately captivated with my own appearance. It was huge and took up the whole mirror. And looking in the mirror at my younger siblings reflection so far behind me, they really looked like little people. They were talking, but all I heard was "Blah blah blah." Vanity coursed through my veins like heroin. I looked like a babe.

Yvonne must have sensed that because she said, "Don't get too cocky. You aren't as pretty as me."

That was when Dad bounced in the door. He set the mail on the counter, kissed Yvonne, took one look at me, and stopped like he had been hit by a freight train.

"What the fuck is going on here?"

"Oooh," Yvette said, acknowledging the F-bomb.

Yvonne tried to ease his mood. "Nothing, John. I just put a little makeup on Mishna." She rubbed Dad's back as she said, "I think she looks great."

"I think I look kind of pretty," I said.

But Dad looked horrified. He searched my made-up face to try to find something good about it, which just made him madder. "You all went a little crazy with the shit."

"Oooooh!" Yvette put her hand over her mouth.

He looked at me again, angrily. "I don't like this!"

"John," she said. "You said Mishna and I could have woman time."

"Young lady time," Dad said.

I tried changing the subject. "Oh, by the way, Dad, at school we are supposed to go to the water treatment plant to see how it works or something," I ran over to my book bag. "So . . . I just need you to sign my slip." I tried to hand Dad the permission slip, but he didn't take it. He actually backed away as I walked toward him.

"Yvonne, you do it," Dad said, and Yvonne came over and signed my slip as he continued, "Goddamn it, Yvonne. I don't like you making her up like that. You know it sends out the wrong message! And she's too young to know about sending out messages."

This was all over my head. "I can wash it off."

But Yvonne rubbed Dad's shoulders and said, "Oh, John. It's just a little makeup for fun." But Dad still looked angry as she soothed him. "Of course I'm gonna teach your daughter to handle herself."

"But . . ."

"John," she said. "Just, trust me."

And Dad let out a yielding, "Okay."

The next morning at hairdressing time, I wasn't listening to any complaints. I had had a pencil in my eye the night before and beauty wasn't free for anyone, not even Yvette. I sat with the three-year-old in my lap and tugged her hair hard and tight, smoothing handfuls of Bone Strait into her hair until it had no choice but to lie flat.

"Ow!" she cried. "It hurts . . . No, no, no. You're—ow!" But I only pulled tighter, confident that Yvette needed to look her best. And to my surprise, after about a minute of screaming, she went back to watching *DuckTales* and completely ignored the fact that my hands were in her hair. I was really starting to understand beauty. And when I was done Yvette had two perfect braids on her perfectly parted head. And if, God forbid, her hair started even trying to stick up, I had fortified either side with two ribbon clips in colors that matched her outfit. She looked neat and tidy, and not the least bit natural. Andre got way more Pink oil than seemed necessary, but his hair looked shiny and neat and twenty minutes later, it didn't look like too much.

That evening when we picked them up, though their hairdos had deteriorated, they'd started out so tidy that they still looked pretty neat. And when the babies got into the car, Yvonne didn't even mention their hair, which was the same as getting a trophy. Yvonne wasn't in the habit of handing out kudos for things that were expected of you.

That night, every time I went to the bathroom, I lingered at her makeup on the counter, looking at her various powders and brushes that had magically made me look like a woman the night before. I wished Yvonne would offer to do my makeup again. I wanted for her to make me look pretty so I could spend hours looking in the mirror. But instead my sister and I cleaned the kitchen while Yvonne spent the evening in the bedroom with Dad. No one emerged all night except for Dad, who came out to make Yvonne a sandwich. And I had to admit, no matter how crazy I had thought she was, and no matter how smart I thought I was, Yvonne had a lot of power. She had the power to make me beautiful, she had the power to make men make her sandwiches, and everyone in our house wanted to be near her—she had mystique.

When we were done cleaning and Anora and the babies were settled on the couch watching TV, I slipped downstairs into the laundry room and the door to my dad's office. I hadn't thought about Dad's business for a long time, but something that night made me wonder. It just didn't seem like the type of thing Yvonne would go for and I imagined "Never go in that room" didn't work on wives like it did on daughters.

I checked to make sure nobody was nearby and cracked the door open. There was no bright light as I opened the door, and when I flipped on the light the only thing lying on the floor was a dirt and some scattered rags. There were no more pot plants and no one had even bothered to clean up and make a room out of it. It was abandoned—just like I had suspected. Yvonne was more than powerful; she was omnipotent.

The next day, I gave Yvette the best hairstyle yet. I saturated her hair with Pink oil, then parted it into the most adorable French braids with matching blue ribbons on the end, which I pinned in so she wouldn't lose them while she was playing. And that night as the kids climbed in the car and got settled, Yvonne said to them, "Mishna sure did a good job on your hair." And I felt my heart fill with joy. I had pleased Yvonne, and we were communing as women now.

Andreus started chattering about what they did at school, but Yvonne corrected them. "What do you say to your sister who did your hair?"

"Thank you, Mishna," Andreus said.

"Thank you, Duck-Butt," Yvette said, laughing at herself. But Yvonne was not laughing.

"Yvette!"

"What?" Yvette said, giggling. "That's what you call her, Duck-Butt." Just saying it made her laugh.

But Yvonne gave Yvette a little swat on the leg.

"Eeeeh!" she fake whined.

"Say sorry to Mishna!" Yvonne commanded.

"But you say it . . . ," Yvette started, causing Yvonne to raise her hand again, so Yvette quickly spat out, "I'm sorry. I'm sorry."

"Don't say it to me," Yvonne said. "Say it to Mishna."

"I'm sorry, Mishna," Yvette said, and gave me a kiss on the cheek.

"Now, Mishna," Yvonne said, changing the subject. "What do you want to listen to?" She pointed to a stack of cassettes lying in the drink holder. I rifled through five tapes I would never in a million years listen to and said, "Anita Baker," hoping it was what Yvonne wanted, too.

"Oooh, my girl Anita," she said. I had pleased her again. And as we dance-drove home listening to "Giving You the Best That I Got" I felt close to Yvonne and her mystique. And to top it off, when we got back to the house, Yvonne pulled me into her and my father's room and closed the door. There, she handed me one of her dresses.

"Try it on," she said. "It's too small for me." I took the silk shirtdress while the rest of the kids banged on the door.

"What?" Yvonne shouted toward the door.

"It's Andre. Can I come in?"

"It's girl time, Andre," Yvonne said as I slipped the dress over my head.

"Can I come in then?" Anora asked.

"It's woman time," Yvonne replied. "We'll be out in ten minutes." Yvonne looked at me in the dress and said flatly, "It's good."

"But what?" I asked. Yvonne hesitated and said, "Nothing, it's just not great."

I walked over to the mirror that was leaning against the wall. The dress was way too big, but it was pretty and fun to wear.

"Can I keep it?" I asked.

"You ain't got the body for that dress."

"Oh," I said, seeing what she meant.

"We gotta get some meat on your bones, Duck-Butt," Yvonne said disapprovingly. "Give me back the dress." And as quickly as I was in, I was back out of her good graces.

A few days later when I got home from school, Yvonne was home and Dad was out with Anora and the babies. It seemed a little odd, but Yvonne decided that we should have a girl's night and sat me down to do my makeup again.

"Isn't my dad gonna be pissed?" I asked.

"It's okay, just tonight," she said. "Besides . . . it's good when men get angry. It means they are invested. They care." I didn't like the idea of her making my father angry on purpose, but she was doing my makeup so I wasn't gonna argue.

We got in Yvonne's car and went to the mall where she bought me a fancy coffee at an espresso place. I told her I didn't drink coffee, so she ordered me an espresso drink with whipped cream and chocolate, which burned a hole in my stomach. As we walked around looking at clothes and trying on perfume, I tried to pretend I wasn't having the sweats as the caffeine attacked my nervous system.

We wandered into JC Penney and I started looking at a pair of earrings at the jewelry counter. But Yvonne wasn't browsing, and rather than look with me, she grabbed my hand and started leading me. I was titillated that she was leading me to a surprise destination. She stopped in the women's lingerie department.

"What are we doing here?"

"We are getting you a bra," she said. I felt completely ambushed.

"What? Why?"

"Because you need one."

"For what?" I asked. I looked down at my chest in its white Vuarnet T-shirt with a pocket, and saw no evidence of any breasts.

"Your dad and I agree we can't have you running around boobless." I had no idea what she was talking about. That didn't even make sense.

"I don't have breasts," I said. But she dragged me over to a rack of bras that were way too big for me.

She began flipping through the rack scratching her head. "You're probably about a thirty-two A," she said as she handed me a lacy padded bra, something that was meant to make me look like I actually did have breasts.

"What about that one?" I said, pointing to a flat jersey training bra.

"That's ugly," Yvonne said. "The other one is at least pretty."

"I'm not wearing anything padded," I said, really putting my foot down. But my little statement landed with a thud. Yvonne's sisterly mood turned to anger in the blink of an eye. "Try on the bra," she growled.

"Okay, okay." And I went to the dressing room and put it on.

"What's taking you so long?" Yvonne said impatiently after a minute or two.

"I don't know how this works," I said, trying to figure out the hooks and straps.

So Yvonne came in with me and helped me figure out how to put the mess of nylon and foam on my flat chest, and when it was all done I looked like I was wearing my mother's bra. Even Yvonne had to admit that it looked ridiculous.

"Well," she said, tapping her fingernails against the dressing room door. "You sure got some tiny little titties." It was then that she literally reached out and twisted my nipples.

We both stood there in shock as she put together that she wasn't fourteen anymore, and that I wasn't fourteen yet. It was embarrassing for both of us.

"Come on," she barked. "Get dressed and let's pay for that."

"You saw how big that was. Why can't I just not wear a bra?"

"Because!" she said. "You'll grow into it. It's part of your mystique." I was terrified. I didn't want mystique. It seemed like too much. I just wanted to look pretty.

When I got home after the traumatic trip to JC Penney Dad and the kids were eating McDonald's. Dad hadn't gotten any for me or Yvonne. I guessed it was because we were women and women didn't need food. It was part of their mystique. Andreus saw me and said, "You look like a babe!" I forgot that I still had my makeup on. In my hand was the JC Penney bag holding the bra that I would, I guess, grow into. I sat down at the table to glom a fry from my sister, and noticed Dad was acting weird. He wouldn't look at me and he kept clearing his throat.

"So . . . ," he finally said. "Did you guys do your shopping, then?"

"Oh, yes," Yvonne purred. "Mishna's practically a woman now." Anora turned and looked at me questioningly. I shrugged, as Yvonne continued, "Pretty soon you'll be moving out."

Ten

FLAGRANT FOUL

SLEEPOVERS WERE LIKE minivacations for me. I got to step out of my family responsibilities and into my friends' homes where I was catered to like a crippled person. Dad wasn't in the habit of asking if he could make me something to eat, or if I wanted him to rent me something while he was at the video store. In fact, the last time I'd had Zwena over, he got her to clean the kitchen after I made dinner. That's why I was so disappointed when all my friends with super, awesome, overbearing, attentive parents decided to have our big seventh-grade sleepover at Oksana's house.

The lure of Oksana's house was that she had the most lax parents of all my friends—when she was staying with her mom, the artist. By the way, her mom's art was intricately hand-beaded penis sculptures. The whole of her house from top to bottom was beaded penises in various stages of construction. You couldn't look and not see a beaded penis. On the mantelpiece there was a completed rainbow-beaded penis, next to a zebra one. On the coffee table sat a damask penis, and in the bathroom over the sink was an argyle penis.

The greatest quantity of peni resided in the kitchen. On this particular Saturday night as I walked through the kitchen to get to the guesthouse out back, I could see she was working on a new series of paisley penises. And by the looks of the place, nobody was gonna be making me pancakes.

I got to the guesthouse and all my friends had already arrived. Lilith—who that year had taken to dressing like Robert Smith from The Cure. Violet—whose bobbed blond hair had the appearance of feathers. Marni—the only girl in seventh grade with circles under her eyes. Eileen—a ridiculously skinny girl with both braces and glasses. Kirsten—who talked constantly about elves and druids. And, of course, Oksana—who hid the covers of her Harlequin romance novels under fake drawn Faulkner book covers.

The great thing about partying with the "highly gifted" is that you know no one is going home with a broken arm or getting bailed out of prison. That night we talked about schoolwork. We talked about boys. We sang Smiths songs. We worked on a riddle. We built D & D characters. We drew our D & D characters. And as the night went on, we got more and more witchy, adding our usual Ouija board and tarot cards into the mix. Fantasy was our primary way of dealing with the budding sex problem. And our obsession with the occult always focused around creating a reality where we were sexier, more powerful, and less allergic.

Around 4 A.M. we finished nipping at an airline bottle of gin that Oksana had stumbled upon in a locked cabinet, and we were getting restless. Marni was giving Eileen the world's most boring tarot card reading and I was designing a city in my mind made out of toothpicks. That's when Lilith had an idea. She closed her spell book and said in a really creepy voice, "Hey guys, let's try to summon the devil."

The air in the guesthouse changed, and suddenly the party came to life.

"How do we do that?" Marni asked.

"I have a spell right here," Lilith said. "A conjuring spell."

Eileen asked, "Can we finish my tarot reading?"

Violet, who had had more gin than the rest of us said, "Fuck your tarot card reading," which surprised us all. I didn't even know she knew the F-word.

I was beyond skeptical about Lilith's magic abilities, but after *The Exocist,* anything concerning the devil creeped me out.

And I said, "Whoa, whoa, whoa. I think this is a bad idea."

"Mishna is pretty reasonable about this stuff," Violet said. "And if she doesn't think it's a good idea, I don't, either."

"Me, neither," Eileen said.

"So what's the problem, Mishna?" Lilith asked.

"I just don't see the upside," I said. "It's creepy and there has to be a better way to kill time."

That was when Oksana explained, "The idea is for Satan to work for you. He'll do, like, whatever you want. Like wishes and stuff."

"Let's go," I said.

Kirsten, in a show of forethought, asked if Lilith had any spells to put the devil back should he get unruly. But when Lilith said no, we decided to roll the dice anyway.

We got some chalk and candles and sauntered over to the church parking lot across the street. It was cold, so we all wore our sleeping bags around our shoulders and shivered as what little gin we had all sipped wore off. Lilith drew a pentagram on the pavement, and Oksana decorated the middle of the pentagram with one of her mom's penis statues.

Then we lit the candles and sat down around our pentagram wrapped in blankets to chant for Satan to appear. . . . Then we waited.

Nothing.

"Let's do it again," Lilith said. "I think sometimes you just have to keep doing it."

So we did it again. This time Eileen interrupted in the middle, "Are we doing this right? Lilith just double-check the book!"

"Don't interrupt in the middle!" Violet said. "Who knows what can happen?"

"Maybe I should do a druid harvest dance," Kirsten said.

"Let's save the harvest dance for later," I said.

Violet, who was following over Lilith's shoulders screamed, "We are going to do the spell exactly how it's written!" This caused her to get winded and need a puff off her inhaler.

Eileen deflated. "This is like my whole stupid life!"

"Oh, well," I said. "Satan's busy."

"That's easy for you to say!" Eileen growled. "Stupid Mrs. Heller isn't giving you a B-plus in English and refusing to change it. Guess stupid Satan won't be changing it, either!"

Kirsten and Marni looked bummed, too. "You guys didn't really think we were gonna see the devil?" I asked.

"Of course not," Marni took too long to say.

"I hate Mrs. Heller!" Lilith said. "She thinks she can mess with everyone's future by passing out B's and C's. . . . That stuff goes on your transcript like forever!"

"Oh, I know!" Oksana said. "Mr. Hammer tried to give me a B in math and my dad went down there and they had a fight and it took the principal to get him to just give me some extra-credit assignments."

"Ms. Miller won't let me take off for elven holidays," Kirsten said.

"Fascist," Marni said.

"Do you guys want to try this again?" I asked.

"Okay," Lilith said. "Let's do it one more time without the penis, and see what happens."

Nothing happened.

But then someone mentioned boys again, and we wound up sitting around talking on the pentagram till 6 A.M. And I say till 6 A.M., because that's when one of the workers from the church found us. He recognized Oksana and woke her mother up to tell her that he had found us at the church doing a satanic ritual. Of course, Oksansa's mom thought it was the funniest thing she had ever heard.

The next day, Dad was his usual three hours late to pick me up from the slumber party. I tried to slink out the door and run to the van, but Dad was already coming up the walk to flirt with Oksana's mom. She wasn't his type, but Dad also wasn't turning down female attention. And when he came into the house the first thing out of Oksana's mom's mouth was, "You're never gonna believe what happened." That was when Oksana's stupid hippie mom, who thought witchcraft was a hoot, told Dad how we had tried to summon the devil the night before.

He didn't think it was a hoot.

And when we got home, punning aside, all hell broke loose.

He stood beside Yvonne, yelling so loudly, he was frothing. "Do you know what kind of family we are here?!"

I knew the answer he was looking for was not "weird."

"We are Christians, goddamn it! Jesus fucking Christ!"

Yvonne added, "You think we go to church every Sunday for our health?!"

"No," I said, and then turned to Dad. "But it's not like the devil actually came!"

"Are you talking back?" Dad asked.

"No."

"You're a teenager now. You need to start acting a little more responsibly," Yvonne said.

"Technically, you have to have the word *teen* in your age—"

"Young lady!" Dad was banging his huge fist on the counter. "It is time you learned some discipline!"

We had been going to a new all-black church called Powerhouse Baptist, and Yvonne thought that a good punishment for me would be to go to Bible study on Tuesdays and Thursdays. But Dad disagreed with her. He decided that the best way for me to learn about discipline and not summoning the devil was for me to start playing basketball. I reminded him about the four-hundred-yard dash, but I guess that had a statute of limitations. Yvonne gave him a litany of other punishments that might be more appropriate: grounding, charm school, chores, community service. But Dad brushed them all aside—a ball and a hoop would straighten me out.

The next week Dad took me down to the Miller Community Center to sign me up for basketball as though he hadn't been planning on it for the last twelve years. But I knew that Dad had always wanted me to play. I was tall, and after the initial disappointment of having a girl, the fact that I exited the womb at twenty-three and a half inches gave him hope that he still might someday hear, "That's a three-pointer for Wolff!"

Although football had been his game, basketball ran a close second. I grew up watching him play a weekly game of hoops with his crew on a league called Tuesday Night Fever. And he *played*. I remember once on his way to the hoop he elbowed Reggie Dee in the nose so hard that he made his nose bleed.

And as Reggie stood in the middle of the court, holding his nose and saying, "Wolfie, what the fuck is wrong with you?" My father just held the ball on his hip impatiently and said in a low flat voice, "Hey . . . I thought we was playing some basketball."

On Friday nights we often found ourselves at high school games watching kids from the neighborhood, whom Dad always seemed to know better when they were winning. "That's Jay-Jay," he would say, pointing to the sophomore who had made a three-pointer. "He's T's kid. I taught him that hook at the R.B. when he was ten." And when he did that, I always thanked God that middle school didn't have team sports.

So we both knew the Satan thing was just an excuse, and that if I could play hoops well, all the embarrassing things about me would become the eccentricities of a baller. Like, "Sure she wears black every day and reads Greek plays for fun . . . but hey—whatever you gotta do to get in the zone." But basketball was Dad's thing. I felt like I had my own things now.

Dad hustled me down the trophy-covered hallway of Miller rec center toward the office. "This will teach you a little discipline," Dad said as he signed the consent form. "Now, what number do you want?"

"Is the number *one* taken?" I asked. Turns out it wasn't.

And as we walked back down the hallway and into the parking lot, I noticed we were the only white people. Dad put his arm around me and said proudly, "Now you're playing for the Miller Satin Dolls."

"What's that? The name of the team?"

"Puh!" Dad was indignant. "The Satin Dolls are an institution."

I asked Dad why I was playing for the Satin Dolls and not the whiter rec center the same distance away, and he said, "'Cause the Satin Dolls are the best. You want to learn about hoops from the seventh best?"

"I guess not."

"That's right," Dad said. "You want to be the best, you have to surround yourself with the best."

On my first day of practice, Dad and I walked into the gym where my teammates were "messing around before practice." Underneath the hoop were five six-foot-tall black girls who must have had a ball in their hands as soon as they pried the tit out, and one five-foot-three point guard who must have shared the womb with a Spaulding regulation. I couldn't believe these girls were the same age as me. They looked like they drove themselves there and had a club to go to later. Dad laced up my shoes painfully tight and sent me over to shoot with the big girls.

I slinked over and stopped at the top of the key thinking that any one of them could kick my ass. And I just stood there watching them make shot after perfect shot.

"Get in there!" Dad said, motioning with his hand.

But I ignored him, and kept watching.

Finally Shawanda, the largest girl on the team, who actually looked like Michael Jordan, turned to me. "Hey," she said in a shockingly low voice. "You on our team?"

"Yes," I whispered.

She passed the ball to me to take a shot. "You play well . . . we won't have no problems."

I took the shot and missed—by a lot. Dad put his hands over his eyes and left the gym. I looked at Shawanda's hulking form looming next to me and said, "We might have a problem."

To which she responded, "Ha . . . ha . . . ha . . ." Her whole body moved when she laughed. Then she smiled, which reassured me that she might kick my ass one day, but today was not that day.

Then our coach, Coach Wheeler showed up. She was this ominous figure in a flat cap and trench coat, holding a clipboard, and I could tell immediately that she was the angriest woman I had ever met. Something inside her had started yelling before she even opened her mouth. She lined us up in the middle of the court and stared us down.

"So," she said curtly. "You all are my team!" She scanned our faces. There were only seven of us, but she was talking to us like there were thirty. "I know a lot of you'all have been playing ball for a long time! Playing that street ball with the boys!" I gulped. "But I'm gonna teach you guys to play like professionals!" *I really shouldn't be here.* "Set up plays . . . zone defense, not just this man-to-man stuff you been doing . . . We gonna have the endurance to full-court press!" She stopped and looked at me, I felt myself turning red. "You, I don't know. You played basketball before?"

"No," I said, trembling. "I've never played on a team before." I watched her rage bubble up in front of my eyes. And I could feel my teammates' disappointment flanking me on either side as they let out a collective silent sigh.

"Well," she said angrily, "you're gonna learn."

"Yes, ma'am."

Then she proceeded to run me till I was nauseous.

When I got into Dad's van that evening, Dad was giddy. He mussed my hair as I crawled exhausted into the back.

"How was practice?" he asked excitedly.

"I'm in pain," I said.

"Well, I had a hard day at work today," Yvonne began. "This woman came in—"

"You met Grace Wheeler, though," Dad said to me.

"Yeah."

"Does she like you?" Dad asked.

Nope. I had managed to drag everyone down on the very first day of practice.

"Too soon to tell," I said.

"Yvonne, you know who Mishna's coach is?" Dad asked her but didn't wait for the response. "Grace Wheeler! She broke all the records at LSU and was on the Harlem Globetrotters."

Great, I thought. *I'm not just out of my league. I'm way out of my league.*

"She was on the Harlem Globetrotters?" Yvonne asked. Even she was impressed.

"Sure enough. She was one of the very first *women* professional basketball players!" Dad said emotionally. I thought he might tear up. "She was a woman who got paid to play ball."

"I don't get it," Yvonne said. "If I had made it like that, I wouldn't be hanging at nasty-ass Miller. I'd be living large."

"Well," Dad said. "That's why Mishna is so lucky."

Coach Wheeler was merciless. She ran, drilled, and push-upped us within an inch of our lives every practice. She also had a tight system for how much water we could drink from the drinking fountain at the side of the gym. And when, one night, she worked me till I threw up, I was told it was 'cause I drank too much water.

But Shawanda patted me on the shoulder and said in her Herman Munster voice, "She shouldn't have given you that last set a' lines to run." I was really starting to like Shawanda.

We ran drills together and learned plays and different defenses. All the plays were built around our biggest strength—Keisha Lee, our five-foot-three insanely talented point guard. She would dribble down the court to us with her two perfect braids bouncing on the side of her head, and hold a certain number of fingers over her head letting us know exactly where she was gonna throw the ball and where it would go from there. And as a team we would get into formation and wait with an animal-like readiness to spring into action. Leslee and

Shawanda, our trusty forwards, got open to catch that ball and drive that lay-up in. I had been appointed the team's center because I was big and didn't move that well. On offense, my job was to catch the ball and get it to someone who could do something with it. On defense, my job was to stand with my big self in the center of the key and block things with my big-ass hands.

At one practice the ball came to me couple times and I took the shots, but the second time I missed a shot, Keisha gave me a frustrated look.

After practice I walked over to Shawanda who was putting the balls away with Leslee. I was feeling bad about pissing off Keisha, to which Shawanda responded, "That's just Keisha."

"She goin' to Duke!" Leslee said with a southern accent.

"What do you mean?"

"We all tryin' to get a Scal-lar-ship!" Leslee said. "But, shoot, I don't care where."

"You mean college ball?" I asked, beginning to grasp Keisha's angst.

"Yeah. We all want to play college ball one day. That's why we play with Grace," Shawanda said, "instead of a nice coach."

Riding home from practice that night I couldn't even look at Dad. I was angry at him for making me a Satin Doll and screwing up an otherwise great team. "I'm glad you're getting along with your teammates," he said. "You know I'm so proud of you. Playing ball with the Satin Dolls. I think this could really be your thing." This just infuriated me more. Basketball was not my scholarship. I sucked at it. And my teammates apparently had their whole futures tied to it. And what was pissing me off was that my dad had planted me right smack-dab in the way of their ambitions like a roadblock.

Anora and friends at the rec center where I played basketball.

"You know, if you got good and wanted to you could do the whole college ball thing."

"I don't think so, Dad," I said. "I'm not very good." And I knew any school that had basketball scholarships also had tailgate parties and drunken assholes that painted their faces.

"You don't know everything," Dad said. "You think you're all head, but you got my athleticism. You never know what you can do. Keep an open mind."

But all the open-mindedness in the world wasn't gonna help me on the court. Within a couple weeks, Coach Wheeler had taken to asking me at every practice, "Wolff! Are you an asset or a liability?" I didn't answer, because I was embarrassed to say I didn't know what a *liability* was. If I had known, I think I would have been flattered that it was a question and not just the statement: "You *are* a liability."

And the day we got our uniforms Coach Wheeler pulled

mine out of the box. "Wolff!" she called, picking up my jersey and seeing the number one on the back. "Is this some kind of a joke?"

I was instantly embarrassed, and I said, "No, Coach Wheeler. It's for number one at something else . . . other than basketball."

She looked at me with her burning-hate eyes and said, "Well, this here is basketball."

However, once I brought that jersey home, Dad wanted me to wear it everywhere: to parties at Lyman's, to the grocery store, to take out the trash. He'd say, "Why don't you just wear your jersey? You're a Satin Doll now." I'd tell him it was dirty, to which he'd respond, "How long does it take to do a load of wash?" Basically it was understood, if he was gonna be seen with me, it would be in a Satin Dolls' jersey.

Yvonne would argue, "John. No boy's gonna be into a girl that walks around in a basketball jersey." At which point Dad just looked at her like she was on crack. There would be no boys.

When the season started, the idea of actual games kept me up at night. I just knew I would screw up and cost the whole team their futures. Luckily, I had an out. I had complained to Dad all through preseason about debilitating ankle pain. The type of pain that starts in the head and increases the more you think about it. Dad himself had had ankle problems and I thought, *Maybe he'll feel just practicing with the team was enough. I learned my lesson. I got my jersey. No game play necessary.*

On the morning of our first game Dad woke me up smiling with my jersey in his hands. He had such hope in his eyes—it was like he was holding a fresh lotto ticket. I almost felt guilty as I limped out of bed dramatically and said, "Dad . . . Wow. My ankle really hurts. I don't know about playing." Then I made a show of walking and wincing. "Yeah, I think this ankle's gonna be a problem."

"That's okay, I gotcha covered!" He magically produced a roll of athletic tape.

"What's that?" I asked.

"We are gonna tape your ankles up," Dad said. "It'll give you the support you need."

Fuck! "Um, won't my game play suffer?"

"Nah," he said, propping my leg up and taking tape off the roll. "I used to do this all the time." He smiled as he wrapped my foot. "Guess you got my ankles!"

I thought I was gonna be sick.

Remarkably, once I took the court and started playing, my fears were quickly assuaged. There was nothing I could do to make this team lose. The Satin Dolls were a well-oiled machine. We set up plays, we stole, we rebounded, we blocked, and we hustled. And the opposing team ran around the court like twelve-year-old white kids that had played three months a year for the last two years, while their disturbed parents ran around trying to verify that we were, in fact, all twelve.

When the game ended, the Satin Dolls all breathed a sigh of relief and there were high-fives all around. We had beat the team we were playing 54–12. It was reassuring to have such a colossal win our first game out. And Coach Wheeler even smiled, deciding to put off telling us about all the mistakes we made until Tuesday practice.

The next week we played a North End team called Queen Anne, whom we beat 62–7. And the following week we beat a team called Laurelhurst 79–2. They naturally scored those two at the free-throw line. A seventy-point lead wasn't gonna keep the Satin Dolls from flagrant fouls.

I, however, played that game like a lady. I shared the ball with my teammates and I tried not to touch anyone I wasn't supposed to. And if I somehow wound up invading someone's space even in a perfectly reasonable basketball way I promptly said, "I'm sorry." This, juxtaposed against my teammate's frothing aggressiveness, really pissed Dad off.

Dad taping my ankle for games meant him later removing the tape, which gave him plenty of time to tell me how disappointed he was in the way I played.

"You know," he said after the Laurelhurst game. "It's like you're playing, but you're not playing. . . . Let me just rip the tape off quickly."

"No, please," I said. "Let's just leave the tape on. I can learn to live with it." I imagined the tape turning into a smelly goo, which could be the next penicillin and win me my scholarship.

"I'm just thinking," Dad continued, slowly ripping tape off my foot. "That you're playing like you're scared . . . you can't be scared of nobody."

Then he whipped out his trusty jackknife. "You want me to cut it off?"

"No!" I screamed. "But you can rip it off quickly."

"You know, you could be a lot tougher on D."

"But, Dad," I said. "The other team didn't even score."

"Still, you're letting your teammates do all the work. You need to get in there. I saw about three layups you could have grabbed instead of Shawanda." At this point I wondered if he even knew who the fuck he was talking to. By not playing, I was being a team player, and *clearly*, it worked. I was sacrificing personal glory for the benefit of the greatest numbers. Duh. And I wasn't willing to mess these girls up so that he could be proud.

But Tuesday after practice Coach Wheeler stopped me on the way out of the gym. "Wolff!" she said. "I'm not sure if you're an asset or a liability." I nodded as though I hadn't heard it a hundred times. "This here is basketball. If you're out there, you play." I guessed she didn't like winning.

"I've been trying to just get the ball to Keisha."

"As long as you guys aren't in trouble, you can take a shot or two."

"I'll gauge it," I said. But what I was thinking was, *Why is everyone so hung up on me play-playing? The status quo is making everyone look good. Coach Wheeler gets her wins, and Dad gets his winner, who cares whether or not I learn to play? Not me.*

The Satin Dolls cared, though. And almost as if instructed, during the next few practices they passed to me, and they didn't grab my rebounds. But it was practice, and that's what practices were for—practicing.

The next weekend we played Green Lake, and all through the first half, when I passed the ball to Shawanda or Leslee, if I had the shot, they passed it right back to me. And as well as having Coach Wheeler shouting at me, I now had Dad telling me to "Take the shot!" or "Grab that!" which made me positively skitzy.

At halftime when the coach let us drink, I caught up with Shawanda and Leslee at the drinking fountain.

"What the hell's going on?" I asked.

"Coach said that we could lean on you a little more," Shawanda said.

"There's only seven of us, you know," Leslee said. "That's a lot of running."

I had never thought of it that way and asked, "Aren't you scared I'm gonna mess up?"

"Nah," Leslee twanged. "You gotta learn someways, right?"

I couldn't wrap my head around how generous they were

being. It was the opposite of what I was used to at school. When I had been the weak link on the math team, Kirsten got me booted because she felt I was holding everyone back. And Violet kicked me out of our quartet when Claudia, a better violinist, became available. These girls needed the city championship like I needed oxygen and yet they were still trying to include me.

"Well," I said to Shawanda, still nervous about it, "Keisha seemed to get pretty mad when I missed that shot from inside the paint."

"We can afford it," said Shawanda. "Just try not to mess up. And grab more rebounds. You're tall."

"Okay," I said, and I headed back to the bench for the second half.

The second half I took three shots and missed three shots, but grabbed a few rebounds and made two shots at the free-throw line. And the whole time Dad and Coach Wheeler alternated screaming at me and covering their eyes. But it's not like I could have possibly held us back. We won the game 79–0, with Keisha scoring fifty-two points and Shawanda scoring sixteen. I scored my two and hustled on defense and didn't incur one foul in the process. And when we left the opposing rec center I thought clear as a bell, *This shit is kinda fun.*

The next week my whole family came to the game. Yvonne, Anora, Andreus, Yvette, and, of course, Dad. And walking onto the home court that morning, I was glad to have my family there. Not because I wanted them to see me—but because my team was pretty amazing. The kind of thing one really has to see to believe.

Upon arriving, Yvonne instantly became impatient and fancy.

"Ooh, John," she said, turning up her nose as they walked in. "You smell that? It smells funky in here. Like too much activator . . . something nasty."

"It's a gym," Dad said. "What do you expect it to smell like?"

"My gym growing up didn't smell like this," she said, putting on her airs. "And look at her teammates. G–H–E–T–T–O. They look like they just got out of juvie."

"Well," Dad said. "They can play like a mofo."

"Well," she said. "Maybe we should go at halftime. I don't feel comfortable here. You know there was a stabbing here in September."

"I'm gonna watch my daughter play a little basketball," Dad said. "If you need to go, just come back with the car in like an hour or so."

Yvonne was angry and said, "I guess I can watch for a little bit." She turned to me, "So bring your A game, Duck-Butt!"

When it was time for me to leave my family in the bleachers and take my place with the rest of the team on the bench, Keisha looked up at my stepmother and stepbrother and -sister in the bleachers and said, "That's your family?"

"Yeah," I said, a little cautious. People didn't always know what to make of our different colors and how they worked. Andre and Yvette were a lot lighter than their mother, so they looked like they might be Dad's, and my sister had curly dark hair so she looked like she might be mixed with something. And I was white as the day is long. As I watched Keisha's and Shawanda's faces as they tried to figure out who was related to whom and how many marriages were involved, I could feel my preppy alabaster sheen warming into something they could relate to.

"Is that your half sister?" Keisha wanted to know.

"No," I said. "That's my full sister!"

"Really?" Leslee said. "You guys both white?"

"Now it makes sense," Shawanda said.

"What?"

"Just your whole thing," she said.

That was when I noticed someone on Montlake, the opposing team, was waving to me. In the middle of their line up of affluent white faces was Eileen Connoly, smiling and waving her arms so I would spot her. I tried to pretend I didn't know her, but I could feel my cred with Keisha and Shawanda diminish incrementally the more she tried to get my attention. Finally, I relented and waved a little wave back.

And as we took the court and I stood across from her in the tip-off she said, "Wow. This is your team?"

"Yeah, this is my team." I was talking to her, but I didn't feel like I was the same Mishna that she knew. I felt like a Satin Doll. "No hard feelings, okay?" I said.

"What?" she said.

"When this is over."

"Yeah, whatever," she said. But I knew she probably wouldn't want to talk to me after what we were about to do to her and her teammates. The Dolls were no longer happy with winning. It wasn't a win to them unless the other team didn't score. Any bit of allegiance in this environment was to those six girls who were better at basketball than Eileen was at algorithms.

As the game began there was a marked difference in my game play. I played more aggressively than I ever had before. I looked at Eileen and her soft, spoiled teammates who all looked like her—like my friends at Oksana's house—like everyone I went to school with. And I resented the fact she was even playing basketball. And the resentment felt so good that I stole the ball from her midcourt and immediately threw it to Keisha.

But the next time the ball came to me, I took a chance on a three-pointer and missed.

At halftime Coach Wheeler said to me, "You're getting cocky, Wolff." But I didn't care. If cocky was the drug I was high on, let it flow. I felt like I was having a good time out there. Either that, or I was mad at everyone, and running and jumping was making it better. And in the second half I thought about Eileen's snobbery about how I had NEVER been to Europe!? And even though I didn't really have to, I elbowed a pudgy girl with my left hand while dribbling with my right. And I did it for the weirdest reason. I did it because I didn't like a white person thinking they could guard me. That was when the referee blew his whistle and I received my—very—first—flagrant—foul. And it was so flagrant.

I wasn't worried about the foul hurting the Dolls. This girl had a better chance of curing cancer than making her free throws. Besides, I had Shawanda and Leslee to grab the rebounds.

Now I know why these girls play basketball, I thought. I felt so strong.

When the game was over we had won 67–2. But on Tuesday we'd all be kicking ourselves for letting that one basket get away.

We had to go down a line and tell the Montlake team "Good game." And as I moved through the line I made sure that I was the last one to get to Eileen. Eileen looked at me, waiting for me to apologize to her or soften the blow of that steal, and what we had done to her team. Every instinct in me knew to conduct myself with humility and try to make her feel better. But I just couldn't and after slapping her hand I said, "I told you . . . no hard feelings."

"Well, it's just for fun anyways," Eileen said.

"For you guys maybe," I said, and we were both quiet for a second. "Well . . . I guess I'll see you Monday."

"Yeah," Eileen said, and walked away. And though I knew I'd pay for my cockiness on Monday, all I could think was, *I really got a flagrant foul!*

Eleven

EXTRACURRICULAR

I LOOKED AT the clock. It was 4 A.M. I had been up almost all night and soon my alarm for school would go off. I had been worrying again, and at this point lack of sleep was a more pressing fear than my previous ones, which I think was the point of staying up all night worrying. It was the third night in a row, and the next day was going to be brutal. The result of these late nights was midday tension headaches that started behind my forehead, and sent me to the nurse Mrs. Wilkins's office. I had written myself a note and had Mom sign it authorizing Mrs. Wilkins to give me Tylenol, but my ass-kicking headaches laughed at Mrs. Wilkins's girly little Tylenol.

Jesus! I thought. *I'm going to be a wreck tomorrow! Even if I fall asleep right now, I'll still only get 150 minutes of sleep.* I tried a number of positions and then looked at the clock again. *One hundred and forty seven minutes of sleep.* The red digital numbers on my alarm clock were taunting me and I finally put a pillow over the clock to stop it from making fun of me. Not only did I have insomnia, but I was aware that I wasn't supposed to have it at my age, causing more worry: maybe I was causing permanent brain damage, maybe I needed it.

I hurled myself out of bed and stumbled into the kitchen of Mom's apartment. I poured myself a glass of milk and was mixing in some chocolate syrup when Mom stepped out of her bedroom in her bus-driving uniform. She grabbed her work bag and saw me standing there, wide awake in my nightgown. Her face radiated concern.

"You can't sleep again?" she asked.

I nodded as I stirred my milk.

"Are you like this at your dad's house?"

"Sort of," I said.

"Well," she asked. "What the hell is keeping you up at night? What are you worried about?"

"I think about how I'm not sleeping."

"Well, why aren't you sleeping? Are you scared of something?"

I thought about it for a second to see if it was gonna hurt her feelings before I said sullenly, "My future."

I think she thought I was gonna say "Bears," because she looked annoyed. "You're twelve!"

"I know . . . But I'd like to have some financial security when I'm older. The rest of my friends are gonna go to great schools and be doctors and lawyers and stuff."

"So will you," Mom said.

"How?" I asked.

This was not a question Mom was ready to face at four in the morning and she tried to sound blasé as she said, "You're poor and smart. You'll get a scholarship or something."

Her lack of concern only worried me more. "But what if I don't?"

My mom was silent. It was not reassuring. Finally she said, "Why do you care about all this stuff?"

"Because *now* is when you start planning!"

"We'll plan it when you get closer to going."

"Okay, but I really want to go to Stanford, MIT, or Penn."

"The University of Washington is a very good school."

"Not to my friends," I said, tearing up. "They laugh at it. And I don't want to be poor my whole life. Poor people go to the University of Washington."

"You sound like a Republican."

"Well," I cried, "I just want to have a lucrative anesthesia practice like all my friends. And at this rate, I can't see that happening!"

"Your dad and I didn't finish college at all."

I sobbed. Loudly.

"Listen," she said in her "don't cry" voice. "When you see the future, what do you see? I mean, what do you envision is going to be so bad?"

"Well," I said, "there's this shack—"

"Whoa!" Mom said.

"Can I finish?" I asked. She nodded. "There's this shack and there's a mattress on the floor . . . no sheets."

"Uh-huh."

"And the mattress is stained like all different weird-colored stains. Like you can't tell what the stains are from—"

"Okay," Mom said. "I gotta stop you here."

"Wait," I said, and spit out really fast, "And I die of hepatitis from bad water. The end."

"Wow," Mom said. "How do you come up with this stuff?"

"How is that not gonna happen?"

"Listen, I have to go to work now. But I think you might have a little bit of black-and-white thinking about how people become rich and poor. Will you call me from your dad's?"

I wasn't sure I wanted to take advice from her. She still had student loans, no degree, and two kids. It wasn't the type of security I was looking for.

"I promise," she said as she headed out the door, "that there are a few steps between Stanford and a shack." But it didn't seem that way to me. My friend Marni lived in a glass palace on the ocean, her dad had gone to Wharton—Dad's friend Randy, who lived in an alley, had gone to the University of Washington. And no one had sat me down for the "crack talk" yet.

"Besides," Mom said, "there are a lot of ways for people to get scholarships. Just do extracurricular activities."

"What's that? Extra . . ."

"Extracurricular activities. Like your violin is an extracurricular activity," she said.

"Really?"

"You do orchestra. Do it in high school."

"I was already planning on it."

"And there are clubs, and student government . . . and sports is huge to colleges."

"Sports? You saw me at basketball. I'm not athletic."

"You are. You get it from your dad."

"I'm not," I said. "And I don't think that would be a factor at the schools I'm thinking of. I think it's just grades and stuff."

"I don't know." Mom rolled her eyes. "Your father had shit grades and even he got a football scholarship to a good school."

That day at school I had my usual tension headache. And I wound up in the nurse's office, as was my norm, trying to take a nap on her corner mattress that felt like it was made out of dog hair and chalkboard erasers. But even if I didn't sleep there, the lying down acted as a reset button for me in a way that really refreshed me. And I thought Mrs. Wilkins and I were getting into kind of a groove—like she really enjoyed my visits.

As I lay there looking up at the popcorn ceiling, I felt

weirdly optimistic. I had never heard of these extracurricular activities before, and as I tried to block out the crushing pain behind my forehead, I made a list on my hand of all the extracurricular activities that might help with getting me a scholarship, shooting down bad ideas as I went:

Soccer—twelve=too late to start
Skiing—too expensive to be great at
Lacrosse—too late, also hate everyone who does it
Basketball—clearly, a no
Debate—awesome, find out what it is
Cheerleading—not pretty enough, in cheerleader
    way—also no splits
Orchestra—check
Insect club—where do I sign?
Football—

I lingered on that one for a long time. Football had worked for Dad. And the idea of running into things really fast seemed like something that would be good for insomnia.

I was drifting when Mrs. Wilkins woke me from my half sleep to send me back to class. As I stretched she said, "I don't want to see you in here tomorrow." And I nodded, a little hurt and embarrassed. I thought we had a connection, but I guessed she was just being a nurse.

That night when I got home to Dad's house, he was wrestling with Yvonne. Andre and Yvette were trying to help their mom win, and were hanging off Dad's arms in a way that begged the question: *Why doesn't he just fling them?* Yvonne had something in her hands that I couldn't see, and as Dad tried to pry it from her, she laughed and squealed, "Don't, John, no!"

I set my book bag and violin down and watched, of course,

wanting to see what was in her hand. But Dad immediately involved me saying, "Mishna, grab her arm!" And instead of choosing sides I stood next to Yvonne, looking like I wasn't quite sure what an arm was or how to grab one. Dad was annoyed with my lack of assistance as he proudly lifted a pack of cigarettes above his head shouting, "Busted!"

"It was just this one time." Yvonne tried to grab them again, but failed.

"Kids," Dad asked, "does Mommy smoke?"

Yvonne put her finger to her lips.

"Yes," Andreus said.

"Andre!" Yvonne cried.

"Busted!" Dad repeated. "You are so busted."

"Dad," I said. He, Yvonne, and the kids turned and looked at me like I was from the moon. It was then I realized I had interrupted.

"I'm sorry. I interrupted." I grabbed my bag and started heading downstairs.

"What is it?" Dad asked impatiently. "You don't gotta huff off."

"Well," I said, unsure now. "Today I decided that I want to play football."

Dad didn't look as stoked as I thought he would, and he and Yvonne said in unison some version of: "You're a girl." And Yvette the three-year-old just started giggling.

"I know that," I said. "But there are, like, girls' leagues, right?"

"Not that I know of!" Dad said. "And even if there were, you're skinny. You'll get hurt."

"She's not that skinny, John," Yvonne said.

"I'm not!" I repeated. "Plus, I've never broken a bone, 'cause I'm strong!" I tried to make myself look more muscular. "And you got a football scholarship to college, right? Maybe if I get good I can get one, too."

"Well . . . ," Dad said, not wanting to burst my gender bubble yet. "Football doesn't start until the fall, and if you can gain twenty pounds between now and then you can play."

"Awesome," I said.

"But if you're suddenly feeling athletic, no need to wait till then to get competitive. Let's get you into a summer sport now."

"I don't want to do track again."

"I want to play football!" Andre shouted, causing Dad to smile uncontrollably. Dad picked him up and kissed him on the forehead, holding him as he continued to talk to me.

"What about summer swim league at Medgar Evers?"

"Cool!" I said. "Wait . . . It's like laps, right?" Suddenly I realized we wouldn't be playing Marco Polo.

"You race. It's a team," Dad said.

"Okay," I replied—sold but not quite sure how I had gotten thrown off football.

"A'ight, then," he said. "You swim this summer."

"And in the fall I can play football?"

"Twenty pounds."

"Wait, wait, wait!" Yvonne said. "You're rewarding your daughter for bulking up?"

Then Dad whispered something in Yvonne's ear, and she laughed a little. I imagined him saying, "Don't worry. She'll never get enough to eat in this house." But it was probably just something about Yvonne's butt, and how big and awesome it was.

I swam on the league at Medgar Evers Pool where we trained and then did little meets against other rec center pools. And I couldn't tell how good I was, but the rest of my team was really horrible—which after being on the Satin Dolls was super refreshing. There were people on the team who were afraid to jump into the deep end, and every race involved a lot of slapping and splashing. So I couldn't really rest on my laurels knowing I was better than people who looked like they were drowning. Still, I found that there was one stroke I was undeniably good at—breaststroke. And I got blue ribbons for it, lots of them. I also got teased to no end, thanks in part to the fact that the coach referred to people who were good at breaststroke as "her breasters."

Still, as much as I had fun swimming, I just saw it as a way-station till I could bulk up enough to start playing football. And I focused tirelessly on gaining weight. After swim practice ended I would go down the street to Thriftway, a very low-priced neighborhood supermarket that sold a generic brand called Western Family. I knew Dad would be late to pick me up, which gave me enough time to buy my bulking agents. I had read the labels, so I knew that the highest calorie content for the cheapest food that didn't make you throw up was Western Family fruit pies—five for a dollar. I tried all of the flavors, and my favorite for bulking was lemon because I thought the sourness of the lemon made it even easier to keep down. Vanilla and chocolate were fun but they actually would make me hurl—and cherry was for dessert. I would consume my pies as quickly as possible on my way back to the pool and hide any evidence of eating them, because I still wanted my pork chop at dinner. But every day when I got on the scale at the pool my weight seemed to be the same. By the halfway point of swimming season, I still hovered around eighty-seven pounds. I began to give up hope of ever getting a football scholarship. And I also spent a good deal of time mentally redecorating my future shack and finding clever ways to work with the water stains.

One night, I was over at Mom's and I got one of my tension headaches so bad that she had to give me four aspirin.

"I'm gonna talk to your dad about your stress level," Mom said. "I think you have anxiety and I think that maybe you should be spending more time at my house now."

"Yes," I said, hardly containing my delight. "Maybe you're right. I'm soooo stressed out."

"Well, I'm gonna talk to him."

I was amazed. Mom had always been a little intimidated by my dad and had always agreed with his custody arrangements. But if she was now willing to talk to him about changing things up, I couldn't be happier. She kept the fridge full and her house was clean and quiet—all things I liked.

The next day when Mom went to drop me and Anora off at Dad's, she said she wanted to talk to him. "Okay," Dad said. "What's on your mind, Diane?"

"Well," she started, all of a sudden getting squirmy, "I feel like Mishna would maybe do better spending a little more time at my house."

"Are you saying you're a better parent than me?"

"No . . . Here's the thing," Mom said, sounding confused. "Mishna has these headaches—"

"What headaches?" Dad asked. "She doesn't have headaches at my house."

"She has them at school a lot."

"You're feeding them stuff."

She paused. "The nurse and I agree. . . ."

"What nurse?"

"The school nurse."

Dad looked at her and said, "It's summer. Mishna's not in

school." Mom stammered, she was losing her train of thought in front of my eyes. It's like Dad was made out of kryptonite.

"Listen," Dad said, grabbing Mom's lower back and leading her toward her car, "this is the first time I'm hearing about any of this."

"Really?" she said.

"Yes," Dad said. "Mishna hasn't mentioned any headaches to me."

"Oh," Mom said as Dad opened her car door.

"So, I'll talk to Mishna and together we'll get to the bottom of it all."

"Okay," Mom said. "That sounds reasonable." Dad shut her door and walked back up to where I was on the back steps. He passed me on his way into the house and said, "Your mom's a control freak." And that was the end of that.

The summer swim league was almost over when, after practice one day, a blond guy named Dan who seemed to work at the pool approached me. His hair was white from chlorine, and had the consistency of cotton candy. And he was shaped like an upside-down triangle. He even walked on the outside edges of his feet, which folded in to make the triangle's bottom point.

"I noticed your breast," he said without a tinge of humor. "If you wanted to keep swimming into the fall, I'd like to try you out on CAST, our swim club."

"Hmmm," I said. "I was planning on trying to get a football scholarship, but I'm not big enough yet."

He snickered in a way I found arrogant. "You might want to consider swimming then . . . on a real USA Swimming club."

"Does it cost money?"

"Yes."

"Oh," I said, dismayed.

I turned to leave as the conversation was over, when he said, "We really need a breaststroker, especially for the relay. The board has talked about scholarship spots. Maybe we can work something out." Then he said the magic words, "Do you want me to talk to your parents?"

"Absolutely!"

So in the fall I started training with the Central Area Swim Club or CAST. In addition to finally being good at a sport, the great thing about swimming was that Dad knew almost nothing about it. Still, when he *would* show up at meets; lack of knowledge didn't stop him from trying to coach me at competitive swimming.

Before I got on the blocks for my events he'd pull me aside from my teammates and say, "Can we just take a second to talk about your race?"

"Yes, Dad," I'd say, waving my teammates along. Then trying to mask my sarcasm, I'd ask, "How do you think we should handle this one?"

"Well," he'd say, scratching his chin. "I think you should take the first lap just real fast."

"Great idea!"

"Then when you get to the second lap—go for it! Don't try to coast off that first lap. . . ."

"Okay, Dad."

"The third lap you just want to give it all ya got." Then he got really serious, "Then on that fourth lap, you just bring it on home—fast as you can."

Then I would go talk to my coach, Dan, who would tell me what my competition looked like and what it would take to get me into the finals. Always telling me to "streamline" and to "explode off the walls." Then he'd remind me, "A winner is someone who finds the absolute limits of personal agony, and surpasses them every day." Then whatever was gonna happen would happen, and I would get a hot dog.

As months went by I got a little bigger, and even though swimming was fun, I was sure that football was more important to college types, and I was eager to solidify my future.

"Dad," I said one afternoon after swim practice, "I think I'm bigger now, and when I checked the scale I gained a few pounds. Hey!" I flexed. "Look at these arms."

"That's great, baby," he said.

"So?" I said expectantly. But he just looked at the road. "Dad!"

"Don't yell at me."

"Sorry, Dad. But you said I could play football—"

"When?" Dad asked.

"That I could play football, if I got bigger!" I couldn't believe he was drawing a blank. "That's why I was swimming this summer . . . 'member?"

"Those boys would crush you, baby," he said.

"Well, I can play with the girls. I'm bigger now!"

"Damn, Mishna," he said impatiently. "When are you gonna get it through your head? There is no girls' football!"

"There is," I said. "There must be."

"Well, there's not!" he said. "Besides, I would never let you play football. What's wrong with you?"

"But you said . . ."

"I never said you could play football . . . that's crazy."

"It's not crazy," I said, not really sure why I was starting to cry. "I want to get a football scholarship!"

"Well, no one is giving them to girls!" he said. "What you ought to do is get yourself a swimming scholarship or something. 'Cause football ain't on for you."

"But," I said, still crying, "nobody likes a swimmer. It's not like you sit down and watch Monday night swimming."

Dad looked up from the road and said, "We don't have that kind of cable."

That night dribbled by slowly. My life plans all shaken up, my fears of the future multiplied as I helped Dad with dinner. And my good ol' tension headache came back in the middle of Yvonne's grace.

But as I picked at my chicken thigh—my purpose for eating evaporated—part of me still wondered if what Dad said about women's football was true. I mean, maybe there were teams and he just didn't know about. Secret women's football teams that met at night and played by candlelight. He didn't know everything and I decided that before I made myself crazy, I should get a second opinion.

So after dinner when I saw Zwena out on the street with Nay-Nay, I ran out of the house. Zwena had started hanging out with Nay-Nay in the last year or so, and after school she would change out of her uniform into something closer to what Nay-Nay wore, which at the moment were big gold earrings and bright-colored jeans. I was always still happy to see Zwena, but I thought she looked ridiculous in her red jeans. And she was wearing cheap hoops so big, it looked like her ears had been handcuffed and were trying to break free before the fake gold turned them green.

Both the girls were about sixteen now, but looked about twenty-two as they leaned against Nay-Nay's father's Caddie and flirted with a light-skinned boy with a fade. Nay-Nay had a bag of cheese puffs and in between bites she would lick the orange powder off her fingers like cheese powder was a delicacy.

"Yo, Zwena," I said, walking up to them and getting my guard up a little for Nay-Nay.

"Hey, violin!" Nay-Nay said, not bothering to take her fingers out of her mouth. "Where is your violin?"

"I dunno," I said. "You must have eaten it." That landed a little harder than I had intended, because Nay-Nay raised her hand to hit me. But when I flinched everyone laughed—and her dominance was reasserted.

"S'up, Mishmash," Zwena said, acting a little more street for Nay-Nay. Then she pointed to the boy beside her. "This here is Ty."

"Hey," I said. "I'm Mishna."

"Don't you go wit' Bijon?" he asked, referring to a light-skinned boy who lived nearby.

"No!" I said incredulously. "He's gross."

"Would you like to?" Ty asked.

"Shut up, Ty!" Zwena said.

"No!" I said. "I barely know Bijon!"

"Okay. Dang," Ty said. "You ain't gotta yell."

"Whatever," I said, dismissing Ty, and then asking the girls, "Hey, do you know any girls' football teams?"

"Nope," Nay-Nay said.

"Maybe . . . ," Zwena said.

"You're tripping," snapped Ty. "There's no girls' football teams, not at Miller or RB or CAYA."

My heart sank.

Zwena said, "I know a girl that played football with the boys, though." She turned to Ty and Nay-Nay. "'Member Shanda?"

"Oh yeah . . . Shanda," Ty said, giving me a glimmer of hope, before adding, "She was a ho."

"She was not a ho!" Nay-Nay said—half-eaten cheese puffs falling out of her mouth. "Why you saying that?"

"Because it's true," Ty said. "She slept with that whole damn team."

"That's what I hear," Zwena said. "She was on that team 'cause she was hoin'." I didn't like Zwena saying *hoin'*. She was a mathlete.

I continued, "Maybe she just really liked to ram things with her head and tackle and stuff."

"Now that don't make no kind of sense," Zwena said. "You're crazy."

"So there are no girls' football teams?"

"What, are you deaf and dumb?" Ty quipped.

"You want to play football, violin?" Nay-Nay laughed. "You better stick with playing your violin and making out with Bijon."

"I met him like once!" I yelled, and stomped back into the house all bummed out thinking about was how I was never going to college. And on top of it I didn't think Zwena liked me anymore.

The next week at swim practice I was too depressed to train. I loafed my way through every workout and stopped eating fruit pies. I was good at swimming, but I didn't really get the point of it anymore. You just swam really fast for the sake of swimming, big deal. It wasn't like football where people give you college money for it, and scream at the TV, and throw parades where mooning and head-butting might occur. By Friday practice, Dan took me out of the pool. He sat me down by a chalkboard where our team mantra was written.

"You want to tell me why you're loafing?" he asked.

"I'm swimming as fast as I can." I said.

"Since when does Sean lap you?"

Since swimming is lame and it's not football.

"I'm tired," I said flatly, but Dan simply pointed to the little chalkboard.

"What does that say?" he asked.

I read aloud, " 'A winner is someone who finds the absolute limits of personal agony, and surpasses them every day.' " *And that's why you're a swim coach and not an anethesiologist. You probably live in a shack.*

"Are you a winner?" Dan asked.

"I guess not," I said.

"Then get out of my pool."

"What?" I asked. "You serious?" I thought he needed me.

"Yes, I'm serious. You're not here to win, and you're wasting everyone's time. Get out of my pool."

"I will," I said, as I headed toward the locker room. Adding, "Also, it's not your pool, the city owns it!"

"Well, I'm kicking you out of it," he said. "Go be a loser somewhere else."

"I will!" I said, getting angrier as a marched away. "And I don't care!"

"Well, that's handy! 'Cause you're kicked off the team! Good-bye."

"Good-bye!" I said, turning around.

By now everyone was staring and I hoped my teammates got a good look at my face, because they were never gonna see it again!

I hit the women's showers and threw my cap and goggles against the wall, liking the way the way the goggles echoed against the tile, and excited to have the whole shower area to myself. I picked them up and threw them again.

"All mine!" I said, turning on every shower and running between them—finally deciding to sprawl out on the giant wheelchair shower bench and luxuriate in a seated cleaning. When I was a big rich doctor somewhere I would have a seat in my shower, too. But as I washed the chlorine out of my hair and felt the warm water trickle down my face, I noticed I was crying, and "all mine" quickly became all alone. And I admitted for the first time that I really loved swimming.

When you're kicked off a swim team, or any team for that matter, you kinda just want to stomp out, get into a Lamborghini drive off into the sunset. But I was waiting for a ride from my dad, which was like waiting for a really moody slot machine to pay. So in order to give everyone the impression that I was long gone, I had to hide myself on the side of the steps above the pool. And when Dad showed up an hour later, he looked like rush-hour traffic had just handed him his ass, so I didn't have the guts to tell him I got kicked off the team.

All weekend I obsessed about CAST. I vacillated between feeling bad for being rude to Dan and thinking about all the names I should have called him. I thought about how good it felt to be on a team that didn't involve numbers. And it's not like I actually knew colleges didn't give away swimming scholarships. I had just been so focused on getting big and moving on that I never bothered to check out what the whole sport was really about. Weirdly, now that it was all over, I was really ready to take swimming seriously.

By Monday morning I was exhausted—I hadn't been able to sleep on Sunday night because all of my neuroses had returned, and I was so distracted I flubbed a pop quiz in math. I took a sad bus ride home instead of going straight to the pool, and when I got home my father was sitting on the couch, looking like he had been there all day. He had the paper spread across the cushions and he looked surprised when I walked in.

"What are you doing here? Why aren't you swimmin'?"

"There's no practice today," I said.

"How come?"

"A pool thing?" I said. "I don't know. Dan didn't say."

"Ah, well," Dad said. "I saved the sports section for you.

There's a thing in here about that girl from Stanford, Janet Evans."

"Oh. Okay," I said, feeling like dirt.

"Says she swims like six hours a day. . . . You could do that."

"Yeah," I said, wishing I had just hid at the corner store for three hours.

"I imagine that would be enough swimming . . . you know, to be the best. She *is* the best, right?"

"Yeah . . . I think so," I said, wondering if Dan called him and he knew I had gotten kicked off the team.

"Well, you train like her, you could be the best," he said, smiling. "I truly believe that." I tried to be a rock, as his eyes filled with pride. But I knew if he said one more word about swimming, I was gonna fall apart and start confessing.

Instead, he stood up and changed the subject. "Well, here's the paper." He grabbed his coat. "I gotta go get your stepmom at school." I wondered if he knew how stupid he sounded when he said that.

The phone rang, and Dad picked it up on his way out.

It was Dan and he handed me the phone before walking out the door.

"Where are you?" Dan asked.

"Home," I said. "I'm banned, remember."

"Bullshit!" Dan said. "You get your butt down here and get in this pool, or you're not going to regionals!"

"But I'm at home," I said. "You kicked me off the team!"

"Listen," Dan said, "I don't have time to argue with you. If you want to be a little baby, stay home. But if you want to be a real swimmer, you get your ass down here!"

I looked out the window at Dad driving away. "I want to be a swimmer," I said. "But Dad just took off, I don't have a ride."

"Oh, for Christ's sake!" Dan said impatiently and hung up

the phone. I didn't know what that meant—if I was off the team or on, or what. I sat on the couch feeling confused and sorry for myself and decided to pick up the article about Janet Evans. She had a swimming scholarship at Stanford, an Olympic gold medal, and she was white. I didn't know if I could achieve all of those things, but I felt a twinge of hopefulness about the future. Like maybe I wouldn't die of hepatitis, my last meal a plate of food-bank cheese with food-bank honey on it—the only two things I got from the food bank that week.

My train of thought was broken by a knock at the door, and as I walked to get it I saw Dan's car out the front window. Janie, one of the other girls from the team, was waiting in the passenger seat. Her mom had given me a ride to a meet once, so I assumed she had gotten him there. I opened the door, and Dan looked a little horrified as he asked, "You live here?"

"Yeah," I said, touched. "You came to get me."

"You know there's like a ten-foot drop out your front door!"

I nodded still unsure if he was gonna lecture me or hug me. But he just stood there looking like an upside-down triangle. "Well, get your stuff and get in the car! Practice starts in twenty minutes!"

On the way to the pool everyone in the car was quiet. I looked at Dan, who was determined to pretend nothing happened on Friday. He was staring so intently at the road that it was obvious he was avoiding eye contact. Janie, who was what Dad would call "spoiled" or "a punk," had been kicked off the team several times now. And, even though she was the loudest girl I had ever met besides Nay-Nay, she respected the ride of silence and didn't say a word.

"I'm sorry," I said, enjoying being important enough to be picked up. "I'm really gonna do my best from now on."

"Don't tell it to me," Dan said. "Tell it to the pool."

Twelve

THE FAMILY RACIST

DAD HAD ALWAYS rigged up everything in our house. You needed pliers to turn on the shower or open the bedroom door. There was a trick to opening every drawer in the kitchen, and the phone was a mess of electrical tape and worked only if you sat perfectly still. But Dad's *Mona Lisa* was the van. This was a cargo van that he transported four children around in. The inside door handles fell off so to get out of the van from the driver's side you had to use a bent coat hanger, and to get out of the passenger side you used a wrench. The two back doors of the van were held closed with a wire wrapped around them, and the latch on them was broken so the wire was actually the only thing holding the doors closed. And for the kids to sit on, in the cargo area were three plastic milk crates—and your crate wasn't attached to the floor, so to stay on it while the car was in motion required a deft sense of balance and a working knowledge of physics. The floor of the van also had ridges, so if there was some water in the back that had seeped in through the not-really-closed back doors, we could while away the hours watching it roll back and forth as the van drove up and down slopes. Needless to say, my sister and I always called shotgun the night before.

The summer after my fourteenth birthday I spent with a family in France. The night I returned, my dad picked me up from the airport in the van. I got off my plane and seeing the hooptie-mobile was a subtle reminder that I wasn't really Continental, and that brake pads aren't for everyone. Dad helped me with my bags but he didn't look particularly happy to see me. He looked anxious and stiff. And as we pulled the jalopy away from airport pick up he said. "Your stepmom wants us all to have a talk when you get home." I was worried it was about money.

The trip to France was something that my French teacher had said would look good on my transcript, and I'd filled out all the paperwork and a scholarship application. My father's tax forms confirmed what I had already known, that he hadn't really had a *job* job in years. And that along with my transcripts bought me an almost full scholarship—except for five hundred dollars. I don't think I had a full grasp of what five hundred dollars was to my family, I just knew it was a lot less than the thirty-five hundred all of the other kids' parents paid. I actually thought they should be grateful because I saved them three thousand dollars. As I sat down for our "talk" I found out they were not grateful.

"We need you to start earning your keep," Yvonne said, smoothing a piece of hair by the side of her face into a finger curl. "You got to go to France, and part of that is that you need to get yourself a *J-O-B*."

"I have a job . . . I do childcare for that Tuesday night group." Yvonne and Dad drew a blank. "PEPS."

"What?" Yvonne looked at me blankly.

Dad used his hands to explicate. "She takes care of the kids during they little meeting, I forgot about that."

"That's volunteer work," Yvonne said, grabbing Dad's hand again.

"No," I said. "Catholic Service Center pays me. Plus, there's Saturday mornings at the Jewish Center. I watch the kids during shul." I was an equal opportunity kid-watcher.

"We mean a real job," said Yvonne. "The type of job you do every day after school. You got to go to France, now you need to get a job."

"Your stepmom is right," Dad said nervously. "You should start contributing to this family." I didn't want to contribute to this family. This family needed a lot of work.

"Well, what about my extracurricular activities?" I asked. "My violin, my swimming, my clubs?"

"You'll have to give some things up," Yvonne said, causing my stomach to fall and my whole body to shudder.

"You don't understand! I need those to get a scholarship for college!" *So I can get the fuck out of here.*

"No, *you* don't understand!" Yvonne said. "You are too old to be not contributing to this household. And since you don't have enough time to work, I say you quit swimming." At this point I was swimming five hours a day.

"Whoa, whoa, whoa!" Dad said. "She doesn't have to give up swimming, does she?"

Yvonne shot Dad a look so neutering, he actually left his body for a second.

"I'm fourteen. Who's gonna hire me?" I asked.

"McDonald's, for one," Yvonne said

McDonalds, does she know who the fuck I am? "I'm pretty sure you have to be sixteen."

"To work at McDonald's?" Yvonne said incredulously.

"Pretty sure," I said.

Yvonne was flustered and got dismissive. "Well, that's not the point! Besides," she said, "no one is gonna check your age." Wrong again, but I didn't say anything. I just sat there wishing that I hadn't gone to France, and more, that she hadn't said the word *McDonald's*. I wouldn't have taken the summer in France if I had known it might end in McDonald's.

Since I was old enough to know it was a shitty job, McDonald's was where I was worried I'd end up. Every time someone joked about McDonald's being my future My friend Violet said that McDonald's was where we'd work if we didn't finish our history presentation. When I missed a geometry problem, and my math teacher said I should practice saying, "Would you like some fries with that order?" I just froze. They thought it was funny because it was so far-fetched, but for me McDonald's wasn't all that far-fetched. I had been fighting it all these years, but I knew if I stopped fighting, my genes would catch up to me like a tailwind no matter where I'd gone to school, and I'd spend the rest of my life on fries.

"Jesus!" I said. "You don't understand." I tried not to get upset. Yvonne fed on upset-ness. "We get like four hours of homework a night."

"That sounds like an excuse," Yvonne said. "I had a job when I was your age, and had time to get pretty good grades. And I'll tell you, I had a lot more family responsibilities than you do. I understood my priority was to my family."

"I'm not having some great time!" I was getting upset anyway so I decided to lay it on thick, "I have a four-point-oh, and I play in two orchestras, I'm in swimming, and I work with underprivileged youth, because I think it will pay off down the road . . . for all of us." The last part made no sense to Yvonne.

"You're underprivileged youth!" Yvonne said. "Or did you not know that?" Why was she killing my American dream?

"Besides," Dad said, "I see you find plenty of time to monkey around here and watch that TV."

"Yeah," Yvonne said. "You could easily spend the same hour flippin' burgers and have made five dollars."

"Do you want a McDonald's employee or an All-American?" This was meant to grab my dad's attention. He may not have related to swimming that well, but he liked the way those words rolled off the tongue: *All-American.*

"Can't you do both?" Dad asked.

"She's manipulating."

"You don't understand," I said, panicked. "I know it doesn't look like it, but I have a plan."

"You have a plan?" Yvonne laughed. "A plan for what? You're fourteen."

"To go to the same schools my classmates are going to."

"Oh, this again," Dad said. "You think you're better than this family."

Yvonne nodded in agreement before declaring, "You're just being racist." *Racist?* I was shocked and recoiled. It was like we were all just having a conversation and she pulled out a hand grenade. "That's right. You got a problem with black people." I could keep talking, but the argument was over, so I started to cry. I had worked too hard at trying to be down to be called a racist.

"I'm not racist."

"Mishna," Dad said. "Get a job."

"You guys are being really shortsighted!" I screamed and stomped off. What I really wanted to say was "ghetto"—"You guys are being really ghetto!" So maybe I was racist.

I raced down the stairs to my room, wondering why I couldn't have my friend Violet's parents. *They don't even talk to her most of the night. She sits in her room and does whatever she wants and nobody makes her clean anything or do anyone's hair or get a job. Her only job is her schoolwork and she doesn't even do that well in history. Or my friend Marni—her parents even take her to Europe every summer and she doesn't have to pay them back. In fact, she gets a HUGE allowance and all she has to do is stomp around and act all depressed. I wished someone would pay me to be depressed—I would do such a good job.*

I jumped into my top bunk and wedged myself into the corner against the cement wall and imagined I was in a Soviet prison. Dad was supposed to have finished drywalling it seven years ago, and now the pebbles in the cement just elevated my self-pity as I pressed my face into cold rock like a Dostoyevsky character. And as the tears poured down my cheeks I realized I was mostly upset about Dad. He had totally let Yvonne call me a racist, and I wondered if there was any way he could really think I was.

That night I had a dream. I saw myself running down a street in the middle of the night. The street was desolate—just abandoned warehouses lining a cobblestone street. It must have been inspired by Michael Jackson videos—maybe "Smooth Criminal" or "The Way You Make Me Feel." I was running fast to get away from something, but I could feel its breath on my neck. I sprinted, trying to resist, but this giant hand reached out to grab my shoulder and pull me back. I finally fell into the fog and became a part of it. But in the fog there was a warm, familiar peace. I woke up thinking about McDonald's.

The next day when I came home from swim practice, Yvonne was sitting in the kitchen with Anora, Andreus, and Yvette. All of them had a Happy Meal.

"Did you get me one?" I asked.

"No," Yvonne joked. "I thought you didn't like McDonald's."

"I like McDonald's food!" I said, feeling hungry and dejected.

"Well, you should get yourself some money." She laughed. I pulled a five out of my pocket and handed it to her.

"Ask your dad to take you."

"Dad, can we go get some food?" I asked. "I'm hungry."

"You're always hungry," he said, retreating to his bedroom. "Make yourself something out of the fridge."

"Maybe you can find yourself some pâté," Yvonne joked.

I opened the fridge. Yvonne, Anora, Andre, and Yvette were still watching me like my hunger was entertainment. Milk. Eggs. Rotting scallions. I looked in the cupboard for some Top Ramen. Nothing.

I looked at my family chowing down on McDonald's in the next room. At this point, Yvonne started laughing again as I closed the fridge and headed for the pantry, where we kept stuff we got at Costco. Triumphantly, I found a box of Jiffy mix and started to make myself some corn bread. Anora, who had finished her Happy Meal, ran into the kitchen to help me. She grabbed the muffin tin out off the shelf and handed it to me.

"Make it in this!" she said. My sister liked muffin-shaped things. I had the skillet out to make hot water corn bread, but decided to put it away to make my sister happy.

"Okay," I said, "do you want to grease it for me?" She nodded and ran for the drippings jar, but at that moment Yvonne had turned on a Jody Watley cassette in the living room and started shaking her hips along with the babies. While I had played basketball, Anora had replaced me on Yvonne's beauty team. So Anora took one look at the dance party in the living room and became instantly disenchanted with corn bread. She dropped the pan and ran off to join them.

"Come on, Mishna," Yvonne said, jokingly sashaying up to Anora, who was dance-walking into the living room. "Come shake that duck butt." I was surprised to be invited, but I was still in the middle of my food project, and hungrier than I was lonely.

"As soon as I get my corn bread in the oven."

"You just don't like black music," Yvonne snapped. "You're racist about music." What she said knocked the wind out of me. There was that word again, *racist*. It made me immediately defensive.

"What are you talking about?" I asked.

"You know," she said, trying to play down the fact she just called me racist again, "you just like that depressing white music."

"That's not true!" I shouted over the music. "Dad took me to see Miles Davis, and I like Miles Davis." I thought I was making a compelling argument and asked, "Would a racist like Miles Davis?"

But Yvonne brushed my argument off without breaking step. "No," she said, "but a really, really white person would." And returned to the bump with my sister.

I had had it. I ran to the living room and screamed, "Just because I don't like Jody Watley does not make me a racist!" Yvonne stopped dancing and the dance party stopped. "She sucks!" I thought standing my ground might put this whole racist thing to bed. Instead, it made Dad poke his head out of the bedroom. He saw Yvonne and me standing across from each other, clearly having some difficulty, and attempted to retreat back to the bedroom when Yvonne screamed, "John! Come here!"

And as he slinked out of the bedroom into the living room, everything in his walk made me wonder, *What happened to my dad?*

Anora turned down the stereo as Yvonne stood with her arms crossed and nostrils flaring. "John, your daughter is disrespecting me and I'm not gonna take it from a kid."

"Dad," I said, tearing up, "she called me a racist!" Surely he had to see how deeply this was affecting me.

Dad looked at Yvonne before saying. "Well, you know, Mishna, you can be kind of snobby about black folks stuff." I couldn't believe he was siding with her.

"But I'm not a racist!" I desperately cried to Yvonne and Dad. I had to make them see. But they were deeply connected in their judgment of me, and looking at me hysterical in the living room they seemed very close. It made me wonder if they had spent the entire time I was in France talking about the "Mishna problem," and I could feel their reality slowly replacing my own, until I said, "Am I?"

I looked at both their faces and neither of them knew what to say. They were neither reassuring nor condemning.

"What makes me a racist?" I asked, not even sure what the word meant anymore. "Am I a racist because I don't want to work at McDonald's?" I asked. "Or because I don't like Jody Watley?" I was completely confused and started to cry again, in a way that just pissed Yvonne off.

"Anora," Dad said. "Take the babies downstairs." Anora grabbed Andre's and Yvette's hands and headed downstairs. Dad turned to me. "You seem to have some different values than the rest of us. . . ."

"What do you mean?" I asked. "That makes me racist?"

"Not so much racist," Dad said. "Just selfish and judgemental." I couldn't believe that was Dad's idea of softening it.

"I'm just different."

"That's bullshit," Yvonne said. "Mishna's judging me, John. And I seriously don't need it from her. I got enough on my plate, I don't need her prissy attitude."

"Mishna," Dad said, "you make any headway on getting that job yet?"

"Since yesterday?" I asked. "No."

"Why don't you get on that for your stepmom and stop causing trouble."

"Okay," I said, wiping my face, "but I don't think I'm a racist."

The next day after school and before swim practice, I went to McDonald's to try to get a job. I was willing to give up swimming or violin if it would just make the house bearable again. Even if everyone I went to school with knew, and I wound up working there the rest of my goddamn life, and my grades and swimming slipped, and I couldn't even get a scholarship to community college, I decided it would be so worth it if I could just not be the problem for a while. I walked past the McDonald's playground, where I had spent so many hours as a child seesawing next to plastic Hamburglar or climbing into the Big Mac tower, and into the restaurant. I scanned the employees. They were all black, older than me, and remarkably intimidating at that moment. I wondered if they would even want to hire a white person, and whether just thinking that made me racist. Were racists just people that noticed color? Or was it expecting that they wouldn't like me that made me a racist?

I held my breath and walked up to a teenage girl who was the most friendly-looking of the bunch. She had two pair of earrings on, a big pair and a small pair, and she looked me up and down before she said an anemic, "Welcome to McDonald's, can I take your order?"

"Are there any openings?" I mumbled, cripplingly scared all of a sudden that she would laugh at me.

"Pardon?" she said in a way that made one of the world's most polite words sound rude.

I said as loud as I could, which was a whisper: "An application . . . for a job?" She broke the tension with a big reassuring smile.

"Oh yeah, you can fill out an application. Let me get my manager." She said it nicely, like we were in the same club.

"Um . . . before you do," I said, "I thought I'd ask . . . How old do you have to be to work here?"

"Fifteen," she said. "But you need a note from your school."

"Oh, okay," I said, trying to sound disappointed. "I'm too young."

"Shoot," she said. "You look seventeen!"

"Thank you . . . You, too," I mumbled, but she had already moved on to the woman behind me and was talking over me saying, "Welcome to McDonald's . . ." before I finished. I guess I wasn't in the club anymore.

I headed out the door, relieved and righteous. I knew I was too young for McDonald's. None of my friends at school had those types of jobs. And the girl behind the counter kind of liked me, so I probably wasn't *obviously* racist to people.

I returned home that night trying my best to look really disappointed as I walked in the door. I let out a little sigh as I set my things down and Yvonne said, "What's wrong with you now, Duck-Butt?"

"Well," I said, letting out another disappointed sigh. "I tried to get a job at McDonald's . . . but I'm too young to work there."

"I don't believe you!" Yvonne said. "I bet if you talked to the manager, you could have worked something out."

"It didn't sound like that kind of a deal," I said. "They said I could work there when I'm fifteen if I get a note from my school."

"Oh," Yvonne said. "Don't act like you're not thrilled."

"I'm not!" I said, lying through my teeth. "I'm sorry," I pleaded even though I wasn't.

But Yvonne had turned on the silent treatment and wouldn't look at me. It was a maneuver that made me desperate to please her. After three minutes of ignoring me and looking displeased, I was cooked. I tried to make eye contact with her, which she rejected. And finally I said, "I'm gonna try to earn as much money as I can this year babysitting. And next year, I'll get a job-job, and quit swimming." I knew I was over-promising, but Yvonne could be gone in a year and none of this would matter. For this moment, I needed things to be okay with her.

She softened a little as she named her terms. "I want you to pay for all your clothes and school stuff from now on."

I was shocked; it was as though she had her terms ready.

"And your swim stuff," she said.

"Okay," I said like a robot.

"And next year you can pay us back for France."

I grimaced a little at that one. I couldn't imagine how long that would take.

"That's a lot of money for a fourteen-year-old."

"You'll be fifteen," she said. "And it's beaucoup bucks to me, too!"

"Okay. I'll try to pay you back," I relented, knowing divorce was real and so was the possibility of either one of us stepping in front of a bus this year. But in the meantime, I couldn't take the silent treatment, and I couldn't take her calling me racist one more time. I just wanted us all to be happy.

For the next week I relished my time in a new way. The fact that I wasn't working made my schedule seem really luxurious. But things were different. Now I knew that no one cared if I did well at school, or violin, or swimming, or anything and I was having a hard time seeing the point. Negative ruminations would creep into my head while I was in the middle of homework or swim practice and exhaust me. And I would have to talk myself into focusing on the small picture, because the big picture sucked.

A week later I was riding in the van with Dad, my sister, Andre, and Yvette. We had just picked the babies up from school, and were headed to the store to get some stuff to make dinner.

Riding in the van when it was more than just one kid was always tricky because of the whole milk-crate situation. My sister was in the front, meaning I was stuck in the back with the babies, watching about a half cup of water roll back and forth. Dad was cursing at traffic, which Andre scolded and Yvette imitated.

Someone would cut Dad off in traffic and he'd say, "Motherfucker."

And Andre would say, "Ooooh! You said a bad word."

And Yvette would say, "Mutterfucka."

My sister and I laughed a little every time Yvette cursed—but Dad had no idea what was going on since he was so absorbed by "how shitty everyone was driving."

Then, Dad ran over something. A rock or a pothole, nothing Dad even noticed, but whatever it was caused Andre's crate to fall over. Then, both him and the crate slid down the inside of the van and out the back doors, which had only been kept together with the wire.

"Andre!" Yvette screamed as he tumbled out the back of the van and hit the street, the back doors swinging freely. But Dad, oblivious, continued driving and showed no sign that he would be slowing the van any time soon. Andreus hit the street in the middle of traffic, and promptly picked himself up and made the choice to abandon his crate and chase the van.

Cars behind us slowed to leave room for a six-year-old boy chasing a cargo van in two lanes of traffic, screaming, "Don't leave me! Don't leave me!"

Anora, being in the front seat, took it upon herself to get Dad's attention and tapped his shoulder and told our dad that the baby had fallen out of the back. But he didn't hear her, and she had to tap him, "Dad . . . the baby fell out the back!"

"What?" Dad said, looking up from the road confused. Anora's eyes motioned to the back of the van, where, out the back two swinging doors, you could see Andre was struggling to keep pace with the truck. My father immediately hit the brakes, and Andreus caught up to us. There was a scrape on his head that was bleeding, but it was unbelievably minor considering. The whole incident took only about thirty seconds, but Andreus was horrified as he poked his head into the back of the van, "You guys were gonna leave me!"

I reassured my very jarred brother as I pulled him into the van. "It's okay. Dad was gonna stop the van—"

But Dad interrupted me. "Mishna!" he screamed. "What the hell were you doing while you were supposed to be watching your brother?"

I was baffled by how it could be my fault that his van was so jacked up, but as we drove home, I tried to get used to the idea.

By the time we got home, I was in big trouble. I still didn't quite know why, but I knew I was. My dad sent my sister and me to my room saying, "I got some stuff I need to deal with." I wondered if Dad was going to use the time before Yvonne got home to try to get Andre to keep the van incident a secret. But it did seem like the scrape on his head would raise a lot of questions.

I was reading a book for school while Anora tried on a one-dollar hat she had bought at Value Village, when we heard Yvonne come in. We looked at each other apprehensively, and went back to what we were doing. Then there was yelling for about five minutes. And finally Dad came down and said, "Mishna, can you come upstairs for a minute? Me and your stepmom want to talk to you." I knew this wouldn't end well.

I walked into the kitchen, where Yvonne was looking the scariest I had ever seen her. She stared at the floor and she was so angry, I half expected that when she looked up her eyes would glow red. They didn't. Instead she looked at me with brown eyes—brown eyes that said, "You hurt me, bitch."

Dad said, "Yvonne and I was talking. And we're both pretty pissed off about what happened in the van today." Yvonne, nostrils flaring, looked away—it made me want to beg again.

"What did I do?" I asked. Yvonne shot me a quick look, registering her disgust at my attempt to play innocent, then looked away again.

"You should have been on your J-O-B," Dad said. What the hell had he told her had happened? Yvonne finally looked over at me to say, "You're so selfish!" She spat it out it so venomously and so calculated that it bore into my head like a hollow-point bullet and shattered me from the inside. I'd thought I had really been making her happy lately, and now she was more pissed at me than ever.

"I'm sorry!" I said, once again not sure what I was sorry for, but sure that apologizing was the way to find out.

"You aren't sorry," Yvonne said, knowing I would have said anything to get myself off the hook. "You don't care about this family. You are too busy thinking about going to France and your fancy school, and what you are gonna be and yourself to give a shit about what I'm dealing with."

Huh? "What?" I asked. "What did I do?"

"You let your brother fall out of the van," Dad said, cementing his version of the story. I laughed, either because I thought he was joking, or out of discomfort. Whichever it was, it made me look guilty.

"That's funny to you," Yvonne said. "Your dad can't be looking out for every little old thing."

"I couldn't have stopped him!" I cried. "He's too heavy."

"Please," Dad said.

Then Yvonne said, "Just admit it. You weren't paying attention." Defeated, I just nodded in agreement.

"You're right," I said, crying hard now. I cried for forgiveness. I cried like it was my job. I cried because I didn't know what was true, but I knew I needed them.

"You spoiled her, John!" Yvonne said. "She's used to crying to you to get what she wants." Yvonne shook her head. "She's a princess."

"Well," Dad said. "She's not a princess at sports—"

"John!" Yvonne said. "This is half your fault!" I was glad to hear that I wasn't the only one at fault. She continued and turned her frustration at Dad for a second. "If you had a job, and didn't need me supporting this whole goddamn family, your van wouldn't be so janky that my kids are falling out."

Whoa. Supporting this whole family? I mean, I knew Dad didn't have a lot of W-2 income, but I thought there were cash construction jobs or something. I looked at Yvonne standing there upset, and she looked like she was about to collapse. No wonder she was so pissed off at me all the time.

This took me a moment to digest, her supporting us; it meant a lot of things. It meant that Dad was only pretending to still be the head of the household. It meant that I really did have to contribute, and it meant that I had probably been judging the hand that fed me. The least I could do to earn my keep was to adore her, like everyone else in the house. I wasn't even doing that right. I was wholly ungrateful.

Yvonne shook her head and looked sad and frustrated, like *she* was gonna cry. "Goddamn it!" she said. "Andreus could have gotten killed."

I looked at Dad cowering beside Yvonne, the big twenty-five-year-old provider and thought, *So, Dad needs to not like me anymore, and think I'm a racist. It's kind of his J-O-B.* And at that moment I was so angry at him, I couldn't see straight. Not because he couldn't get it together to provide for us, but for keeping me in the dark about what was really going on.

"I'm so sorry," I said, still crying but not with the same commitment. "It's all my fault. I wasn't paying enough attention to my brother. I was thinking about myself."

"Tell me something I don't know," Yvonne said. "You better get with the program here, or step off. You really need to make a decision, Mishna." She looked me right in the eye. "Are you a part of this family or not?" She was talking to my soul.

"Okay," she said, straightening her hair and walking toward the bedroom. "I'll let your dad punish you." And with that she said something to Dad with her eyes and retreated to her bedroom, where Andreus and Yvette were waiting.

"I'll deal with you later," Dad said, running after her. But I had a feeling that he would put it off until Yvonne reminded him to punish me. I returned to the bedroom, to my Russian prison, and began to do something very white. I got "depressed."

Three days later, I was woken up in the middle of the night. Yvonne stood over my bed leering angrily until the searing heat of her rage woke me. I jumped out of the top bunk and followed her.

"What is it?" my sister asked from the bottom bunk.

"Go back to sleep," I said, walking out the door to what felt like my next battle.

Upstairs in the kitchen, Dad was groggily leaning against the counter. So we'd both been summoned for this 2 A.M. Spanish Inquisition. I could not wait to find out what I did this time. I waved at Dad wearily; then Yvonne put her finger in my face.

"Where is my shirt?" Yvonne demanded. I stared at her blankly. This was not at all what I'd expected. I was ready for racist or disrespectful, but thieving came from left field.

"What?" I asked.

"My white shirt!" Yvonne said. "Don't act like you don't know."

"Mishna," Dad said. "Just tell her where the shirt is and we can all go to bed."

"I really want to help here—," I said, but I was interrupted. The shirt was just a jumping-off point.

"It's not just the shirt!" Yvonne said. "It's your entitlement! You think you can just walk around here and get into anything you want. You have no respect for other people's property."

"I don't even know what shirt you're talking about! We don't even like the same clothes."

"What are you saying?" Yvonne said. "You know more about fashion than me now 'cause you went to France? You're French now?"

"No," I said.

"When are you gonna pay us back, anyway?" It was too much all coming at once. I started to cry again.

"Stop your crying," Dad said. "Just tell Yvonne where you put her shirt."

"I don't know where the shirt is."

"It's probably in your room somewhere in some pile. You don't treat shit right." She took a pause. "You know, if you had asked me, I'd probably have lent you the shirt. . . . That's the fucked-up thing." My tears were useless. I had no idea what this shirt was. I had never worn her shirt, but none of that made a difference. I was supposed to be wrong.

"I'm sorry about your shirt," I cried. "You're right, I stole it. I don't know why I did it."

"Where is it, then?" she asked.

"I lost it," I said, causing Dad to throw his hands up.

"You lost my shirt!" Yvonne said. "See, John."

"It's my fault. I raised her wrong."

"I'll pay you back!" I begged. "Out of my babysitting money . . . I'll pay you back for the shirt. Just please, forgive me," I pleaded, but it was just a show now because this was the game the three of us played.

"It's not the shirt," Yvonne said. "It's the lack of respect. Do you know how hard I work? I'm doing everything I can to make things nice for all of us. And you don't even care!"

"I'm sorry," I said again. "I care. I love you, Yvonne! I really love you so much."

"You make it very hard for me to love you back," she said, the tears starting to roll down her face.

There was a weird tension in the air. Something had broken and it was uncomfortable. "Go to bed, Mishna," Dad said, trying to act all business, "Tomorrow, I want you to find Yvonne's shirt."

Things felt too weird. For starters, there was no shirt. But I knew now that it wasn't about that. It wasn't even about me. It was about them. And whatever it was, it was more than I understood and I had seen too much of both of them. And at that moment I felt like the oldest person in the room.

Yvonne was still crying. As I walked downstairs, I looked back at her and she no longer looked powerful. She looked really frail. She caught my eye in the stairwell.

"I'm sorry, Yvonne," I said, "I'm really, really sorry." I was apologizing for my father. And as he held her close, while she cried on his chest, I skulked away.

The next morning at school I was deliriously tired. And during passing period, Lilith found me in the hallway, "Mishna, are you okay?"

I looked up at her as though I were in a trance.

"Jesus!" she said. Lilith loved drama. "Family stuff?"

The only picture of Dad's house. It was taken after I moved out and the "porch" was built, up to the front door. I don't know who that guy is."

I nodded, faced Lilith, and said quite out of the blue. "I need to move out today. I need to go to my mother's house." I didn't know where it came from, but apparently the look on my face was alarming enough to make Lilith say, "Yes, Jesus. I'll go with you. Just let me get my coat."

But I couldn't wait and walked out of the front two doors of the school and onto the steps with Lilith following me, dumbfounded. I wasn't going to call my mom, because she would just get all scared about dealing with my dad. I wasn't gonna talk to my dad, because he would talk me out of it. I was just gonna get my shit and get the hell out.

On the bus ride to Dad's house, I must have been a little spaced out because I missed my stop and Lilith kept saying, "Where are you?" I was just maintaining the distance I needed to fend off the horrendous feelings of disloyalty that were threatening to make me get off the bus and go back to school.

When we walked up my street and approached the house in silence, I looked at it and suddenly realized what a shit hole it was. With the gravel and sand and broken glass in the front yard, the barbed wire in the back, the ten-foot drop from the front door—at that moment I saw the house, not from my perspective, but from Lilith's. Ours was the worst house on the street—and maybe the neighborhood. We had even managed to out-ghetto the coke dealer who lived down the street.

Lilith saw that I was paralyzed. "Let's get your stuff."

She pulled me up the steps and I relocated my resolve. Lilith's perspective of my house fortified me. Even when I saw Andre's Big Wheel and felt like a horrible sister, I looked over at her and she had a strong look on her face that said, "We gotta get you out of here." And I pressed on down the unfinished cement stairway into our room. And, as Lilith followed me down the stairs looking a little appalled, I realized that I had never actually had a school friend in my house before.

We grabbed some garbage bags out of the pantry and started shoving my clothes into them. I was gripped with panic that Dad or Yvonne would come home early, but it took a surprisingly lot less time than I thought to pack up all my stuff.

"What about this?" Lilith asked, picking up my sister's Value Village hat, and I lost it for a moment.

"I can't do this," I said.

Lilith grabbed two bags in one hand and my arm in the other and said, "Yes—you—can! You'll see your sister when she visits you and your mom." Lilith put a bag in my hand and hustled me up the stairs. "Now let's get out of here."

I called a cab, and Lilith and I shoved all my clothes into the trunk of the taxi, and as we sped away from the house, I was even more vacant than I had been on the way there. I wasn't sad. I wasn't angry. I felt hollow, and it was a relief.

That afternoon when my mom got home she was surprised to see me standing in her kitchen making a sandwich. Lilith had gone home already and when she saw the bags leaning up against the door to my room she said, "What's going on?" as though she didn't already know.

"Can I stay with you?"

"What about your dad?" she asked, obviously unsure if I was allowed to be there.

"I don't want to live with him anymore," I said. "Can I just live here all the time?"

Mom looked at me and looked at my stuff. She looked concerned but said reassuringly, "Okay." Then she paused and asked, "Do they know?"

"Not yet. But I think they'll figure it out soon."

"Well," Mom said. "Do you want to call?"

"No," I said, feeling unusually self-assured. "What I want to do is eat this sandwich in front of the television."

"I think you need to call your dad," she said as she handed me the phone. "I don't mind you living here full time, but your dad needs to understand that it's your decision."

"Why? Why can't you talk to him?" I asked pointedly.

"Because of our agreement," she said nervously. "I'll be up in my room when you're done if you want me." And she left the room.

I looked at the phone for a second and then dialed the number. It rang a few times and then Yvonne answered.

"Hi, Yvonne. It's Mishna."

"I'll get your dad," she said, and got off abruptly.

Then there was silence for a few minutes.

"Hello," Dad said. "Where are you?"

"I'm at Mom's."

"You need to come home. We can work stuff out with you and your stepmom, but you need to come home."

"I'm gonna stay here, Dad. I have all my stuff, and I'm not coming back to live there." I was terrified. I was worried that Dad was gonna just storm over and show up angry and yelling. And I knew that if he did, I would have no defense against it. But he didn't get angry. He just slowly and quietly started to cry. I was baffled.

"Why?" he said. "Why?"

"I make everyone miserable. I always seem to be making everyone upset."

"Why?" he repeated. "I just don't understand why you're leaving me."

"I'm not leaving you. I'm just moving."

"You know," he said, still sobbing, "you can come home tonight if you change your mind."

"Okay, Dad."

"Please, come back. We can work it out!"

"I'm not going to."

"I'm gonna come get you." He was talking to himself now. "I'm just gonna get in the van and come over there, and we'll go get some coffee at the place on Fifteenth—"

"I won't."

"Please," he begged. "Please."

"Dad . . ."

"Please . . ."

"Okay, Dad," I said. "I'm gonna hang up now." And I set down the phone. I saw my mom in the hallway where she had been listening.

"Was he upset?" she asked timidly.

"Yeah. But not angry," I said. "He was crying."

"Whoa," she said, looking impressed with me. "How did you deal with that?"

I looked at my mom, disappointed that she couldn't have made that phone call for me, even after all these years. "I just did."

Thirteen

WHAT'S THE MATTER WITH WHITE PEOPLE?

"THIS IS LIKE the greatest thing I have ever tasted," I said to Violet, ignoring my turn on *Mike Tyson's Punch-Out!!* in order to focus on my Hot Pocket.

"Really?" Violet said. "I think they taste like barf."

It occurred to me all of a sudden that she was saying that I liked to eat barf. But the way the hot cheese mingled with the doughy goodness and the tomato sauce, I wasn't about to succumb to her pickiness and in between boxing rounds I proudly held up my Hot Pocket saying, "Best barf I ever tasted." And knowing they had a freezer full of them, I added, "How many Hot Pockets do you think I could eat?"

"I don't know," Violet said, coughing. Violet always had a cough. She lived in a huge modern cedar, glass, and steel thing in the woods, and I sorta thought all that glass and metal made her house extra chilly.

"I bet I could eat all of them," I said. "Do you dare me?"

"No," Violet said impatiently. "I don't want to dare you to eat all the barf pockets."

"What's your problem?" I asked, even though I already knew the answer—nothing. *What could possibly be her problem?*

"I'm a little depressed these days," she said. "No big deal." Making me actually want to barf. She had a cool house, a Nintendo, and freezer full of Hot Pockets. What the hell did she have to be depressed about? She even had a family of raccoons that visited the backyard. How could anyone be depressed when they had raccoon friends?

"Or maybe stressed out," she added. "I have a lot on my mind."

This ought to be good, I thought.

She continued, "My mom and dad haven't been getting along that well, and yesterday I heard Dad talking about moving out."

I got a weird joy from hearing her say this. It was a bad joy, the kind of joy you wouldn't want anyone to know about.

"They're just always in this weird space with each other, and they act like my sister and I don't exist." I really thought she was being a baby, but I needed her to see the upside of all this.

"It's a good thing that your parents don't pay attention to you," I said. "You can just do your own thing and eat Hot Pockets and stuff."

"I want to run away."

"Don't be a retard! You have a great house. . . . Just hide in the family room. No one ever comes down here. Get really good grades and in four years, you can be sooo out of here." I finally paused the game. "You're in IPP. You'll get into an amazing school somewhere in New England, and your parents will pay for it."

"I don't think I can make it four years."

I saw her tearing up and I looked her in the eye, serious as a heart attack as I said, "You can fucking make it."

"You don't understand. No one cares about me." I looked

at her sitting in her Generra sweater, with the eighty-five-year-old violin that she owned set down sloppily next to her new computer.

"If no one cares about you, why do they buy you all this stuff?"

"Because they feel bad because they're never around."

"Sounds rough."

"You don't get it because you're poor!" she said. She had never said anything like that, something mean meant to shut me up.

But I was feeling surprisingly thick-skinned that day. "Thank God I'm poor. . . . You'd never see me whining because my parents bought me cool stuff and then left me alone to do whatever I wanted. And you know why?" I asked, and then answered my own question, "Because it's awesome."

"It's not as awesome as you'd think," she said, resigned, but I wasn't letting it go.

"Are you kidding? We have just played three violin duets, spent three hours on Nintendo, we have a check for a pizza . . . and I still haven't seen either of your parents all night."

"Okay," Violet said, cracking a smile. "You have a point."

"And it's almost time for *Next Generation*. Who has it better than you?"

"I get it. I get it," Violet said, and grabbed the controller of the Nintendo. "I guess I was just looking at it the wrong way." She laughed and coughed at the same time.

"Man," I said to Violet, who was back at Nintendo. "You should get that cough checked out."

My social life was the best part of living with my mother. When I wasn't swimming, studying, or carbo-loading, I was spending the night with people richer than me. It was like staying in a hotel. Nice bed, clean sheets, new sights. I seemed to gravitate toward a relatively depressed crowd, because the more depressed my friend was, the more expensive my company was. I liked good dinners, video games, boats, and horses. I liked houses on the water or with wooded acreage if possible. Having both was, of course, ideal. Short of that, having a parent that adored me was a plus, and having a parent who saw me as a charity case and wanted to take me under their wing and improve my station made you my BFF. My friend Eileen's mom would sit me down and we would talk about music, politics, and how Eileen could improve her grades. Whereas Dana's dad might talk to me about when they all lived in India, and whether or not his son would ever get his shit together and act more like me.

As for my friends themselves, I had a growing irritation with them that was getting harder and harder to hide. I didn't think they really appreciated their parents, and it was amazing how much love and support they expected for being relatively inert. They took things for granted, they whined about cold and hunger like it was gonna kill them, they went to therapy, and they nursed ridiculous crushes on homosexual celebrities.

A few weeks after my stay with Violet, I decided to try out staying with Marni Madison. She was the first of my friends to start smoking and in the years since we all had tried to summon the devil, her verbal skills had improved and now she talked like a third-grader. I had the hardest time with her out of all my friends, because I knew she lived in a beautiful glass house on the sea, and yet she dressed like a homeless person. She woke up every day with what I can only imagine was a direct ambition to look like a wet rat. All she owned were these hideous yet overpriced long gray cotton sweaters that were meant to look "raw." Once she bought a new one, she'd stretch out the sleeves and have one constantly in her mouth. When she talked to you, she stared into the middle distance.

And at this point, spacey didn't even begin to describe it—she was catatonic without the commitment.

The impetus for a weekend visit came about when she walked up to me on Thursday in the hallway. She stood next to me vacantly, and I thought she had forgotten why she wanted to talk to me until she took her sweater out of her mouth.

"What are you doing this weekend?" Marni asked, putting her sweater right back in her mouth when she was done.

"I don't know," I said. "I think I might get together with some people, or maybe just watch TV. Depends how I feel."

"Oh," she said, but didn't walk away.

"Why? What's up with you?"

"Well . . . My mom told me I could take the sailboat out on my own this weekend if I wanted to."

My ears perked up immediately. *Sailing—I like the sound of that.*

"Yeah?" I said casually.

"Yeah. I could bring a friend," Marni said, unsure.

"Maybe I'd be into that."

"Well," she said, "it was just an idea."

"No! No!" I said. "I'm warming up to it. . . . I could use some air myself."

Marni got excited, which for a moment made her seem normal, but she caught herself and put her sweater in her mouth and said, "Cool." Then spaced out until the bell rang. I had to admit part of my eagerness to stay with Marni was also curiosity. I thought that over the course of a sleepover I might understand what it was that made her so weird.

Oddly, the person I was actually feeling the most connected to these days was my sister. She would come and stay with Mom on the weekends and I was embarrassed how much I looked forward to it. She had gotten the other scholarship spot on the swim team—another born breaster. So now I got to see her every day at swim practice. We would play together in our lanes after practice, submerging ourselves all the way to the bottom of the pool and walking on the bottom like astronauts. Or arching our backs and trying to jump out of the water like dolphins. Then afterwards, we would shower off and dress together. Then I would head back to Mom's, leaving Anora waiting in the pool lobby for Dad, who would be late to pick her up. I was always a little sad to leave her, but never worried. She had endeared herself to all the lifeguards there. And when I left, she usually jumped behind the attendant's booth to watch TV with Tony, a black man in his forties, whose job it was to tell us to be quiet.

I would return to my mother's house and to my room, where I could practice, eat, talk on the phone, watch TV, study, or draw unicorns until bedtime. Sometimes I used the time to plan my weekend and whose house I was gonna stay at if I didn't have a swim meet. And I thought about Dad—not at all. Which was handy because since I had left, it seemed I was dead to him. And I was just like my mother—a leaver.

I arrived at Marni's house at around eleven on Saturday morning. I was supposed to be there at ten, but Mom drove around in circles for a while because she couldn't believe that there was a house on that particular stretch of beach. In fact, I was also surprised it wasn't protected land. I got out of the car still unsure if we were at Marni's house or if it was some wildly bougie caretaker's house in a state park that paid their caretakers seven figures.

The door creaked open and Marni appeared slumped over in the entryway. "Hey," she said anemically, and slowly motioned for me to follow her into the house. I waved back at Mom to let her know she didn't have to stay. But she had already taken off, intimidated by the prospect of having to meet her parents. I followed Marni up the terrazzo stairs and into her living room.

It was an airy house with huge picture windows, but somehow it still seemed dark. There was a big screen in a side area that was on but no one was watching. And in spite of the TV blaring CNN, the house was eerily quiet.

"Where are your folks?" I asked.

Marni shrugged.

"Well," I asked slowly, "when you woke up this morning were they here?"

"Of course," Marni said, quicker than usual. "I just don't know where they went. They might actually be here."

"Do they know I'm here?"

"I told them," she said. It all felt a bit odd, but everything about Marni was odd, why shouldn't her home be, too?

"Well." I slapped my hands together. "When do you want to take the boat out?"

"Oh . . . It's too choppy today. I don't think I should."

"But I came over here because we were gonna take the boat out," I said. "I really want to do that."

"Why?" Marni asked. "Is that the only reason you wanted to hang out with me?"

I felt guilty immediately and really ashamed. "No. I just thought that's what you wanted to do. I don't care what we do. . . . What do you want to do?"

"I don't know. . . . Hang out . . . talk."

Yipes!

"We can watch a movie on the big screen, right?" I said.

"No, let's just go to my room." And she walked me down the hall to her lair of sadness.

The rest of the afternoon went as followed: Marni told me about how her parents don't touch each other or her, and how her dad runs the house like it's a business. Then around noon her dad walked into her room to tell her that she "lacked talent and character" in front of me. Then she got even spacier. Then we talked about the band Skinny Puppy. Then her mom came in and held up some pink blouses she had bought for Marni. Then Marni told her she wouldn't wear them and that her mother should return them. Then her mother cried. Then her mother asked me what I thought of the blouses. Then I tried to comfort her mother while Marni crawled into her sweater like a turtle. And by late afternoon her dad was gone, her mom was drinking, I was watching sitcoms on the big screen, and Marni was *actually* catatonic.

"Hey, Marni!" I had now been trying to cheer her up for about a half hour. "You want to watch *Saturday Night Live* later?" I tried to make it sound like the best thing that could happen to a person.

"Ughn," Marni said without taking her sweater out of her mouth.

"I'll take that as a yes!" I said.

She took the sweater out of her mouth and said clear as a bell, "Do you ever just feel like it would be better for everyone if you didn't exist?"

I thought she was being a terrible host.

She continued, "Not to kill yourself—just not existing."

"Yes," I said. Then trying to ease things, "Sure."

"Not like I do."

I really didn't want to fight about it and said, "How 'bout something to eat? I'm hungry."

"I'll go ask my mom to take us to Jack in the Box."

I thought about that a second "Wait, your mom who's in the living room?" I said. But what I meant was, "Your mom who's been drinking since four and is passed out on your Italian sectional?"

"Yeah," she said, and took off to wake her mom.

"I'm sure we can find something to eat in the fridge. I don't have to go anywhere."

"I like their curly fries," she said, and bounded out of the room.

Ten minutes later I was in the backseat of a swerving, careening piece of glass and metal helmed by a drunken housewife. After four tries, and at my behest, Marni's mom finally found the headlights, which I had to point out were different from the turn signal. Oddly, Marni seemed more easy and relaxed in this possibly life-threatening situation than she had all day, and as Mrs. Madison made right turns that left skid marks, Marni conversed relatively normally with her about history class and what her mom might cook for a potluck later in the week. I had to admit, except for the driving, Marni's mom really was more fun to be around when she was intoxicated, and barely resembled the hysterical woman from that morning.

Of course, I was relieved when we peeled into the drive-through at Jack in the Box in one piece. And it seemed like Mrs. Madison had sobered up a little during the ride. That's when the lady's voice at the drive-through said, "Welcome to Jack in the Box, can I take your order?"

And Marni's mom said, "Why the fuck not?"

That night Marni and I started to watch *Saturday Night Live* but wound up getting too tired and fell asleep in Marni's room. She had a trundle bed that we had to push a pile of dark clothes out of the way to open and it took us twenty minutes to find some extra bedding, but ultimately I fell into a deep restful sleep.

That is until I was awoken in the middle of the night by Marni's dad coming into her room, flipping on the light, and yelling at Marni about how he had to move her bike in order to park his car, which quickly escalated back into the earlier conversation about her lack of character.

Marni was rattled again and went into her bathroom, while I put the pillow over my head and tried to go back to sleep. But then I had to pee and, thinking Marni was just smoking, thoughtlessly barged into her bathroom.

I flung the door open to find Marni was not smoking. Marni was cutting herself. She was slumped over the tile floor of her bathroom with an X-Acto knife making a series of short marks in her left forearm.

I was too stunned to say anything, but I think my face said it all because Marni immediately got defensive and said, "It's okay. I'm just relieving some stress." And from the looks of her arm, she wasn't new to this form of pressure release.

"Stop that!" I demanded. "What the fuck?"

"I'm sorry."

"What the fuck?" I repeated.

"Why didn't you knock?"

"Why are you cutting yourself? I don't understand why anyone would do that to themselves."

"I don't know!" she said, confused. "It just makes me feel good. It's not what you think. I'm not hurting myself."

"I think you're making your arm look like shit, and you might want to wear short sleeves one day."

"Doubtful," Marni said, and then realizing that wasn't the point, said, "Well, I guess you're gonna go now."

"No," I said, knowing there was no way in hell that I was getting my mom out of bed at this hour and there was equally no way I was getting back in a car with hers. "I'm gonna stay. But you gotta give me the knife."

She silently handed over the knife. "Don't tell anyone."

"No," I said, unsure whether I was lying, "I won't."

"Promise?"

"Okay, okay."

"Say you promise," she said, and looked at me expectantly.

I didn't know what to say and said, "Um . . . I still really have to pee."

"Say it," she said.

"Okay, Marni. Jesus . . . I promise not to tell anyone." And Marni slumped out of the bathroom.

The next day I got into the car with my mom, both physically and emotionally exhausted. I threw my bag in, and she asked, "So, how was sailing?"

I didn't want to get into it, so I just said, "Tiring." And climbed into the backseat and fell asleep until the car's pulling into the driveway woke me.

Mom and I walked into the front door and she instinctively ran to the bathroom, arriving as Anora was pouring the last of a gallon of milk into the bathtub.

"Whoa, whoa, whoa!" Mom yelled as Anora finished off the bottle and tossed it aside. "What are you doing?" I caught up to Mom and stood behind her in the bathroom.

"Mish!" my sister said.

"Hey." I waved.

"You haven't answered my question!" Mom said to Anora.

"It's a milk bath," she said. "Yvonne said it keeps your skin young."

"You're eleven," Mom said.

"You're never too young to start taking care of your skin," she said, as though quoting Scripture. "Oh yeah . . . Mom can you get me some cocoa butter when you go to the store?"

"Aren't you just gonna undo all that skin softening when you go in the chlorinated pool?" I pointed out.

"Huh?" Anora said, then, "Hey, Mish, do you want me to leave my milk bathwater for you when I'm done?"

"I don't want your cold dirty milk water."

"Anora!" Mom said, getting back to the matter at hand. "I don't care what Yvonne says, milk does not grow on trees!" She tried her best to seem intimidating. "We need it for cereal!"

But Anora wasn't the least bit fazed by Mom's order and said a placating, "Okay," before taking off her clothes and getting into her bath.

I went to my room and tried to go to sleep but thought about Marni instead. I didn't know what to do. I knew Marni needed some help and although I wanted to give it to her, I was smart enough to know I was in over my head. I was even a little angry at her for inviting me over and sucking me into her problems under the guise of sailing. I felt bad for being angry, but didn't she know I had my own problems? I was deep in my thoughts when my sister started hollering for the lotion as though if someone didn't bring it to her right away, she was going to die of dry skin. I got back out of bed and found it for her in her room.

"Here." I handed her the bottle in the bathtub.

"I miss you," she said.

"Let's have this conversation later."

"Why don't you come back to Dad's house? It's super yucky there without you."

"I would think it would be better."

"Well, it's not," she said. "It's yucky and Dad and Yvonne are always mad at each other, and all I do is clean and take care of the babies."

"You could live here, too."

"No way. I couldn't do that to the family. I mean, don't you feel terrible?"

"Nope," I said.

———————

On Monday at lunch I looked for Violet. Her divorce self-pity was preferable to Marni's creepy secret. Unfortunately, Violet was absent, and Marni caught up to me in the lunch line. We sat down together and it was instant weirdness. The fact that I was the keeper of her secret made her feel much closer to me than she actually should.

"Hey, Mishna."

"Hi, Marni," I said, suddenly feeling engulfed with responsibility.

"I'm really depressed," she said. "I have been since you left."

"Oh?" I said. I just didn't want to get into it. "You should probably talk to the counselor or something."

"Yeah," she said. "I think sometimes I just cut so I can feel something."

"Lilith!" I said, seeing her across the room. "There's Lilith."

"I thought maybe just you and me would have lunch," Marni said.

"Well, I already waved."

The rest of the week Marni tried to have lunch with me, and every day I pulled a third into the mix. I felt bad for her, but I knew that if we did any more hanging out one-on-one, I wasn't gonna be able to keep her secret for her. It was too heavy.

By Friday, things with Marni had calmed down and she didn't seem to have the same sense of urgency. For the time being she was acting like herself, and promised me twice during the week that she wouldn't cut again. But now Violet still hadn't come back to school and Lilith was worried.

"Calm down, calm down," I said as Lilith paced the hallway outside the cafeteria. "Why are you so worried about Violet?"

"Are you kidding?" Lilith said. "Her parents have their

heads so far up their asses that she and her brother and sister could light the place on fire without them noticing."

"Really?" I asked. "Are they that bad? I mean, I've spent the night there a lot, things never seemed that weird."

"Have you ever met her dad?" Lilith asked.

"No," I said.

"Well . . . ," Lilith said.

"I never thought that was that weird. I guess it's weird. I don't know."

"Of course it's weird!" Lilith said.

I was getting impatient with this conversation. I didn't want to play witch hunt with Lilith. I didn't know Violet's parents well enough—and I guess that was her point. "Well," I said, and sort of changed the subject, "have you called over there?"

"Of course," Lilith said. "No one picks up."

"Well, I'm sure everything's fine. She's probably just sick or something." I was irritated and walked away.

That weekend I spent alone. Anora was at Dad's and I didn't feel like socializing. And for the first time in a while I thought about Dad's house. I guessed part of Marni's problem was that her parents weren't really involved *and* she was an only child. And I guess Violet's parents weren't around enough, either. The one thing I could say about Dad's house was you were never lonely there—he didn't work too much, and the house wasn't uncomfortably nice. You never thought you might get in trouble for sitting on something or breaking anything, because everything was shit being held together with shit. Plus Anora was there, and Andreus and Yvette were awesome kids, really. At least everyone at Dad's house seemed like they were trying to have a good time. As a matter of fact, I had always been the killjoy. I guess I never appreciated just how hard it must have been to live with me. And for a few minutes

I missed being a big sister and I missed Dad and I missed the old house. That was, until my new friend Kendra called and asked if I wanted to help her pick out a new dressage horse.

On Monday there was still no Violet, and Marni was gone from school, too. It was bizarre. My friends seemed to be disappearing like teenagers in *Friday the 13th*. I walked up to Lilith in the hallway, who was putting on black eyeliner in a mirror with a picture of Morrissey taped to it.

"Hey, Lilith," I said. I could tell by the look in her eye she was waiting to tell me something. Her lip was almost trembling with anticipation.

"You heard from Violet?" I asked.

"Oh yeah!" Lilith said, almost pissed off. "Her fucking parents didn't even notice she'd been walking around with pneumonia for like three weeks!"

"Jesus Christ," I said.

"That's not the half of it," Lilith said. "She was, like, telling them she thought she should get her lungs checked out. Like for two weeks. The girl has asthma, for fuck's sake."

"Oh, my God," I said slowly. I knew that cough sounded nasty, but I had no idea. "Is she okay?"

"No!" Lilith said. She loved this kind of stuff. It gave her an excuse to be righteous. "It gets worse. . . ." She closed her locker door and turned to face me. She took a deep breath and paused for maximum effect. "Her lung collapsed. She's in the hospital."

"That's like pretty bad, right?" I said.

"Yeah!" Lilith said. "It's really, really bad."

"I don't get it," I said, shaking my head.

"What's not to get? No one in her whole fucking family cares about her. . . . I told you."

"I know you said that, but I didn't really get it," I said apologetically. "I mean get it, get it. I'm sorry."

"Urgh!" Lilith grunted indignantly. "Her stupid parents are fighting with each other in her hospital room. You know, it's sick! Truly sick." I felt sick. And I felt like the crappiest friend that had every lived. *Why can't Violet just have problems like being hungry with the phone turned off? Or plain ol' no money?* That would be a simple problem that I would understand and could help out with.

The next week Violet was back in class, looking a little worse for the wear, and avoiding the smokers on the stoop out front. But Marni was still nowhere to be found. And as much as I kept thinking I should call over there and see what was up, after Violet I was scared that it might be something horrible—like she was killed in the passenger side of her mother's car on a drunken late-night run to Jack in the Box. But no news was forthcoming and by the end of the week, I saw that as a good sign—and cynically reassured myself that if something tragic had happened, they would have called an assembly. But the fact that I was even worried about these people was weird to me. I had spent the last six years being jealous of them.

A few weeks later I had a swim meet. Mom had dropped me off, and I didn't ask her to stay. Though inhaling chlorine in a damp environment was my idea of a great Saturday, she worked seventy hours a week and I respected her desire to take a nap or eat sitting down once in a while. She provided, she fed, and she went to the trouble of making my life about as free of drama as humanly possible. We had a good thing going as long as I didn't ask her to stand up to Dad for me.

I walked into the host pool and saw Lilith, who was on another team, sitting against the wall with her teammates. Normally I would walk over and say hi, but seeing my sister over by my teammates was more compelling to me. She was walking around the pool deck in a T-shirt with African colors on it and a silhouette of an Egyptian monarchist couple holding their newborn African prince. And as I walked up to her, she threw her arms around my neck and said, "Sissy!"

She had come with Dad, whom I hadn't seen since I'd left, and I looked over and noticed him taking a seat in the bleachers with the other parents. He looked lonely and out of place. He took a seat near a girl named Teagan's parents and started a conversation with them even though I knew he didn't like them. When he saw me, he got excited and waved as though nothing had happened between us. I waved back. I was happy that I existed to him again, but it also felt weird—like I didn't want to let down my guard. And for the rest of the morning, as I warmed up, stretched, and prepared for my events, I could feel him watching me and wanting to be included. And I knew he was proud and sad.

When it was time for my last event, he grabbed me on the way to the block like he always did when he came to a meet. He squared off my shoulders to him and looked me in the eye and said, "I want you to come off the block real fast."

I didn't know how to handle it, so I just said, "Okay."

"Then on that second lap, don't give up," he said. "That needs to be real fast, too."

"Yeah, sure," I said.

"Then the third lap—" But I stopped him. I felt myself loving him as he was standing there, and I needed my bad feelings back or I was going to cry and ask him if I could come home. Instead I let my anger at him well up like nausea. I thought about the van incident and the business with Yvonne and the shirt. And I could feel new resentments growing inside me like muscles, making me strong.

"I know what I'm doing, Dad!" I said. "I don't need you to tell me how to swim."

"I'm your father," he said.

"Yeah!" I said. "Well, I'm the swimmer, and I already have a coach! Go coach Anora!" I saw him getting hurt and then angry, and I was scared for a moment. But he didn't lash out at me.

He just threw up his arms and said, "A'ight," and turned and walked away. I walked the other way, inflating my anger, pumping it like lead as I walked past my coach over to my lane and got on the block.

I did poorly—not only that, I was conscious of what I was doing wrong as I was doing it. I was hovering over myself in my lane watching myself late on the start and then taking one stroke too many on the turn, all the time thinking, *That's gonna cost you at the finish.* And to add insult to it, when I went to get out of the pool, there was Lilith standing above me. And no matter how much I knew she understood that everyone has a bad race sometimes, no one wants to eat it in front of their friends.

"Hey," she said.

"I really bit that." I was embarrassed and hoped she didn't think that was the best I could do.

"Eh," she said. "Let's get some chips."

I looked across the pool and saw Dad and Anora palling around in the bleachers. And I was glad Lilith was with me because I wanted to look popular.

"So," I asked awkwardly, still half-looking over at my sister and Dad as we walked over to the concession stand, "how have your events been going?"

"Killer," Lilith said, "I got a personal best in the hundred fly."

"That's cool," I said. "What's next for you?"

"That's it till finals," she said, tearing open a bag of barbecue Lay's.

We sat on a bench by the trophies, eating chips, when she

casually said, "Oh, so guess what . . ." and I knew whatever she said next would be bad news. Lilith then told me that she had heard through the grapevine that Marni's parents had put her in the nut house.

"What?" I asked. "You gotta be kidding me."

"Well, they called it something else, but basically they had her committed."

"Not a theraputic community?" I asked. "Like where Jenna got sent for stealing her dad's prescription pad?"

"No, dude. Not rehab. Crazy-hab. Institutionalized, like the song."

"But Marni's not crazy. She just has shitty parents." The princess who lived in the glass house on the sea was not a princess at all.

"I don't know," Lilith said.

"Trust me," I said. "You'd be crazy, too, if you had her parents." And I suddenly wanted to get away from Lilith and everyone she worried about. I no longer felt like I could navigate the kind of problems my friends had. They seemed much worse than being poor. I looked around the pool deck at all these preppy swimmers and I felt so out of place in all this whiteness.

"Excuse me," I said to Lilith, "I'll catch up with you later."

"Where are you going?" Lilith said.

But I was already walking away and just said, "Sister."

When I found Anora, she was sitting on the bleachers quietly watching our teammate Janie, a blond, eighty-pound fourteen-year-old dance around with her Walkman to an NWA song. She bobbed her neck and moved in a little circle as she sang. I don't think she realized just how loud she was, because she had her headphones on:

"*'Cause she's gotta bunch of kids nappy heads and all dirty . . .*"

She pumped her hands to the beat, indicating that she was a

gangster. She was completely lost in the music and her Walk-man as she closed her eyes and sang,

"And she's getting pimped by a mhhmph whose thirty . . ."

My sister and I both knew the song well enough to know that *mhhmph* was the N-word.

The next line of the song Janie forgot, and sort of mumbled but came back in to say way too loud, *"But I heard that she sucks a good dick!"*

I watched her bounce around the pool deck a bit more, singing about how big her dick was and then I turned to my sister and said, "What the fuck is the matter with white people?"

My sister didn't even look at me but just shook her head and said, "I-do-not-know."

Fourteen

THE LAKE

SUMMERTIME. We had two swim club workouts a day, which meant Anora and I lived in the water together. In the one year since she had started swimming, Anora was such a presence on the team that I seemed like her shadow. The upper-middle-class decorum that surrounded us in and around the pool had little to no effect on her. She wore her Polo puffer and corn-rows, she didn't deal with people she didn't feel like dealing with, she tuned out their grunge music like she was allergic to it, and she swam like a motherfucker. And as a result people worked to please her, and those that didn't, couldn't stand her. Either way, she didn't care. In fact, the only person she seemed interested in impressing was me. Why, I had no idea. I was faster, but she was well on her way to breaking all of my team records. And now that we didn't share a room, we had nothing in common.

Summer also meant it was time for CAST to do their annual swim across Lake Washington. This was a 2.7-mile swim, which wasn't that much for us in the pool, but adding cold, waves, and boat traffic made it a palpable challenge. Anora seemed pissed off by the very idea of swimming across the lake for fun.

"Why?" she asked when Dan announced the swim. We had finished practice and he was standing on the bulkhead like Caesar.

"Did you ask why?" he asked, amazed at Anora. He often found things she said amazing. "Are you really a swimmer? You're asking me why we should swim across Lake Washington as a team?"

"Sounds awesome!" I said to Ari and Janie, who were in my lane. I had been geeking out on the idea of a lake swim since Dan had mentioned it, and I already saw myself winning it.

"It's not a race, Mishna," Dan said, reading my mind.

"What do you mean it's not a race?" Ari said.

"There's a boat alongside so you can't break ahead of the rest of the team."

"What about the last leg?" I asked.

"You can do whatever you want with the last leg."

"Kiss your butt good-bye," Ari said, looking at me.

"I'm not doing it," Anora said.

"It's not optional," Dan shot back. "There's no *I* in team."

"I'm sorry," Anora said. "I just don't understand why I would do that. Especially on a weekend."

"Just to finish a swim across the lake," I said sarcastically. We didn't do anything just to do it. There was always winning involved.

And Anora announced to everyone, loudly, "I'm only doing it because Mishi is doing it!"

That weekend I had a dinner with Dad. It had been six months since I had lived with him, and over the previous month I had started agreeing to a couple dinners during which Dad took me someplace that was convenient for him, but not particularly wonderful for me, and always left me stranded for hours longer than I wanted to be and not wanting to have dinner with him ever again. On this particular night he announced as we got onto the on-ramp of the interstate that he was taking me to the Sarge's house in Tacoma, a military suburb of Seattle. The Sarge was Yvonne's father, who was a veteran and not particularly fond of white people or my father. He lived in a split-level ranch house, and it always seemed surprisingly big for him, considering I never saw him anywhere other than the kitchen and a leather La-Z-Boy in the den. It was like the rest of the house was haunted by the ghost-of-marriage-past, and he was able to keep the spirits at bay by staying in rooms with TVs.

Yvonne adored her father and doted over him, constantly cleaning and organizing things for him. When she wasn't doing that, she was telling him what he needed to be doing for this or that little health problem he had.

But that night when we walked into the front door of Sarge's house, Yvonne was not parenting her dad at all. The second we walked in the house, I could sense there was something off.

"Goddamnit, Yvonne! Just give me the shirt!" we heard Sarge spit from the kitchen. We made our way into the kitchen to see Yvonne pleading with her father while standing over a pile of his clothes.

"Sarge," Yvonne said desperately, "this is how I always fold your shirts." It always seemed odd when she didn't call him Dad.

"Yvonne, why you such a problem? I never taught you how to fold a shirt! Or you stupid?" Sarge asked as he freshened the yellow tumbler of rum and Coke he had been walking around with. Anora, Andre, and Yvette watched silently.

"I'm doing it right," Yvonne said again.

"You ain't doing anything right," he said. "You come over

here like you're helping, but you ain't helping! I got a way of doing things!"

"Dad," Yvonne pleaded, "this is how I fold. This is how Mom folded. We all folded your shirts this way."

"Don't you patronize me!" he said. "I'm your father! Tell me, what have you done with your life that I should listen to you?" He trailed off. "Messed-up little girl done messed up your life."

"Dad, don't be that way," Yvonne said, sounding fragile. "I'm doing really good with John."

Then Sarge repeated himself, "Mess up your life!" Dad looked worried. "And another thing . . . You just never had no kind of standards for yourself!"

"That's enough, Sarge," Dad said. "You been drinking, and you've upset Yvonne."

"Oh, let her be upset! She always upset about something."

Dad just stood looking really big and way too close to Sarge, and said in a low voice, "Either you put an end to this . . . or I will." Dad's authority surprised me. He had always been eager to please Sarge, but there was no eagerness in his voice and no threat either—just the facts.

Sarge got quiet as he decided whether to chill or fight Dad. After an electric thirty seconds, Sarge's angry disposition relaxed and he laughed, "Shoot . . . You all ganged up on me tonight!" And smiling, he grabbed a box from under the kitchen counter.

"Cigar?" he asked Dad.

Dad accepted the cigar, and at the same time he took Sarge's bottle of rum and put it out of reach on a high shelf. And Yvonne took a deep breath and went back to folding.

Sarge looked over at me. "Hey, girl. You back around?"

"Yes, Sarge. Sort of."

"Oh. Your dad been so sad without you around. You know he talks about you all the time." I looked at Sarge, surprised. "You don't believe me? Always 'Mishna won city championships for swimming.' 'Mishna got straight A's.' What else, John?"

"Mishna plays the hell out of that violin," my dad said.

"I'm not that good," I said, but I was relishing the compliments, even secondhand.

"Come on," Sarge said to me deviously. "You can help me cook."

"Is that dinner?" I asked, pointing to the pot on the stove.

"No, your dinner is on the grill outside. That there's for me. Come take a look." He watched as I bent over the pot and gave it a stir. I saw the familiar sight of broth and entrails and knew immediately that he had brought me over there to try to gross out the white girl, but I was more grossed out by the smell of cigars and rum on him.

"You know what that is?" he asked.

"Yes," I said, brushing it off. "They're chitlins."

"What did you say?" The humor dissolved instantly and the angry guy was back.

I cowered a little. "Chit-lins?" I said nervously.

"Little girl," the Sarge explained, "those are a food that have been with black people for generations, and you're giving it some slave pronunciation." He looked at me sternly. "They're called *chit-ter-lings.*"

"Yeah," I said, knowing he was inferring racism. "But everybody calls them chitlins."

"Everybody who?" the Sarge asked.

I kept silent.

"Chitterlings," Sarge snapped. "You don't believe me, we can look it up in a dictionary."

"Sarge!" my father warned him.

"Chit-ter-lings," I said slowly.

But my sister was fearless, and sitting at the table, she cried out clear as a bell, "More like shit-lings!"

I looked over at Yvonne, who was giggling to herself a little over her father's wash. And it was good to see her smile.

When it was time to take me back to Mom's house, Anora came with me and Dad. She was super excited that it was the three of us in the van and kept bouncing in her seat, saying we should go somewhere else before I go back to Mom's.

"Like where?" Dad said, open to the idea.

"Dancing!" my sister screamed, not getting that in the book of things that I would never do, dancing with my little sister was number two. It came right after going dancing.

"I'm going to bed," I said, really busting my sister's bubble so that she folded her arms and pouted.

"Hey," Dad interrupted, "your sister told me you all's team is swimming across the lake."

"Yeah," I said. "It's gonna be pretty cool, I guess."

"Well," Dad said. "I want to swim with you all." I couldn't imagine what was making him want to do something so crazy.

"I don't think that's such a great idea, Dad."

"Why?" he asked.

I could think of a million reasons why my thirty-nine-year-old dad shouldn't get into the water with a dozen twelve to eighteen-year-old swimmers. In fact, the first ten reasons started with the word *herniated,* and then you could just fill in the blank.

"Well," I said. "We swim a lot-lot. And we are pretty efficient at it. Plus, our endurance . . ."

"Why don't you worry about your own self?"

Now Dad was just pissing me off. It was so completely

ridiculous to think that an old guy who didn't work out that regularly could get into the water with twenty athletes at their peak and not expect to hold us up. I was gonna be the one stuck waiting with him while Ari and Janie swam to glory.

I urged him to be reasonable, explaining that none of the other parents were going to try to swim with us.

"That's 'cause they aren't in the kind of shape I am," Dad said.

"But you're not a swimmer!" I said. "I'm a swimmer! I do this five hours a day! Every day!"

"That's fine," Dad said. "I won't try to swim with you."

"Okay, okay," I said, knowing that I was going to lose this one, and my best bet was to start negotiating. "But if you get too far behind—" Dad looked hurt and incredulous that it would ever happen. "—will you get in the boat so that we don't have to wait for you?" He looked at me like I was being mean, and not totally realistic.

"Don't worry about it," he said, which not only didn't answer my question, but also brought up a new one: "Who the hell does he think he is?"

The swim started at our teammate Teagan's house because she had lakefront property. There was her awesome house, then behind the house a backyard, and then where the backyard would have ended, there was a dock and a boat. We arrived on the late side, and as we entered her living room, most of my teammates were already jacked up on root beer and bouncing off the walls.

"Mishna and Anora!" someone called, and then everyone repeated it as we filled our hands with chips and plopped down on the couch. I started communing with my teammates while at the same time sizing them up as competition. Ari and Janie were there, and they were the likely favorites. But there was also a dark horse in Teagan who wasn't necessarily the fastest, but worked hard and probably had more endurance than any of us. I was trying to gauge how much of a role endurance was going to play in the last leg, but my eye kept being drawn to Dad across the room, looking quiet and out of place. He didn't talk to the other parents much, but instead walked around Teagan's very glass living room, admiring the view and looking like a kid who had been left out of tag. He was about as far from cool as I had ever seen him.

Anora walked over to me with a can of Coke in her hand and looked at Dad and saw something completely different. "Aren't you glad we are all doing this as a family?"

"Um, no," I said.

"Why?" my sister said, tilting her head to the side.

"Aren't you afraid Dad won't be able to keep up and we'll all be stuck treading water every five minutes while he tries to catch up to us?"

My sister thought about it for a second. It was clear she hadn't even considered the idea.

"If Dad can't make it, that's his problem," she said.

"But," I said, trying to make her see, "if we waste energy treading water and being cold, I won't make it."

"You have to make it," she said, grabbing my arm and cozying up to me. "You're my mommy."

"I'm not your mommy," I said, throwing her arm down. "I'm your sister,"

"Okay," she said, grabbing my arm again. "Sister-mommy. Either way, you have nothing to worry about. You'll beat us both."

"Why can't this just be our thing, though?" I asked.

I looked back over at Dad, who was now picking up a large glass award Teagan's dad had won for business-something-or-other and weighing it against a two-liter bottle of Coke he had in the other hand. He saw my sister and me looking at him, and he smiled. Then he jokingly made a bludgeoning motion with the award, indicating that you could really kill a person with it, and my sister and I laughed.

"All right!" Dan said, clapping his hands. "Enough horsing around already. This lake isn't gonna swim itself."

"Is your fly gonna zip itself?" Janie asked, and Dan looked down at his zipper.

"Got you!" Janie pointed and laughed. "Made you look."

"Hey," Dan said, upstaged. "Remember, we came here to swim today . . . not to party."

And Janie looked at me like "what a dork." I smiled back. I actually lived for this stuff.

So we suited up and began wading into the lake. It was an overcast day, which made the lake seem even colder. And as I looked at the dark green water underneath the gray sky, my enthusiasm for the swim itself vanished.

"It's cold," I said to Dan.

"Nah," Dad interrupted, jumping in the water and taking the first few strokes. "You'll heat up once you start swimming." I dunked my head and goggled up. Next to me Anora carefully put her cornrows in her swim cap.

Teagan's mom and Ari's dad got behind the wheel of the boat and took off. The rest watched us through the panoramic windows of Teagan's comfy living room for a few minutes as we began swimming away from shore, and then began freshening their drinks and returning to their conversations. They looked so warm and dry.

Dad and Anora pulled up to my side. It was the beginning of the swim, and they both seemed a little too ambitious. But I let them keep pace with me, thinking that I could afford to slow down a little. I'd just save my thunder for the last quarter mile. My plan was to swim with the group till we got close to the other side, then break away from the herd and sprint to shore. At that point no one could yell at me about swimming ahead of the boat. And knowing my teammates the way I did, I was sure I'd have some competition. Any way things shook out, I was definitely gonna kick Dad's ass.

But keeping pace for Anora and Dad proved harder than I thought. Anora had two speeds: racing and slow. Whereas my natural tendency was to gain speed, and I unconsciously sped up a little. Then I saw that I was losing my sister and Dad, and had to slow to what seemed like a snail's pace as I waited for them to catch up to me—just to have the same thing happen all over again. Swimming this way, I also became painfully aware of how tediously long 2.7 miles could be. And rather than being afraid I'd tire out, I was afraid I'd lose my mind.

Then the boat cut its engine about seven hundred yards out, and we made our first stop to let everyone catch up. Ari and Janie were up ahead and they promptly stopped as they had been instructed. And me, Dad, and Anora quickly caught up to them and stopped, too. The water was choppier now and very cold, but Dad's face was beaming as he clumsily treaded water, and Anora looked as happy and energetic as if she were waiting to start the swim. I had no idea what I looked like, but I already felt tired—not from the swim but from pacing myself, and worrying about my dad and sister, who seemed utterly unconcerned with my sacrifice.

The next leg of the swim I didn't worry about Dad and Anora, and swam at my own pace. I felt like kind of a dick for leaving them behind, but we would all catch up at the next stop. I tuned out guilt I had about leaving my family and tried to enjoy the swim—pulling through the lake, feeling the weightlessness that you feel only in water and the grace of swimming well. I listened to the sound of my own breath in my ears as I glided into my zone. I was one with the lake. I was a fish. It was me and the water. And then the boat pulled to a halt again for our next break.

We had stopped near the middle of the lake. And because a lot of boats came through, there was a giant buoy that we could all grab on to and take a real rest. This time my father was way, way back. He plodded along one stroke after another with a form I could tell must be exhausting him. I was tired just watching him, and thought, *He has to be working at least twice as hard as me.* And for some reason I began to worry that he might come in last. *Well, he does have a really even pace,* I reassured myself. *And he's not last.* A seven-year-old named Wesley was behind him.

Bobbing along in the water, hanging on to an edge of the buoy with the rest of my teammates, we started to get really cold, and it was a very unpleasant wait. The wind was blowing, making big waves and knocking the boat around, but mostly it was causing our top halves, which were out of the water and grabbing the buoy, to get really chilled. And the more uncomfortable we got, the more I thought my teammates might be resenting Dad. And as the minutes passed, I started to get mad at them for the resentment they may or not have felt, and I wanted to make sure Dad was going to get enough rest before we started the next leg.

"Dan!" I yelled. "You're gonna give them a rest, right?"

"A little one," he said. "But there are twenty of us hanging off a buoy right now, and we have to keep moving in this cold, or our muscles will tense up."

"Okay," I said nervously. "As long as they get a second to catch their breath, you know?"

"Don't worry about it," Dan said, which was easy for him to say.

Dad and Wesley finally swam in, and Dad grabbed the buoy next to me. He smiled at me, exhausted, but so happy to have held his own with the team. And little Wesley doggy-paddled from where he had landed on the buoy over to Dan and tugged on his arm.

"Dan . . . I wanna go in the boat," Wesley said in his little-boy voice. I immediately panicked. With Wesley in the boat, Dad was last. I looked at him next to me—his pale white body grabbing on to the buoy while he gulped air, he looked like one of those bodies they fish out of the water on crime shows.

"You sure, Wesley?" Dan asked.

"You sure, Wesley?" I echoed. "You don't want to just try to do one more leg, buddy?"

"Yes, I'm sure!" he stammered through little blue lips. "I wanna go in the boat!" So Dan gently handed Wesley up into the boat, and Teagan's mom handed him a blanket, which he immediately wrapped his little body in and smiled. Wesley didn't need to be a hero.

"Okay!" Dan shouted. "Enough sitting around. Let's get back to it." And we all found acrobatic ways to get a push off the buoy, but I was worried about Dad drowning at this point. He was just too exhausted and he obviously couldn't keep up with us. My sister swam by me and did a little butterfly, kicking up a splash.

"Isn't this cool, Mishi!" she said. "I didn't think I was gonna like it, but I never get to swim with you in the same lane. Isn't it fun to swim together?"

"I think Dad's too tired," I said.

"For what?" she asked.

"To keep going!"

"Mishi!" she replied. "He's practically surrounded by life-guards, and he can always get in the boat. He's not gonna die or anything."

"But he's last."

"No," Anora pointed out. "Wesley is last. I mean he's in the boat. A person who finishes definitely beats someone in the boat."

When it was time to stop again, just as I had thought, Dad was last. He was at least fifty meters back as he hurled his stiff arms one over another. The team seemed patient, but I looked dubiously at my sister,

"He's not gonna get any rest," I said, watching his tired arms slap at the water.

"No," she said. "Not really." And with her limitless reserves of energy, she started doing front flips in the water. She stopped and asked me, "Do I look like a dolphin when I do that?"

"Exactly like a dolphin," I said. Then returning to Dad, "Doesn't he look tired?"

"Exhausted," she said.

"I would have gotten in the boat by now."

"Maybe," she said, doing another one of her dolphin flips.

I watched with anticipation as Dad crawled toward us. I was anxious to see what kind of state he was in when he stopped, and thinking maybe he'd be ready to get in the boat. But when he finally reached us, rather than try to cop a little rest with us, he just kept swimming past us. He knew we'd been waiting for him for a long time and he wasn't gonna keep us anymore. And then Dan shouted, "Time's up, move out!"

Why is he doing this?

The next leg of the swim I was rattled. I swam close to the center of the herd, but only out of habit. I was letting my arms and feet do what they do in water with this particular group of people and freed my mind to wander back to Dad. I knew he must be very far back now. Cold, alone, and so tired. But he couldn't be thinking that. There's no way he could be doing what he was doing without total control over his own mind. The swim was hard for me, and I did it every day.

When we stopped again I could see the shore. It was a little landing with a sandy beach and tall grasses growing all around it. I imagined myself sprinting toward it, Janie and Ari on either side of me. I saw us racing up the beach and them trailing as I ran into the tall grasses and threw my arms in the air victoriously. Me ruling—them drooling. And then I felt my sister's voice pulling me out of my fantasy.

"Look at Dad," she said. And now she was worried. I pulled my gaze from the sandy line of beach and pointed it 180 degrees in the opposite direction.

"Oh, my God," I said as I saw him.

"You think he's gonna make it?" she asked.

"I don't know," I said, unable to draw my attention away. It was like watching a train wreck. He was weak. He was exhausted. He was in agony. And physically, I felt tired but fine. I wondered if there was any way of carrying him on my back, but I guessed that defeated the whole purpose. I felt the utter powerlessness of being unable to do anything to get him to that beach, and totally astounded by his effort to keep up with us all. I imagined that if he was swimming with guys his own age and who didn't swim five hours every day, he would look pretty good. And then I realized, *He isn't trying to beat guys his own age. He's swimming against me.* And he looked like he might drown just to make a point. And as much as I wanted to beat Ari and Janie, I just couldn't sprint in to shore now. I needed to get my dad out of the water.

I swam over to Dan. "I'm cold," I said. "I'm getting in the boat." I thought maybe if I got in the boat, Dad would take another twenty strokes and get in. Point proved, no drowning necessary.

"What?" he said incredulously. "What are you talking about? You're being ridiculous. You're almost there!"

"I don't care," I insisted. "I want to be dry. I want a blanket. I'm getting in the boat."

"I would expect this from Janie," he said. "But you, Mishna?" I knew I couldn't take much more of this . . . and I interrupted him.

"I know I'm lame. I know I'm a pussy. I know I'm a loser."

"Yeah!" he said. "Your own dad is gonna beat you!"

"Them's the breaks, I guess," I said, and swam for the boat.

In the background I could hear Anora asking, "What's Mishna doing?" And when I reached the fiberglass side of the boat, there were no helpful arms or ladders coming down to assist me.

"Hey!" I said. "Coming up."

"Why?" Teagan's mom said, still not throwing down a ladder.

"Yeah," Ari's dad said. "The shore's right there. Just finish it."

"I'm cold," I said. "Too cold."

"You're just being stubborn," Teagan's mom said. "If you're cold, swim it fast."

This quitting thing was harder than I thought.

"No!" I said. "I've really decided. I'm getting in the boat."

"If she wants to quit, let her quit!" Dan screamed. "But just know, Mishna, if you quit, now, you'll never stop quitting!"

I looked at Dad, his every stroke said, *I'm here, Mishna. I'm still here. It doesn't matter what you do—I'm right behind you, I'm still here.*

"I'll have to live with that," I said.

Teagan's mom said. "So you have to come up? There's no way you can finish?"

"*N-O!*" I said. And a rope ladder was lowered.

I climbed into the boat, but I got none of the compassion that Wesley had gotten. I had to find my own blanket and place to sit. Teagan's mom and Ari's dad just glared at me like I was letting everybody down, but they could never understand. My dad had come to me on my turf and across 2.7 miles of water so that I could hand him his ass. He had surpassed the limits of personal agony. He was the winner.

Just as I got situated Anora came splashing up to the side of the boat.

"Hey, sissy," she said. "What are you doing in the boat? You aren't gonna finish?" Ari and Janie were right behind her. Everyone was getting in on it.

"But Mishi," Anora said, disappointed. "I need you to swim with me. Who do I swim with now?"

"You swim with you," I said.

"Wimpy wimperman," Ari said, antagonizing me.

"Just make sure you kick Ari's butt," I said to Anora.

"I will," she said. And splashed him in the face.

Dad finally caught up with the group. He looked like someone who had been breaking rocks on a chain gang all day—only wetter. He took one look at me up in the boat and got confused.

"Oh, no," he said. "What's your problem?"

"She's cold," Anora said.

"I'm cold," I said.

"That's 'cause you don't eat enough," he said. "Now get out of the boat."

"Nope," I said. "It's over. Once you get into the boat, it's over."

"No," Dad said, fighting for air. "It's not over. You can get back in."

"Yeah. But if I got back in now, I would have gotten a rest

in the boat that none of you got. . . . It's over," I said. "You guys win."

"Come on," Dan said, trying to draw the gathering attention away from me in the boat. "Enough horsing around. If Mishna wants to be a little baby, she can."

"Come on," Dad said. I was worried he was wasting energy talking. "Just get out of the boat." I looked over and saw my teammates already swimming away. Dad sat there, treading water and looking up at me.

"You can do anything," he said. "You're my daughter."

I looked him in the eye and said unflinchingly, "I just can't make it." I watched him ponder that statement, and a cool came over him that I recognized as him before Yvonne. "You do it for me. Okay, Dad?" I said.

"Okay, baby," he said, serious but smiling. "I'll see you after." And he splashed off with a renewed energy. He looked tired, but he didn't look like he was going to die. He looked like he was gonna make it to the other side. He actually looked like he was always gonna make it to the other side whether I got in the boat or not.

Up ahead, Ari, Janie, and Anora were already quickening their pace for the sand. And from the boat I watched as they sprinted in, pushing each other out of the way to be the first to set foot on shore—doing what I loved to do. The three hit the shallows at the same moment, but Janie didn't have the reserves that Anora and Ari did. And in the final moments, I watched Anora elbow Ari, causing him to fall back into the water as she emerged from the lake a winner. Then she flung herself down on the sandy bank to carefully take her cornrows out of her cap one by one. And I was warm and dry under my blanket in the boat as I watched my dad far behind, plodding along until he finally reached the shore and flopped onto the sand triumphantly.

That evening we went to McDonald's. Anora was so stoked about how well she did with the race and kept doing her little victory dance, occasionally interrupted by singing the phrase, "Can't touch this." But Dad and I had left it all in the lake. I plopped into our booth and watched Dad try to set down his tray with shaky arms. And when he went to sit down in the plastic chair, he moved like his back was made of bruised bruises. But that didn't stop him from smiling.

"Well," he said, "hurry up and get some calories in you all. You lose a lot of calories from the swim, but you lose even more from the water."

"You really owned it out there, Dad," I said.

"Ahh, you know . . ." Dad shrugged.

"I couldn't make it."

"You could. You just didn't!" he said.

"Can't touch this!" Anora said her mouth half-filled with fries already. "Do-do-do dun-duh dun-duh . . . Can't touch this!"

"Anyway, we're all out there to have a good time, and I think we did that." He stuffed a Filet-O-Fish in his mouth. But I could see he was still smiling even while he chewed. He was feeling good about himself.

The eating took over and we were all quiet, which was helpful for me, because it quelled the jealousy I was feeling. I wanted to be big about everything, but I wasn't quite big enough. I couldn't fully accept not having finished the swim. I'd done it for my dad, but it was completely unnecessary. And even worse, since I'd gotten in the boat, I was actually starting to believe my own story—that I was a loser that couldn't even make it across the lake.

I was deep in thought when I realized my sister for some reason needed to dip her fries into my ketchup and kept leaning over me and making a big show of it. After watching her do this four times, I grabbed her wrist and she looked me in the eye and whispered a high-pitched, "Mama." It caught me by surprise and I laughed. It was the kind of laugh that catapults you out of your head and back to your family and the ambience of Rainier Valley McDonald's.

I pointed to my ketchup. "Can't touch this."

She laughed and tried to wrestle her wrist loose.

Dad looked over at us and went back to looking at a man dressed as the mascot Hamburglar heading out to the playground. He asked the air, "Is that Darnell?" Darnell was the son of a woman who lived around the corner from us. Dad had coached him at football for a season at the community center.

"I don't know how you could tell," I said. "He has that big head on."

"He moves like Darnell. He had that bad right shoulder," Dad said, still trying to make out the guy in the furry head. "But I don't know why he'd be dressed as a cartoon character."

"Least he has a job," Anora said, and although she was absolutely busting on Dad, he somehow found a way to make what she said a joke about jobs and not about him. Dad went back to studying Hamburglar, and Anora looked at me giddily to see if I picked up on her joke, but my face was not amused.

"Well, that's what Yvonne says," she said to me under her breath.

Dad stopped looking at the mascot and looked over at us again. "What are you guys talking about?"

"Anora was just telling me about finishing the race."

Dad nodded and smiled.

"Dad," I said.

Something about the tone of my voice made him avoid eye contact he picked at a spot on the table, "Yeah."

"I just . . ."

"You're not coming back from your mom's house. That's okay."

"What?" I said, realizing I wasn't ready to have this conversation yet. Things were still too raw between us. "That's not even what I was gonna talk about. I love you and Yvonne and the family."

"I know . . . I gotta let you go." Dad started to tear up but he wouldn't let himself. He got up out of his seat still looking at the mascot, and said to the air, "You win."

"I don't understand," I said, but Dad was headed toward the playground and had detached from the conversation.

"I'm gonna go see if that's Darnell!" he shouted back, and he was out the door. I couldn't believe he was just walking away on that note. He strode out the glass doors and across to the playground as though nothing had happened. Anora just shrugged, as confused as me. She laid her head on the table and closed her eyes like a wind-up toy that had run out of wind-up. I looked around McDonald's, and maybe it was because I was so physically exhausted or maybe it was everything that had happened in the last few months, but I felt warm and totally alone—like I was in a sleeping bag. It was very quiet and I saw Anora on the table and Dad talking to the mascot outside, and I was truly free. And I had no idea what to do with all this freedom. I could try out for the football team, I could join the ski club, I could practice violin every day—none of it mattered.

Dad walked back in and threw himself down at the table. "That wasn't Darnell," he said.

"What?" Anora said, waking up from her fake sleep. "You woke me up."

"Stop with your playing," he said. "I was gone like a

minute. . . . Anyway, that wasn't Darnell, it was another guy that I don't know . . . Joe something or other." And as quickly as it had come, the silence vanished.

"Sorry, Dad," I said.

"For what?" he asked defensively.

"That it wasn't Darnell."

"Come on," he said. "Get your stuff, let's go."

Dad started hustling Anora and me out of the restaurant, but I was glued to my seat. I didn't want to leave McDonald's and I didn't want the day to end, because I didn't know what came next. Dad was gonna be fine. Just like Dad was gonna make it across the lake. I was worried about me.

On the cold van ride back to Mom's, I looked out the window as I left the Rainier Valley feeling insecure and free floating. It was like heading into the first day of school after Dad had shoved me off with the vague direction, "You be you." Dad must have felt my fear over on the driver's side because he looked over at me and smiled. It was a reassuring look that set me at ease. Even though he was dropping me off at my mother's, and when we'd see each other again was vague, his eyes read, "My girl."